Praise for Late

"In *Late Bloomer*, Melissa Giberson establishes her voice as a brave truthteller. By sharing her most life-altering experiences with unfiltered authenticity, she delivers an emotional tale of identity, sexuality, motherhood, and forgiveness."
—JULIE CANTRELL, *New York Times* and *USA Today* bestselling author of *Perennials*

"Melissa Giberson has written an incredibly important book about truth telling. In this story, she's searching for her own truth, moment by messy moment. Bravo to her bravery. Shedding societal expectations is not easy, and the path to authenticity is rarely smooth. Reading Melissa's journey will give so many people hope that there's sun at the end of the storm."
—JULIE BARTON, *New York Times* Bestselling author of *Dog Medicine: How My Dog Saved Me From Myself*

"Melissa Giberson's *Late Bloomer* is a beautifully written memoir. The author, with vivid recall, takes us from her journey as a young wife and mother, to the realization of her same gender sexuality, and then to her search for her authentic self as she restructures her life. While at times heart-wrenching, this book is also an honest and compelling read."
—CARREN STROCK, author of *Married Women Who Love Women and More*

"An unsparing and timely look at sexual identity and awakening in midlife. Giberson's brave, honest, and heartrending account of the realization that she must be willing to dissolve her marriage and family in order to create and live an authentic life will have you turning pages late into the night."
—MICHELLE THEALL, author of *The Wind Will Catch You* and *Teaching the Cat to Sit*

Late Bloomer

FINDING MY AUTHENTIC SELF AT MIDLIFE

MELISSA GIBERSON

SHE WRITES PRESS

Published 2023
Printed in the United States of America
Print ISBN: 978-1-64742-519-7
E-ISBN: 978-1-64742-520-3
Library of Congress Control Number: 2023905993

For information, address:
She Writes Press
1569 Solano Ave #546
Berkeley, CA 94707

Interior Design by Tabitha Lahr

She Writes Press is a division of SparkPoint Studio, LLC.

All company and/or product names may be trade names, logos, trademarks, and/or registered trademarks and are the property of their respective owners.

Names and identifying characteristics have been changed to protect the privacy of certain individuals.

Dedicated to all the Mama Bears.
And to my cubs—I am never anywhere without you.

I arrived in this world with a hole—literally a big, gaping hole—in the roof of my mouth, which milk would leak up through and then down out of my nose. Surgeons at Columbia Presbyterian Medical Center in New York closed the hole, but it would be a half-century before I felt whole.

 Author's Note

This memoir is my story. I relied on memory, preserved emails, texts, photos, and discussions with others. Many names have been changed or omitted and those that have not, have generously given permission to use their real name. This book reflects the recollection of events and the emotional accuracy to the best of my ability.

I was a late bloomer.
But anyone who blooms at all, ever, is very lucky.
—Sharon Olds

 **Chapter One**

"It has been said that something as small as the flutter of a butterfly's wing can ultimately cause a typhoon halfway around the world."
—CHAOS THEORY

I stand there, frozen, as if the sight of a naked woman is something I've never seen before. I'm captivated by the smoothness of her bare skin, her curves. I watch as her hands glide down from knee to ankle and back up again. She's methodical—painting her flesh with lotion, leaving no part of the canvas untouched. I'm stone-still when a thought surfaces that is, at least to my conscious mind, a first. It's a question that will ultimately usher me across a threshold and into a journey of self-discovery:

Am I gay?

It's a quiet May morning, and I'm at the Young Men's and Young Women's Hebrew Association (YM-YWHA). I'm no stranger here; less than two miles from my house, the Y is a staple in my family's life. It's where my daughter had her first swim class at six months old; it's where she and my son have gone to preschool, attended day camp, and played sports; and it's where I worked off my post-pregnancy weight. It's also where my previous employer rented space, making it my shortest commute ever. Reentering the workforce in the same building where my son attended kindergarten enrichment classes was the secret solution to ease my guilt about working, after admitting that being a stay-at-home mom wasn't a good fit for me.

I've spent considerable hours in the Y's auditorium attending my kids' dance recitals. Countless more in the café with other moms with whom I have little in common aside from the fact that we're all Jewish and raising kids. This Y hosts annual book fairs where I've purchased Judaic children's books, holiday expositions where I've bought Chanukah gifts, and other events that have transformed the lobby into the Lower East Side of Manhattan, replete with hot dog carts, vendors selling potato knishes, and the sounds of *Fiddler on the Roof*–style Klezmer music.

The Y is also, now, where I'm learning to run. My personal goal is to one day complete a 5K. Music from my iPod helps me keep stride, while my lap counter ticks off every turn around the indoor track.

Running is new to me, and new has recently become appealing to me. I'm forty-four years old, and I've spent my life being averse to change. I like familiarity. I lived in one childhood house, one apartment pre-marriage, and one more apartment as a newlywed—that was it before my husband and I bought our current house, which we've now owned for eighteen years. I've seldom changed cars or jobs, and I return to the same vacation spot repeatedly. I have been with the same man since I was twenty years old.

Lately, though, change is enticing. I'm engaging in activities that are completely out of character for me—and I'm doing them without giving much thought to whether or not I should (in and of itself out of character for me, as I tend to overthink everything).

Shrills of squeaking rubber on a glossy floor spill from the indoor basketball court, while the aroma of coffee competes with the stench of sweat. Down the hallway, the smack of chlorine announces the natatorium is nearby. Upon entering the main gym, I am met by the thumping of runners on treadmills, the clang of weights dropping to the floor, and blaring rock music.

I've just dropped my backpack on the narrow wooden bench in the locker room when I catch sight of the woman, one foot propped on a stool. There's no one else here. She applies moisturizer to her bent leg in what seems like slow motion. The sensation evoked within my body reminds me of when I first saw Tom Cruise and Kelly McGillis make love to Berlin's "Take My Breath Away" in *Top Gun*. The mesmerizing scene lingered in my mind for weeks, months. It was 1986, and I was a college freshman who'd never had sex.

The woman stands with her back to me. She's naked and I'm spellbound. I can't see her face, but that doesn't matter. My body is paralyzed; my thoughts muted. I'm staring but can't turn away. It's as if I've entered a tunnel in a rainstorm: I'm experiencing that same eerie-but-calm quiet that takes hold as you pass inside, and the water stops pelting the car.

Snapping out of the fog, there's one thought: *Am I gay?*

I tear my eyes away from the woman, step away from the locker-lined alcove, and text the same three-worded question to Raia.

Trying to be funny, she responds, "No, you just like ME."

We never discuss it again.

It was one year ago in June, when Raia first entered my life as gently as a butterfly lands on a flower.

It was the end of my workday, and I was heading out to play softball in a modern-day adult version of *The Bad News*

Bears with a bunch of other forty-something women and men from my temple. I had been looking forward to the game all day.

My car keys were already in my hand when the colleague with whom I share the orthopedic therapy room stopped me and asked if I could help her make a custom splint.

I glanced toward the exit, then at my colleague, then at the woman seated quietly at the horseshoe table—a patient who'd recently had wrist surgery. Exhaling, I put my work bag down and took a seat across from Raia, a woman I'd one day refer to as my catalyst.

From across the eighteen-inch-wide table, she looked right at me—right into me. I'm typically uncomfortable with direct eye contact, yet I gazed right back. Her eyes drew me in. I struggled to look away. Our eyes locked, hers begging me to help her, mine probing, *Who are you?*

Raia owned a second home ten minutes from my office and was an occasional patient of the medical practice where I work as an occupational therapist. I vaguely recalled having met her two years prior. She returned to the office a few more times over the next couple weeks, and on her last visit, when she was discharged from therapy, she invited me for a drink.

Those times I'd worked with her directly in the previous couple of weeks, she'd shared stories of her family and a recent breakup with a woman. I didn't hesitate to accept her invitation—and before leaving the restaurant-bar that evening, we exchanged phone numbers.

Knowing she was from New England, I asked for her recommendations on where to spend my time while waiting for my son, who would be attending a weekend camp event in Massachusetts soon. Per her suggestion, I drove east to Northampton and then meandered over the border to Vermont. The weekend was a marathon of texting and talking with her on the phone. Unable to find a hotel, I slept in my car overnight but jolted awake, like Pavlov's dog, at every ding of her incoming texts.

By October, we were engaging in hours-long phone conversations every day. Whenever she returned to her New Jersey home, typically for work-related reasons, we'd get together for dinner. There was nothing out of the ordinary in our interactions—except the level of intrigue, which far surpassed any I had experienced with another person in many years.

Over dinner on a Thursday night in December, Raia looked at me across the table and said, "I'm very attracted to you, and I think you are to me."

I sipped my mojito, needing to cool down the rush of heat flashing through me at her words. No one had ever said anything like it to me. Lost at what to do, I said nothing. I recognized my desire to spend time with her, but that was as far as I'd taken it. We continued with dinner and left her words lingering.

After dinner we returned to my car—it was parked nearer to the restaurant than hers—not ready to part ways. It was getting late but there was no mention of the time. Once we were inside, Raia, without warning, leaned over the SUV's center console and kissed me. Like flashbulbs popping, three consecutive thoughts burst into my mind: *I'm kissing someone other than my husband—I'm kissing a woman,* and *This is the most incredible sensation I have ever encountered.*

Again, I said nothing.

She made a joke: "We're not crossing a line . . . just moving it a bit." Then she kissed me again.

I didn't resist. In fact, I delivered tacit consent in my reciprocation of what became a longer, more intimate kiss. Her lips lingered on mine in a delicate, skillful way, brushing over them repeatedly, pausing only briefly to explore my mouth or gently bite my lip. We moved in unison as I followed her lead.

We stayed in the parked car, kissing, for hours. She kissed me unlike anyone had ever kissed me before. My hands held her smooth face, drawing her nearer. I wanted to be close to her, to feel her skin on my skin, and her soft, long hair wrapped in my fingers. Sensations awakened inside of me that I hadn't known existed; it was an otherworldly experience that I didn't want to end. The restaurant had long since closed. The fogged windows were no barrier against the glare from the LED light poles standing sentry around us. Mine was the only vehicle in the parking lot except for the street sweeper trucks.

Deeper into the night, the intrusive ping of my cell phone from the backseat broke the trance. Annoyed, I responded to my husband's text, assuring him I was okay, that Raia and I were talking.

"Do you need to leave?" Raia asked.

"No," I said, and we kissed a little longer.

Finally, at 3:00 a.m., I drove her to her car in the adjacent parking lot and said good night.

I floated home on a cloud.

I slipped quietly into bed, next to my sleeping husband. I stared at the dark ceiling, my eyes as wide as my intoxicated smile, her fresh citrus scent lingering in my nose. I replayed the night in my mind—the graze of her supple lips against mine, the gentle touch of her hand on my lap.

The next day her morning text read, *Do you have any regrets?*

No, I responded, and asked the same question of her.

Not at all.

I separated the event from my life, like an exotic island in the middle of the sea, miles from the mainland. The moment stood apart from anything else I'd known, including my marriage and my presumed sexuality. My relationship with my husband had been on cruise control for years—it was vanilla.

Our physical sex life was satisfactory, less the emotional intimacy I'd never felt with him. We kept to our designated sides of the bed except during sex, and that was almost always initiated by him. The vast space between us, once occupied by small children, now felt sterile. He left early for work, and I enlarged myself on the sheets, spreading out, consuming the empty space. On weekends, while he slept, I stealthily eased off the mattress, relishing in the quiet time it afforded me to work on the kids' scrapbooks. Lately, I'd been heading to the gym.

After that night, our routine life continued, except that my experience with Raia was a constant presence in my orbit—unseeable but everywhere, like air.

Two weeks after our first kiss, Raia invited me to her New Jersey home. From the couch, I watched her flutter about the house with a nervous energy, unpacking her luggage. I wanted to take her picture, to capture her in some way, but was too embarrassed to try.

There was no kissing this time. Her back was sore from the hours-long drive.

"Do you want a massage?" I asked.

We sat on the couch, and after warming the lotion between my hands I began—gently kneading tense muscles, my thumbs tracing the hard edges of her shoulder blades in circular motion. Applying long, firm strokes down the length of her back, my palms pressed along her spine before fanning outward and rounding her sides; I didn't want to miss any permissible skin. My hands drank up the time on her body as though they were parched. Her silky skin was hypnotizing, her hushed sounds of pleasure seductive.

When I stood to leave for a scheduled appointment, she planted a gentle kiss on the back of my neck. My knees buckled.

Our phone conversations continued, but I didn't see Raia again until February. Even as the sexual tension grew, I refused to examine what that might mean about my sexuality. My attraction to her was palpable, my distraction exhaustive. Simply recalling her passing touch sent electrical currents throughout my body. I thought of little else except standing at a threshold and being beckoned to cross it. I existed in two worlds—married with children and unable to imagine a different life yet pulled to explore the place beyond the threshold where this woman dwelled. I shared my increasing interest with a trusted friend, who cautioned, "Don't go there—don't touch," perhaps knowing that once I crossed the line I wouldn't be able to return to life as I knew it.

Intrigue surged into an all-consuming hunger. Whatever stirred, taunting and tugging within me, couldn't be ignored. I considered my time with Raia as an opportunity to reveal something about myself—an unasked question begging to be answered. I imagined regret if I didn't follow through.

Still, no inner dialogue about my sexuality accompanied this increasing urgency. Instead, I dwelled on the fear I had of letting the moment pass—my anxiety that if I did, it would never return. I wondered, too, about having sex with her. Would I know what to do? I didn't consider the implications, or how my life might change if I acted on my feelings.

It was a February morning when I was at Raia's house for the second time. We were on the couch, and she kissed me. It was as easy as a song whose lyrics you know by heart. My hands knew their way around her body as if they'd been there before. My fingers followed her lines and embraced her curves with such ease that she asked me whether I'd had sex with a woman before. Having only ever known the coarse skin and scent of a man, I found her scarcely detectable fragrance of sweet perfume and the softness of her skin irresistible. Her body was like a delicate clay I longed to caress into shape. Being with Raia was as effortless as breathing, exceeding any expectations I imagined.

Yet I resisted her touch. Though embracing her felt vital, it seemed wrong to be touched so intimately by someone other than my husband.

Later that day, I struggled to remember anything from the morning. It was as though those few hours had been erased, and all that remained was a gap of time in my day that I couldn't account for.

"What happened this morning?" I whispered into the phone.

"What do you mean?" Raia asked.

"I can't remember anything."

"You're scaring me," she said plaintively.

By the time I picked the kids up from school, my memory had restored itself. The images came flooding back like a deluge—the couch, the kiss, her body, and all the accompanying, indomitable feelings. I desperately wanted to experience her again.

And so began a four-month affair with my "catalyst."

I didn't think of it as an affair. I didn't examine or label it at all, in fact. Rather, I instinctively safeguarded it like a prized possession. I knew intimacy with anyone other than my husband was wrong, yet nothing had ever seemed so right. I didn't think about what being with a woman might mean about me. I didn't see anything different happening in my life "after." At times I thought I could stop, but soon after resolving to do so, I would find myself craving her again.

During one phone conversation, she declared, "You're not leaving your husband."

Of course not, I thought, wondering why she would make such a comment. I built walls around this unnamed actuality, along with the feelings I couldn't explain, while my life proceeded normally outside of the fortress I constructed to hold my secret. Telling no one about this other world—this place I was only temporarily visiting—I imagined my life as it was before would soon resume.

I failed to see the change that was already occurring.

A few weeks after that first sexual encounter, Raia and I made dinner plans to celebrate her birthday. I bought her a CD and a miniature balloon and hid them in the trunk, then stopped home to see the kids before meeting Raia at her house.

Rushing to leave, I didn't notice my flat tire until my husband, who'd followed me out to the driveway, pointed it out. *OMG the time, I don't have time for this!* I thought frantically—and, desperate to get to her house, I lost focus.

"I'll fix it for you," my husband said, already opening the trunk. He paused, looking inside. "You got her a balloon?"

"Something small for her birthday," I said.

He changed the tire while I paced the black asphalt. I could see him looking at me. Surely, he'd spotted the gift bag next to the metallic balloon on a stick. Would he peek into the bag? I marched around in a tight circle, not daring to leave the proximity of the car. Or him.

He finished the job and I left with no more than a cursory thank-you, conscious of the time and not wanting to get stuck in traffic. Raia and I had so little time with one another.

A few weeks later, we managed to spend a Saturday together—a rarity, since she wasn't often in New Jersey on the weekends. We spent the day in New Hope, an LGBTQ-friendly town known for its boutique stores, restaurants, and the canal running through it. We walked the narrow, tree-lined sidewalks, visited the eclectic shops, and enjoyed both lunch and dinner together. I took her picture, wanting to memorialize the day.

She half-jokingly suggested we hold hands, but I refused, fearing being seen by a client or an acquaintance.

My husband texted, far more than usual, about a variety of mundane things that day. It seemed he was finding every reason he could to message me. Irritated by his interruptions of my time with her, my responses were curt.

When Raia and I got to spend time together, I drove home resentful. I longed to spend the night with her, to sleep next to her. I no longer resisted her touch. I was all in.

Once home, I avoided going directly to bed. I hid pajamas in the office to change into.

Some weeks ago, my husband found me on the couch. He stood in front of the built-in wall unit he'd constructed, shoulders forward, hands in his pajama pants pockets.

"I think I'm losing you," he said. "I think I'm losing you to her. There's a look in your eye when you talk about her. It's the same look you had when you were falling in love with me."

"We're just friends," I said flatly.

He didn't push me to say more; we left the conversation there.

My body tensed, but I couldn't know what he suspected. His implication threatened the existence I knew, the only life I believed I was meant to have. I wasn't ready to go there.

I'm still not ready.

Raia says we're playing with fire, but I continue ignoring her warnings. I'm staying present, letting the feelings devour me. She's concerned about my husband, doesn't want him to get hurt.

"You have to keep sleeping with him, so he doesn't detect a change," she said at first—but when our wedding anniversary came this month, she confessed that the idea of me having sex with him bothered her and probed for details. I told her it was obligatory sex that I got through by imagining her in the bed.

She concocted a scheme so she wouldn't be such a mystery to him: She would call the house so he could hear her voice, like she was any other friend of mine. My job was to make sure he was the one who answered when she called.

When the agreed-upon day and hour arrived, I stayed outside to ensure my husband answered the phone when it rang. I rode my bicycle up and down the street, needing to pass the time and work off nervous energy but not wanting to venture too far away. When he flagged me down, he commented only that her voice was deeper than he'd imagined.

Still my husband didn't press the issue—but he *was* gathering evidence. As I was heading out to have dinner with her on another night, he stopped me before I got to the door. Standing in the mudroom, he hugged me goodbye—an unusual gesture made all the more unusual when he lingered by my neck, his nose in my hair.

He was home early from work after I picked up the kids from school a week or two later.

"You left your email open," he said, and admitted he'd read an email I recently sent to Raia about the joy I was feeling. "If I died today," I wrote, "I would die happy, I know what's been missing."

I explained I was ecstatic having a close female friend again.

Despite these encounters, I never questioned our affair until the night a few weeks back when we were in her bedroom and she shouted, "Oh shit," and jumped off the bed. The throw pillow we'd accidentally pushed over the edge of the bed had caught fire from the candle on her nightstand. Hot ashes sprayed onto my naked legs as she beat the burning pillow against the ground and left bantam burns scattered on my skin, including one on my hip whose shape resembled the state of New Jersey.

For weeks I've thought about what could have happened, entertaining images of the bed bursting into flames, of more serious burns scarring me for life, of me dying in a blaze that would leave my children motherless. My reddish-brown scars are visible proof of my indiscretion. I diligently care for them, using scar pads to expedite the healing.

I no longer change my clothes anywhere but behind a closed door. My husband won't see my legs in the light of day until we are on our beach vacation months from now.

 **Chapter Two**

"All journeys have secret destinations of which the traveler is unaware."

—Martin Buber

I met my husband in high school; we started dating during my second year of college. He was the quintessential nice guy, a Boy Scout raised with good manners who wasn't afraid of public displays of affection—a coffee-drinking, classic car–loving, lake-fishing, Sunday football–watching kind of guy. He was six-three to my five-foot-five, handsome, and universally acknowledged as a great guy. His happily married parents presented a novelty for me; their family birthday and holiday celebrations resembled a December Hallmark movie. A closer look would eventually reveal that they had their fair share of dysfunction, like any family, but their glossy surface held great appeal for a girl who had weathered her parents' traumatizing and contentious divorce a decade earlier.

A fight with my mom and stepfather prompted me to move out of my childhood house after college, but I couldn't afford rent on my own. We hadn't wanted to cohabitate before marriage, but the certainty of our intention to marry eased the decision to do so. Early red flags appeared in our relationship, but our friends and family pressed us to get engaged; then, after we did, they chided us for taking too long to plan the wedding. Once we married, all anyone asked about was when we'd buy a house and start a family. The path was clearly marked, steering us both toward that certain future. We bought a family-size car knowing kids would ultimately arrive. A year after we married, we purchased a four-bedroom house on a corner property in a suburban town, walking distance from the local elementary school and just over a mile from the YM-YWHA.

I remember standing on the blue-gray-and-red flagstone walkway looking at the house that would become our home. It was as I'd imagined it would be: tree-lined street, manicured lawn, sidewalks along which I would one day push a stroller and later escort my costumed kids as they trick-or-treated around the neighborhood on Halloween. I printed kid-friendly recipes, bought and stored away children's books, read parenting magazines, even kept a folder full of useful tips, like painless ways to remove splinters and why to keep a red washcloth in the freezer. There was no question we'd raise children in this house.

We hustled those first few years. My husband tackled multiple home projects when he wasn't working his day job or the second job he'd taken to ease our financial strain, while I immersed myself in graduate school. Adhering to the adage *it takes a village*, seeds were planted for the community I envisioned my future children growing up in. We hosted backyard BBQs for the neighbors in June and delivered poinsettias to them in December. In contrast to my childhood neighborhood, instead of observant Jews walking to temple twice a day, dog-walkers and joggers occupied the street, herds of deer crossed my front lawn, and cardinals and blue jays sang from mature trees dotting the block. On Friday nights, from my porch I heard the high school band playing at football games in the fall, and Little League announcements from the Boys and Girls

Club on Saturdays in the spring. In the summer, patio fire pits scented the night air and the days smelled like fresh-cut grass. Moms schlepped their kids to the town pool for swim lessons on July mornings, soccer on weekends starting in September.

We had been married five years, and my graduation was approaching when I got pregnant. I studied for my boards in the rocking chair I would later use for breastfeeding. I was four months pregnant when I interviewed for my first full-time position in my new career and already unable to button my dress slacks.

Once my daughter arrived, however, returning to work full time was inconceivable.

My days as a new mom were seemingly endless. Long drives to the beach just to have a destination became routine. I wrote through my feelings, returned to therapy, and stared at the phone—willing it to ring, forgetting that the few people I knew had careers. The next Gymboree class couldn't come fast enough.

Nights were no better. Becoming a dad triggered my husband's depression about having lost his mom the previous year, before we conceived. The loneliness was as bad when he was home as when I was alone. I signed on for per diem work; most rehabilitation therapists hated working Saturdays, but I bounced out of the house like Tigger from *Winnie the Pooh* when I had a shift.

A long stretch of gray skies prompted a spontaneous drive with my husband to Florida, and then a last-minute decision to stay behind with the baby while he returned to his job in New York. My husband was a hands-on dad. Proving that I could take care of my daughter on my own felt vital. Being a mom was my life's greatest test. Failing wasn't an option.

Desiring an opportunity to feel relevant—and to snag a photo-op so my daughter would one day know I'd done *something* important in my life—my first Mother's Day landed us in Washington DC for a gun control rally. I came home from the demonstration feeling no better than I had before. *How can I feel this inadequate for a role I spent years preparing for?*

Trying to tame the emotional upheaval stirring in me, I asked my husband for a trial separation before our daughter was one year old. He reluctantly agreed and stayed with his dad—but I missed being a family, and within a couple weeks I asked him to come home.

Soon, our young daughter announced my pregnancy by wearing a T-shirt that read, "I'm the big sister." This bolstered my vision of a family of four—until I suffered a miscarriage, which felt like a trap door opening beneath my feet.

My husband was soft and sweet afterward—and with no expectation of sex, we thrived as a couple for the next two months. We resumed couples' counseling, and I clung to hope.

In the final month before I was cleared to conceive, it all changed. He removed our wedding picture from his wallet and his wedding band from his finger and kept unpredictable hours. There were nights when I didn't know if he had come home at all. Suspicious, I poured baby powder on the front step to check for footprints in the morning. Desperate to get pregnant again, I initiated sex, a rare occurrence, and we conceived the first time we tried post-miscarriage. It would be a long time before we had sex again.

His behavior was vexing, and this baby announcement came without the creativity of the first two. "Do you even care that I'm pregnant?" I shouted after one of those nights he disappeared.

Two days after revealing my news, none of it mattered. On September 11, 2001, after dropping my daughter at daycare near our home, I headed to my new part-time job thirty minutes away. I hadn't been paying attention to the chatter on the car radio, so when I reached my destination, a school, and found folks buzzing about an incident in Manhattan, I was caught off guard.

People were hurrying about, unsure how to proceed with the day. A teacher walked up to another, asking, "Can you reach him?'

"No," the second teacher responded, frantic.

What is happening?

The television in the auditorium provided my first glimpse of the plane hitting the World Trade Center Towers. I called my daughter's daycare immediately.

"The children are okay," the director told me. "They're in the bathroom with their heads between their knees as a precaution."

"I'll be right there." I raced to find the highway, wishing the streets were more familiar, but also thankful to be in New Jersey and not my other job in New York—the bridges were all closed.

I found I-80 and sped back to my town. At the daycare, I scooped my two-year-old up from her crouched position with singular focus. We had to get home.

Once in our family room, I turned on the television, then turned it off again. I didn't want her to see those images. *I* didn't want to see them.

My husband came home hours later, but it wasn't until the next morning that we received the call about his brother. He was both a firefighter and the chauffeur that day, meaning he'd driven the firetruck to the scene. Everyone on the truck was missing. The chauffeur was supposed to stay with the truck. He hadn't. He'd last been seen running into the burning building.

My husband insisted on going to the site, determined to find his brother. I begged him not to. He searched the rubble several times over the next few days, until restrictions were enforced preventing public access. I reached out to his other brother for help after an acquaintance phoned to tell me that my husband had obtained firefighting gear so he could go to the site, and another called saying that he was getting into fights.

I imagine that, combined with the weight he'd carried since losing his mom, the survivor's guilt he was experiencing about losing his brother was more than he could manage—but back then, home alone, pregnant, and caring for a toddler on my own, all I could do was wonder, *Where the hell is he?*

By October, I was six weeks pregnant. It was early evening, time to tuck my daughter into bed. I picked up the ringing kitchen phone and heard my husband on the other end.

"I'm not coming home," he announced matter-of-factly.

"What do you mean?" I asked slowly, not understanding.

"I mean I don't know if I want to be married, if I still love you," he said.

My stomach clenched. "You want a separation?"

"Yeah, I guess so."

I slid down the floral wallpapered wall and landed on the vinyl floor, the corded phone in my hand, my thoughts circling the facts: *pregnant, a two-year-old, my husband just left me.*

Arriving early at our next scheduled counseling appointment, not knowing if he would show up, I exhaled relief when his car pulled into the parking lot.

We entered the building for our meeting with his individual therapist. I learned later that she encouraged him to cut his losses and start over. I'll never know why she broke from the norm of neutrality, but at that session, I cried, "My family means everything. There are pictures all over the house, nothing is more important."

She scoffed, "So take them down."

I went to every prenatal appointment alone. I took my daughter apple picking that fall and, as I watched other families posing for pictures at the pumpkin patch, wondered, *Will that ever be us again?*

I worried about the baby. My doctor assured me that babies thrive under stress; I wondered if mothers did too. Even as I heeded advice from an attorney to protect myself, I secretly hoped my husband would come home.

Only two people knew our marriage was in trouble, and my mom was not one of them. I didn't want her thinking less of him when he came back. The life I'd envisioned and created was falling apart, and I was determined not to let that happen.

My husband returned home just before the holidays. Trying to repair our marriage, we continued with therapy and took a family vacation to reset ourselves. I quit my part-time jobs, immersed myself in motherhood. I was steadfast in my determination to provide a stellar childhood for the kids, one they'd be proud to imitate for their own children.

Years passed, during which we busied ourselves with mini adventures that filled the pages of bulky scrapbooks. At playdates, house parties, PTO meetings, school events, and moms-only Mahjong games, I tried finding common ground with other women. On game night, after the women left, I lingered in the family room watching TV shows featuring gay characters.

My soul unsettled, I searched for means of quelling my discontent, seeking a way to become the mom I yearned to be. I landed on a two-year session at my temple.

Sunday mornings were spent with a dozen other adults sitting around U-configured tables in a classroom surrounded by scenic posters of Israel, Hebrew alphabet wall charts, and whiteboards adorned with Israeli flags and simple words like *Shalom*. We studied Jewish history, learned to read right to left, discussed the Torah and Jewish sages. Never having received a formal Jewish education as a kid, becoming an adult b'nai mitzvah was a personal achievement and provided me with the means to help my kids with their Hebrew studies. I was assigned the task of interpreting a passage from Leviticus—"you shall not place a stumbling block before the blind . . ."—and I wondered what obstacles we put in our own way.

Although nourished by the intellectual stimulation and stronger connection to Judaism the course provided, I craved more. After returning to work, I enrolled in a year-long post-graduate program to immerse myself in anatomy and diagnoses. I ended up partnering with a gay woman. During our time together, I steered conversations away from our prescribed studies to personal musings about why we need labels about love. Stories she shared of her wife sparked pangs of envy, but I didn't try to understand why my own marriage lacked the same passion.

When I encountered Raia that June, one educational commitment had been completed and another was a few months off. My kids were twelve and ten. I'd been married eighteen years. Planning my daughter's bat mitzvah was my current priority. I carved out pockets of time for myself while the kids were in school, with friends, or at assorted activities—but not many. In addition to running them to temple and Hebrew school, softball and baseball games, martial arts, art and dance classes, volunteering requirements, piano lessons, and other kids' b'nai mitzvahs anywhere from New Jersey to New York, Connecticut, and Massachusetts, I had returned to couples counseling with my husband. Fighting to make our marriage work seemed to be an ongoing endeavor.

It's May, eleven months after Raia appeared in my office and a few days after the incident in the locker room at the Y. The phone in my bedroom rings: it's my cousin telling me my uncle has died.

This is unexpected, even though our family patriarch had been battling Alzheimer's for seven years. I've always envisioned him saying the blessing over the bread at my daughter's bat mitzvah. Telling my daughter takes a few tries; between gasps for breath and swipes at my runny nose and eyes, I finally get the news out. She's the only other person in the house and needs me to drive her to her softball game.

I phone Raia, still sobbing.

"Oh baby," she says, "I wish I was there with you. Breathe." It's the first time she's used this term of endearment since our affair started three months ago. Her words fill the empty spaces in me. I wish she were here too.

The tsunami of emotions unleashed can't just be about my uncle. Giant waves carrying my every suppressed and repressed thought and feeling are surging, crashing through me. I know I'm in trouble. If I don't get help, I will drown.

The rabbi responds to my request for recommendations of female therapists, but neither is taking new clients. One recommends a male counselor. I send emails to random professionals specializing in sexuality; no one responds. Nothing in my life fits anymore—my clothes hang off me, my home is no longer comforting, my car is now merely a container for my tears.

By the time I reach an available therapist, he tells me the first appointment he can give me is for a day next week.

Thoughts of other means of escaping my pain enter my mind. It's Memorial Day weekend, so my pleas for an earlier meeting are futile. I'm told to seek help if I think I might hurt myself.

The long weekend looms like a gorge I'm not sure I have the strength to cross.

July. The kids are in camp; I'm in Provincetown, Massachusetts. Raia has spoken often about this gay community, so I'm here to ponder the question of my sexuality. I've seen the therapist a couple times, but when I talk about Raia, he mocks me. "That's not a relationship," he tells me, openly laughing.

I must figure things out on my own.

It's my first time on the Cape, and as soon as I pull into the woman-owned bed-and-breakfast where I have a reservation, a sense of peace comes over me. Perhaps it's the Tom Sawyer-like woman in white coveralls who's standing on a ladder and touching up the paint on the yellow colonial house. I feel different, lighter, and at ease, as if I can breathe again. I wonder how long it's been since I last exhaled.

I set off to find the lesbian beach—but after settling onto my blanket, I realize I'm surrounded by retirees and families with young children. Soon, I pack up my gear and return to the inn.

In the privacy of my room, I google anything related to same-sex attraction.

It's my second day in Provincetown. Following the instructions from the woman at the B&B, I head left of yesterday's spot.

The beach is practically barren. From my blanket I see two women walk by, stop, and turn in my direction. One looks familiar. As she nears, I recognize her from work. My heart quickens. When we first met some months ago, she shared that she gifted herself a divorce from her husband on her fortieth birthday upon realizing she was gay. I consider this now when she finds me sitting alone on a coast six hours from home in a town known for its gay population.

When she and the woman she's with—she introduces her as her partner—join me on this largely unoccupied seashore, I tell her that my husband is at home remodeling our primary

23

bathroom and I wanted to be out of the way. This is mostly the truth. As we're chatting, one of the comedians who frequents the Provincetown clubs approaches, hands us a postcard promoting her show, and says, "You know the lesbian beach is that way, right?"

She points down the shoreline while I avoid eye contact with my acquaintance.

Returning to Herring Cove on my third day, I go even farther left than the previous two days. Halfway down the blue-matted footpath skirted by tall grass and beach roses, the serene water of the Cape Cod Bay comes into view. Stopping where the mesh meets the sand, I breathe in salt air—generously infused with coconut suntan lotion—and take in the scene.

Stretched before me is a landscape of colorful umbrellas and blankets set against a backdrop of rocky sand with an interminable array of women. A panorama of same-sex couples as wondrous as the cone-shaped lilacs, silky yellow rosebuds, and sweet-smelling lilies delighting me when I step into my garden on a spring morning. All my life I've been watching the cotillion through the window; suddenly the door is open and I'm inside the ballroom.

In between trying to find the gay beach in Provincetown, my all-consuming random search of the Internet ultimately leads me to a book called *Married Women Who Love Women*. The author's name is Carren Strock; I find her website and email her.

Responding that afternoon, she advises me to be sure before I say anything to my husband. "Once you put the words out there," she warns me, "you can't take them back."

Driving home from Provincetown, I stop in a bookstore thirty minutes from my house. My feet shuffle in place at the customer service desk, and I wipe my sweaty hands on my pants like a tic. In a low voice I order the book, claiming that it's for research and insisting that it be delivered to the store.

A couple weeks later, I'm back, asking if Carren's book has arrived. I'm desperate to read it, but the salesperson tells me it's been accidentally shelved.

I spend what feels like eternity on the floor, searching the store's paltry LGBTQ section for a paperback that isn't there. My nerves are fraying. I'm worried that someone from my temple, or one of my mom's friends, will recognize me as I search the stacks. I might as well be displayed on a stadium jumbotron screen when the clerk announces the book title over the loudspeaker.

Finally, another employee retrieves a copy from the back room. As if I've just been handed the Cullinan Diamond; I practically run out of the store with it.

I tuck the book away in my car trunk, hidden as though it's the nuclear codes, and read it in scanty increments of time in parking lots of neighboring towns over several weeks. Page after page, I devour poignant stories of women who echo the same feelings I've experienced since meeting Raia; it's as if they've transcribed my thoughts into print. Still, I am not convinced I'm gay. Perhaps Raia is merely the exception to my otherwise heterosexual existence. After all, I'm married with two kids. I can't possibly be gay.

One week later, I'm on Fire Island, another well-known destination for the LGBTQ community. My eyes are wide open as I wait to board the ferry and stay that way as we slowly propel across the bay to the little island with the biggest rainbow flag I've ever seen.

I'm looking at women in a way I have never looked at women before, other than Raia. I notice some of them looking at me too. Unlike in the gym locker room, I'm intentional about my actions and paying attention to my feelings—looking for signs that might answer the question I've been asking myself since that fateful day.

Sitting on a sandy beach towel, I watch the women around me. To my right are six women who are sharing a blanket, laughing, and drinking wine from clear plastic cups. One woman kisses another and then talks about her husband with the rest of the group, bewildering me. An attractive redhead crosses by my beach camp to socialize with them. I overhear her name, Toni. She frequently looks my way; I try not to get caught looking at her. She tells the group about a show that's happening later, and I decide to check it out.

At the outdoor venue, I'm a zebra in a corral of Clydesdales. Alone at a picnic table, picking at a salad, I see Toni. She's tossing a football with some women, moving closer to me with each catch. After one close pass, she's behind me; she puts her hand on my shoulder, squeezes it gently, and apologizes for her friends. Her touch ricochets throughout me.

These feelings don't make sense. An invasion—a coup within the walls of my own body—is underway. I know I need more help.

 **Chapter Three**

"The beginning is always today."
—MARY SHELLEY

Without telling anyone, I take the bus into New York City, a trip I haven't made alone since moving to New Jersey. The bus stop is only a mile from my house, but the walk feels longer. I've passed these Cape-style houses countless times, yet nothing looks the same anymore. The wait for the bus seems eternal. I hide behind the scratched plexiglass shelter, afraid of being noticed by another mom or neighbor who might be driving by. I've taken this bus often with my kids. The excitement of a day in the city fed my dream of providing them with adventurous opportunities. Now I ride the bus alone, in secret, in search of answers to a question that might destroy all those dreams.

On the bus, I'm indifferent to the activity around me— oblivious to the blur of familiar stores. I peer down through the dirty window. I gaze into the cars driving alongside the bus. People on their phones, changing radio stations and sipping Starbucks coffee. People whose lives are going on normally while nothing about mine is normal.

I'm heading to meet a rabbi. Two years ago, I read an article about the fifty most influential women rabbis in America. One name caught my attention because she's gay and an advocate for the LGBTQ community. I'm desperate for her help, but she said she's unavailable for the next two full months, so I agreed to meet her assistant, who's also a gay female rabbi.

I traverse graffitied construction corridors; I pass news-stands, high-rise apartment buildings with fire escapes, low-risers with colorful murals, homeless people with their belongings in shopping carts, others with their stories scribbled on cardboard signs, and bicycles and dogs chained to metal poles during my twenty-minute walk from Port Authority. A woman dribbling a basketball brushes by me. Would I have noticed her before? A bass drum pounds in my chest as I maneuver around manhole steam and ignore the blathering of passersby on their phones until I reach my destination.

I'm laser-focused when I arrive at the Chelsea synagogue. A slender, bearded man with glasses greets me, tells me the assistant rabbi is unavailable, says he's the rabbinic intern and offers to meet with me instead. I stare blankly at him; my lips part but no words come out. My arms dangle lifeless by my sides. I've reached out to therapists, even contacted a *New York Times* best-selling author and sexuality experts I've seen on TV. I've been searching for a woman, one knowledgeable who can help me. Instead, I've ended up with this guy—who's younger than me, whom I know nothing about. But I've come too far to turn back now. He's all I have.

We sit at a large conference table adjacent to the lobby. People hustle in and out of their offices. There's no privacy. No sense of security for what I'm about to share. No matter—for the next hour, I sob all over the wooden table. Words burst out of me. I tell him about Raia, about these feelings unlike anything I've experienced before, about questioning if I'm gay but knowing I can't be gay because I'm married to a man and we have children and a life, the only life I know, the only life I can envision for myself. And I'm planning my daughter's bat mitzvah.

What if I'm gay? What does this mean for my kids? For my husband? For me?

I've barely taken a breath as I've released my story in a rapid New York pace, like I'm a contestant on *Chopped* and the buzzer is about to ding, signaling time's up.

I put it all out there. This is foreign territory, the words I say are unrecognizable even to myself. The emotional roller coaster I'm riding has derailed. He listens patiently, says very little, and when our time ends, he hands me a piece of paper.

I take the note, but it can't go home with me, it's a smoking gun. I study it, attempting to memorize the names on the paper, and then once outside the temple I toss it into a metal trash can, along with any clear vision of the future I thought I had until this moment.

On this otherwise beautiful July day, I'm alone in Manhattan, feeling like the Atlas statue from Rockefeller Center—carrying the weight of the world on my back. I sit on a bench overlooking the Hudson River before heading to the LGBTQ community center and an LGBTQ visual arts museum. I wander aimlessly around the West Village and pass a lesbian bar with a sign on the door reading DRAMA with a red line through it. What's to become of my life?

I have lunch at a corner bar. A rush of questions swarms in my head. What if I really am gay? Wouldn't I know if I was? Is it fluidity, a change based on circumstances? After all, I met Raia two years ago. What was so different about the second time? Did the latest problem between my husband and me create a pathway that hadn't been there, or open one buried so deep it was previously undetectable? We resumed therapy due to a recent breach of trust, but we've survived similar tumult before. Our commitment to our family, to our kids, is strong. What will the repercussions of this be for my family?

The questions keep coming, but no answers materialize. Does this explain my passion for defending the rights of the

LGBTQ community? What of the random comments I've made over the years? In graduate school I once said to a friend, "Watch, I'll be the one who figures out she's gay in fifteen years." It was a genuinely casual comment, but I've never forgotten having said it. That was fifteen years ago. Once, after being intimate with my husband, I uttered, "This is how I know I'm not gay." The oddity of the comment didn't escape me, yet I shied away from probing any deeper.

I think about how much I loved *The L Word* after accidentally discovering it during one of my hotel stays in Philadelphia. But it was a good series—even my husband watched with me, after he first semi-jokingly asked if there was anything he should know.

None of these occurrences over the years raised red flags. None prompted me to become introspective or reflective in any way. Not until now, haphazardly wandering the streets of Manhattan on the heels of pouring my heart out to a stranger, trying to catch a glimpse of a life that was once mine but now feels detached and unattainable, do I realize that I've already crossed that threshold. I am newly on the other side of it, utterly lost and alone.

 **Chapter Four**

"*It's your road, and yours alone. Others may walk it with you, but no one can walk it for you.*"

—Rumi

I email one of the organizations whose name I recall from the piece of paper the rabbinic intern gave me, which now lies among empty coffee cups and discarded sandwich foils in a New York City garbage can outside of the Chelsea temple. Cautious in my pursuit of communicating my needs without revealing anything too personal—or being too specific, given that my husband has already searched my computer at least once—I send off an obscure cry for help.

Almost immediately, the bolded email appears. Hannah runs a group in Manhattan for Jewish women who identify as gay. She deciphered my cryptic message; she offers to meet in person as soon as possible. It's the first semblance of hope I've felt since this began.

Two days later, the glass door of the Starbucks closes behind me, quieting the noise of the busy New Jersey thoroughfare. I find the short-haired woman in her midthirties who rearranged her schedule to meet with me. Seated at a table near the window with her laptop and tea, she bears a resemblance to Demi Moore in *Ghost*.

I sit down. Hannah talks—my stiff shoulders soften like a stick of cold butter coming to room temperature. I listen to the story of her ultra-orthodox upbringing and arranged marriage at age eighteen. She tells me about having children soon after getting married, struggling with her sexuality, and taking her children—leaving behind the ironclad religious sect, a courageous move that left her excommunicated from both the community and her family of origin for years. She talks about her current relationship with a woman, showing me pictures on her laptop. Then she invites me to share my story.

I tell her everything, as I did a couple days ago with that intern. I barely get the words out when I plead, "I don't recognize my life anymore, what's going to happen to my future?"

Hannah introduces the "The Parable of the Trapeze" and says, "Imagine an acrobat hanging from a bar who, in preparing to move from one bar to the next, must let go of the first bar briefly, leaving her momentarily suspended in air, entirely unsupported."

I listen, but all I can see is me alone, glued to the platform, knees pulled tight to my chest, trembling. In my version of how this might unfold, I never make it to the next bar.

Nothing makes sense anymore except that any decision I make will profoundly impact the people I love. All our stories will be altered if I address this question.

Hannah needs to leave but promises to reach out to a woman with a similar story who may be able to help.

Meeting this woman has been akin to breaking ground. While I can't know what will happen next, I do leave our discussion with some relief. I'm not alone anymore.

Shira, Hannah's friend, contacts me the next day. She's volunteered to be my guide on this journey. Shira has lived a similar story: married to a man, raising children, and struggling with her personal truth. Now divorced and partnered with a woman, she pledges to send me an email every day.

"It's a frightening time," she says, "as lots of assumptions are being rethought. I'm happy to share my story if you think it will help."

"It will," I say. "I have no one to speak to. My kids are coming home from camp soon. I worry about them seeing me sad and picking up on changes between their dad and me. It's overwhelming thinking about the impact this could have on them. I'm the child of an ugly divorce, and my fear is having my children witness this too."

"I remember experiencing so many of the feelings you are describing," she says. "It was an agonizing time." She suggests a support group for gay women in an LGBTQ center in central New Jersey, the same one she attended years earlier.

Meanwhile, the rabbinic intern from NYC emails me another name: the cantor at a temple not far from my home. Within one week, I will have met with Hannah, exchanged emails with Shira, met with Cantor M, and experienced my first LGBTQ support group. It's a scaffolding of support reminiscent of an energy truck convoy rolling in to help other states during a power outage.

Two days after my first conversation with Shira, I hold tight to Carren Strock's words about being sure before saying anything. I'm shaking when I tell my husband that my noticeable funk is a resurgence of unresolved feelings from childhood issues, likely triggered by the kids reaching the age I was when my own parents divorced. Relying on his agreeable nature, I announce that I'm going to a support group for survivors of difficult childhoods. He doesn't ask for more details.

It's an hours-long drive to the LGBTQ center that Shira recommended. The car rests in stop-and-go traffic, while my body trembles and my mind buzzes. I don't know what to expect and mysteries rattle me; I prefer to be prepared.

Arriving early, I sit in the cramped waiting area. People trickle in slowly, and a young volunteer introduces me to every person who enters the reception room. I consider going home. Instead, I take a seat inside a cluttered, nondescript room with white metal folding chairs arranged in circular fashion.

The group leader, an attractive woman in her early thirties, says she's substituting for the usual moderator. I drove so far to be here for help, and this person is just a stand-in?

There are six or seven other women here, but as the newcomer, all eyes are on me. I'm sitting pretzel-style in the folding chair, arms wrapped tight around my trembling torso to hide my wedding band and hold myself together. I mostly stare at the floor. I don't know what I'm doing here. I don't know who these people are. I don't even know who *I* am anymore.

I'm here but not present and engaged. It's like I'm watching a foreign movie with no subtitles: people are talking but they all sound like the teacher from Charlie Brown.

During a lull I blurt, "I need a therapist. I've been secretly talking to a male therapist for a couple weeks because no one else was available, but he isn't supportive."

Every person in the room opens her wallet and retrieves their therapist's card. The group leader recommends IPG, an organization specializing in LGBTQ issues.

Shira and I have arranged to meet after the group ends. She and her partner find me in the center's lobby. We're exchanging generalities when her partner looks at me and abruptly declares, "You did nothing wrong."

Just like that, like she can see through me—confusion and

guilt infiltrating every pore of my body, lit up as if under a black light. How I needed to hear those words. How I wish I could believe them. I'm wandering alone in another country with no knowledge of the language. I can't comprehend anything going on around or inside of me. I don't know where I am, and I don't know where I'm going. And no matter where I look, I see my children in the periphery.

A few days later, Shira sends an email detailing her divorce. She writes that because she didn't believe divorce equaled a family breakup, she and her ex continued to coparent. She has a roadmap of where this might lead, but I'm not ready. Still, I file her words, like all the other words people have told me, in a lockbox in my brain.

I meet with Cantor M soon after meeting Hannah. She's engaging and supportive. We talk about my kids and my daughter's fast-approaching bat mitzvah. In her office, she tells me about her life with her wife and their young children. A life like mine—except with two women. Her wife is a therapist with IPG, the organization mentioned at the support group, and Cantor M suggests a specific therapist there. It's like opening the wrapper and finding the golden ticket.

The golden ticket's name is Lynn. Clutching a pillow on the couch in her small office, my eyes drift often to the pictures of her son—a year younger than my daughter—and her dog on her desk, reassured by knowing she's a mom. At our first session I say, "I'm submerged in thick mud, trapped. My family is standing on the edge of the mud pool but I'm too far away. I look for Raia, but she isn't there. At times I get pulled under, like I'm in quicksand, but mostly I'm suspended, knowing there's nowhere to go."

I'm getting better at telling my story, but the emotions still sit on the surface, like algae. I want to stay there until I've told Lynn everything, until a solution is found. I couldn't possibly know at this first session what's to come—that I will meet with her once a week, sometimes twice; that she'll be my lifeline when I send urgent emails, needing to process between sessions. I couldn't possibly predict that there will be times I'll appreciate her frank honesty when she says I look like crap, or that I'll welcome her gentle nudges when I can't get out of my own way.

Months from now, I'll arrive for my appointments and head straight to the cabinet where she keeps the Oreos, my treat for making the hourlong drive. I'll be drowning in guilt during one of those sessions, reporting to Lynn how my daughter has asked for a pair of glitter shoes, and I've said no—if this is the beginning of the end of my marriage, I'm not sure what my financial future will look like. I'll talk about these glitter shoes longer than they warrant, but seeing the impact all this is having on my kids will be crushing. They're collateral damage, and the guilt of what they're losing because of my predicament will feel suffocating.

Lynn will ask me how much the shoes are.

"Twenty dollars," I'll answer.

She'll sigh. "Buy the shoes, Melissa."

Mornings are the worst. I wake up only to find my nightmare is just beginning. Facing a rugged mountain I don't know how to climb, I'm reluctant to start my day—as if doing so makes it real again. Regardless of any gains I made the previous day, mornings reset the chains, and I'm starting over.

I often lie here in bed remembering being a college freshman in upstate New York. My roommate, a proficient skier, introduced me to the sport. The unusually frigid conditions that first time meant fewer people at the resort, but the sight of the diehard skiers with icicles in their beards and eyelashes made me question our decision. After painstakingly walking to the base of the mountain (no easy feat in those heavy, rigid boots), I caught my breath, gaped at the intimidating beast, and asked, "Isn't there a smaller one we can start with? A bunny slope, maybe?"

"This *is* the bunny slope," she said.

Every morning now I wake up with this same feeling: frozen in place, gawking up at Mount McKinley from the very bottom of the valley.

Before getting out of bed today, I check my email. Seeing the bold text of an unread email provides a momentary reprieve from the anguish of a new day. Shira's stories and words of wisdom feed me.

One week after meeting these women, a human chain encircling me, I open an email from my husband. He wants to talk after work. He knows the kids are spending the night with my mom and asks me to be honest, to tell him what I haven't been telling him.

My stomach tanks hard, like a ballast. This is the midnight phone call no one wants to receive. I'm not ready for this; I'm still unsure myself.

The clock is ticking—he'll be home soon.

I send an emergency email off to my support system. Cantor M's response arrives quickly. She suggests imagining what could happen if I don't tell him, to let go of the outcomes I want and face the reality I have. Warning me that he might be angry, she gives me instructions on what to do if I fear for my physical safety. She suggests that he is also in a place of great fear and pain. Last, she writes, "But in the end, your life has already changed, and so has his, that's why he wants you to be honest with him. He already knows."

These words echo in my head.

My husband and I sit on the aging, sagging couch in the family room. I'm unprepared, trembling, and my palms sweating. He's waiting on me. I can't look at him. I fidget with a Rubik's Cube, the colorful, rotating puzzle that mimics the twisting and turning of thoughts occupying my mind—holding me hostage.

I take a deep breath, exhale slowly. "I'm struggling with my sexuality," I say.

"I know." His gentle response is delivered with a tinge of relief that the words are out there.

He rises, walks to the half-bathroom several feet away. Behind the closed door, I hear high-pitched crying like I've never heard from him before. My heart throbs as if trying to break out of a tourniquet, wanting to beat freely again. He returns to the couch and sits next to me, his left knee touching my right knee.

"I don't want this," I say, choking on the words.

"You don't have a choice."

We're both crying. I say I'm frightened; he says he's here for me. I explain the significance of the Rubik's Cube, and he reaches for it.

"You can't fix this for me," I say, not giving it to him. "I need to do this on my own."

We agree not to say anything to the kids until after the bat mitzvah. Life will proceed as usual for now. It's unspoken, but we both know that our journey as a married couple has just drastically changed course.

 **Chapter Five**

"Until you make the unconscious conscious, it will
direct your life, and you will call it fate."
—CARL JUNG

Two weeks later, I'm driving into Manhattan. The underground tunnels, traffic, and confusion mirror what's
happening in my head these days. I've accepted Hannah's
invitation to attend her monthly group.

I talk to Raia while I drive. Our conversations are waning,
and—like pretending to be asleep next to your spouse when
the dog whines early on a rainy morning—we never discuss
if I'm gay.

"What are you doing in the city?" she asks.

"I'm going to a support group about sexuality."

"Those groups can be hardcore," she says. "Be careful."

I don't understand but I don't ask for clarification, either.

I enter the large JCC building, plodding along as if unsure of
my destination. I push the button for the lower level and stare
into the busy lobby, waiting for the elevator doors to close.
The empty box hiccups before descending.

I walk the long, windowless corridor with dragging steps,
as if heading to a medical appointment to review biopsy results.
The children's pre-K classroom now doubles as a group room

for Jewish women struggling with sexuality, gender, and religion. I pause at the threshold, remembering when my kids started their school journeys in a room just like this.

I don't know what to do with my hands as I wait for the group to start. I avoid eye contact and make myself small. Tonight, everyone shares her story—painful sagas of divorce, unaccepting parents, troubled relationships, and how to manage the holidays filling the air I imagine was occupied by the sounds of joyful children mere hours ago.

I'm awed by Hannah's ease of being. Will I ever be at peace that way?

When the time is up, a woman approaches me offering her support. We exchange contact information and once again I leave Manhattan, feeling detached from my life but less alone.

On Saturdays I attend Cantor M's morning chanting group at her temple; it's novel, and it gives me a reason to slip out of the house for a while. Seeking solace from my faith, longing to get out of my head, if only briefly, I sit with strangers in a circle. The cantor offers a mantra—"From here to there, each step is a journey"—and I cry. I cry so easily these days.

Lately, I've been scouring the internet in search of other means of emotional support. I recently started exploring Meetup, a platform for meeting new people. And I do need to meet new people; the loneliness is abysmal, it swallows me up daily. Raia and I don't speak much anymore; she's pulled back, and I'm focused on figuring out who I am.

I sit at the kitchen table pushing Cheerios around in milk, replaying the question: *Am I gay?* Before now, my internalized identity—created from a lifetime of stories about myself, along with the absorbed values and messages from my external environment—seemed a given. To question it now means not to rock the boat but to blow it out of the water.

My kids are on that boat.

I'm on the only path I ever envisioned; I need to see this as a detour, not a recalculation. The repercussions for getting it wrong are too big.

Days after Hannah's group, I amble down the front walkway of my house to get the newspaper. I'm halted by the thick fog blanketing my street. Dewy mornings like these often transport me to other times and places; this time it's to Raia's lake house. I linger on the slate path, staring at the pale blue house across the street, lost in my own haze. I see the white-shuttered house where my neighbor, Grace, lived until recently. She's the only other person from my old life who knows why I'm struggling. She detected a problem early in the summer, but I didn't say anything until after the conversation with my husband.

I didn't use specific words when I asked, "Did you know?" She nodded. "Yes, darling, I knew. I always knew."

Her comment made me wonder how people could recognize in me what I couldn't see in myself.

My husband trusted Grace too. He spent so much time at her house, in fact, that her kids and some other neighbors thought they were having an affair—she will tell me this later.

I bawled when she told me they had sold the house and were moving out of state. Grace was a trusted adult my kids adored. Her daughter and my son were best friends. Where will his safe place be when he finds out about his dad and me? Who will my daughter turn to for advice when she's not ready to ask me? How much more will my kids lose that will crack their foundations?

I stand on the walkway staring at Grace's old house, which is slightly blocked by the large climbing tree in which my kids have spent hours. I wipe my eyes with my sleeve and head inside.

"We're going on a road trip!" I announce to the kids when I walk into the house. "Let's go see Grace."

It's a spontaneous decision, quickly approved by Grace, and one that I deem will be good for all of us. The kids need to see their friends, I need a friendly face and a hug, and we could all benefit from a change of scenery. Plus, we seldom shy away from the opportunity for a getaway. Over the years we've covered many miles along the East Coast, from Florida to Maine. I'm grateful for the distraction, and for the easy time alone with my kids.

They're excited. I'm excited. We pack our things and get in the car.

When we arrive at Grace's, there's an email from Shira in my inbox. She tasks me to answer a question quickly, without thinking about it.

If you do nothing, will you regret it in twenty-five years?
Without hesitation I know the answer is yes.

The trip is good for us, but Shira's question lingers. I mull it over again and again. The consequence of my easy answer tugs on my heart with every interaction I have with my kids.

The next couple weeks are like rolling a log in the woods. Each day begins anew with the arduous task of managing my feelings. I rely entirely on the messages of the women who are showing up for me. They impart their wisdom and share their confidence that I will get through this painful period. They remind me to breathe and to take one day at a time. Cantor M writes, "Continue to breathe and remember we all face difficult transitions in our lives, you are not alone."

Hannah writes, "a caterpillar must struggle against its own cocoon to become a butterfly. Stop fighting the feelings. Allow yourself to feel the pain and the fear and then dust yourself off. Go on with your day. Most of all, breathe."

When one day at a time feels unmanageable, they instruct me to take five minutes at a time. Remember, they say, you and your family are healthy and safe. I seek practical advice for how to prepare for the inevitable next stage and replay Shira's words: "Yeah, this sucks."

The train is picking up speed. I don't see an end or exit anywhere. My husband is hurting. My kids are about to inherit the childhood I had. I allowed myself to become dependent on my husband and I'm scared I can't make it on my own. I tell Grace, "I don't have the strength for this. I know there's no way back, and I can't stay here, but going forward scares the hell out of me." I'm suspended in the messy middle, fearing I'll become the bad guy, the one responsible for turning everyone's life upside down. *What if I lose them all?*

I analyze those random comments I've made over the years. I think about Eve, my friend in graduate school—the happiest time of my life. We accented our emotional connection with words like *soulmate.* When I told a therapist about her, she questioned our relationship, raising a flag about my sexuality. I thought her old-fashioned for not understanding that two women could be close and not be gay. And yet I ached for Eve like I would have a lost lover when our friendship ended. My short time with Raia has shed new light on that experience, along with the missing emotional connection between my husband and me.

All I have hangs on this retrospective and prospective journey; I need to get it right.

It's a few days after returning from our road trip. I'm suffocating. My skin doesn't feel like mine, a drum plays in my head, and my heart runs laps in my chest. I call out sick from work. The unending thoughts of my sexuality and the increasing lack of contact with Raia feels like I'm detoxing. I beg Shira to call me.

"Heterosexual people don't question whether they're heterosexual," she tells me. "When you're living a life that doesn't feel true, when you're married to a great man but can't figure out why it doesn't seem right and what can be wrong with you, when you don't want to put your finger on what it is because you know it won't be easy, you probably have the answer."

"Is that really true?" I ask her.

Exasperated, she says, "Melissa, you're head-over-heels in love with a woman, what more proof do you need?"

I don't argue with her assessment, nor do I entirely agree with it. I question if I'm in love with Raia, but I'm certain that I love the feelings roused in me when I'm with her.

"Is this it?" I ask. "Do I already know? And if so, how do I move on from here? How do I help my children? How does one remain in a world that hasn't changed even as you have changed?"

I consider my intrigue with the LGBTQ community, my longing to be near gay women, and my immediate comfort with them. The fact that how I look at men, including my husband, has changed. The answer clicks into place like tumblers in a safe. When I dare to look far into my future, I see a woman as my life's companion.

Shira's story correlates with mine. She also made unusual comments with no impetus to question her presumed sexuality. Like me, she developed an emotional connection to a woman she pined for when the woman moved away, and still she never considered the possibility of being gay. She is credible and straightforward.

Her candid words about Raia are the defibrillator paddles to my cardiac arrest; I'm shocked into facing my truth.

I am gay.

Claiming it is terrifying and liberating, a final acknowledgment that there will be no turning back.

 **Chapter Six**

"You must do the thing you think you cannot do."
—ELEANOR ROOSEVELT

Having crossed the hurdle of claiming my newfound identity, I immerse myself in the gay community between the busyness of bat mitzvah preparations.

There are signs that my daughter knows something is awry. She drops occasional clues but never outright asks. I remind her that she is safe and loved. I plan for our annual family vacation to the Outer Banks (OBX) of North Carolina. Guilt consumes me, knowing it will likely be our last time vacationing there. Already, my children's story is changing.

All moms ever want is to protect their kids; although struggling ultimately helps them cope with life, we never want to see them hurt. But I see the hurt coming, and I am the cause of it. I try convincing myself they'll be okay, but my heart breaks knowing how painful this will be.

One afternoon, when I pick my son up after school, he bounces into the car already talking. "This is the best day!" he exclaims, then tells me he got accepted into the school program he wanted and made weekend plans with friends—"and the bat mitzvah's almost here too!"

I look at him in the passenger seat. "Enjoy this moment, honey," I say. "Remember, life is like boogie boarding. There are pauses while you wait for the next wave, but it always comes, because the ocean never stops."

I'm preparing them for the pain that's coming. My job is to protect them, not be the source of their hurt. I feel like a guy who sets fire to the house and then calls 911.

When I knew where my life was going, the mantra was "after the bat mitzvah." Now that day is only two weeks away.

Bat mitzvah planning is accelerating; the to-do list is endless. I worry about how the kids will respond, even though we've agreed to tell them only when we're on the other side of it. I feel like a fraud planning this important celebration. I avoid people from my local community who detect my anxiety and make assumptions about the cause, asking if I'm physically ill, pregnant, or stressed about the bat mitzvah. People have offered me Xanax so frequently that I become self-conscious about how I must be presenting. I decline every time, and retreat from this suburban niche a little more each day.

October is the home stretch for the bat mitzvah, a coming-of-age ritual my daughter has been working toward since the third grade. It's her moment. Amid finalizing the menu, making the video montage, ordering flower arrangements and party favors, buying dresses and prayer shawls, figuring out seating charts, and putting the finishing touches on the speech I will deliver, Raia calls, stopping me in my tracks.

After two months of silence, she invites me over.

Afraid the invitation might be short-lived, I drive to her house hurriedly, bringing the video montage along with me—I need to preview it today, time is running out. Trembling, I watch it with Raia. On the same couch where I crossed the threshold into another world from which I would never return, I sit on a bridge between my two worlds, watching images of my children's lives go by to music I selected. Tears fall as

Martina McBride sings "In My Daughter's Eyes" against the backdrop of my daughter's life in photos. I relive all those ordinary and extraordinary moments that have comprised the many years I've willingly given to my cherished children—and I wonder, *Will they hate me for what I'm about to do?*

I'm due at the temple for another rehearsal, so I ask Raia if I can come back later. She agrees, and I leave.

From the back pew of my temple's sanctuary, I listen to my daughter, and the girl with whom she'll share the day, read their speeches. Their charge is to interpret the Torah portion "Lech L'cha," the story of God telling Abram to "leave your land, your birthplace and your father's house and go to the land I will show you." It's about a journey.

My daughter's speech begins: "If you knew something bad was going to happen, would you want to know so you could be prepared, or not want to know?" She answers the question for herself, saying yes, she would want to know. I believe she's talking to me.

The other girl talks about donating a portion of her gift money to an LGBTQ cause. I know nothing of her connection to this community. My eyes open wide, my mouth goes dry. Shaking, I send a text to Raia.

No response.

I try again.

Nothing.

The pressure mounts. I feel like I'm in a tunnel as chattering children rush by me in the crowded hallway outside the rabbi's office during dismissal. I crouch outside the rabbi's door, my head in my hands, the din overpowering me. I'm overwhelmed by the cacophony, can't catch my breath.

Seeing me there, the rabbi pulls me into her office. Sobbing, I sit on the floor, slumped over my crossed knees. I'm rambling, jabbering about why "she" isn't answering her phone. The rabbi assumes I'm stressed about the bat mitzvah. She tells me to pull myself together.

I drive back to Raia's house, sensing it might be my last opportunity to see her.

Those last moments with Raia are like standing in your empty house as the moving truck drives away with all your stuff. You take a last look around, replaying your life there like a home movie.

She's talking about her new girlfriend.

"It's unfair to her," she says. "I want to give this relationship a real shot, and I haven't been able to because of my feelings for you. I'll always care about you, but you're unavailable."

I knew about her girlfriend, and I know she's right: I am unavailable. I also know that whatever we have—had—could never have been sustainable. She's not interested in signing on to be with a woman who has kids, and she has too much guilt about my being married. And I'm not about to change my life for her.

I know she's not the one I need to be with; I need to figure this out on my own, not just get absorbed into her world. This is ultimately about finding myself.

Still, it hurts.

It will be eighteen months before I hear from her again.

 **Chapter Seven**

"There is a time for departure even when there's no certain place to go."
—TENNESSEE WILLIAMS

I t's October twenty-ninth, two days after my daughter's bat mitzvah, and the last of the sleepover guests have gone home. A rite of passage for her and the first declared mile marker on my personal journey, kickstarting the task of dealing outwardly with the *massive* weight I'm carrying. The agreement between my husband and me for moving forward has always been TBD, post–bat mitzvah. And here we are. We've carried on as if inside a snow globe, but the mini glass terrarium is cracking—reality calls. I envision the conversation taking place over the winter break.

On this day, though—October twenty-ninth—Hurricane Sandy, which will be recorded as the deadliest, most destructive hurricane of the 2012 hurricane season, lands on New Jersey. After surging through the Atlantic for several days, it arrives, packing a mighty punch that knocks the power out. I lose all connection to the outside world. My work and the kids' schools are shut down indefinitely. Everyone is unreachable; I'm disconnected from my support system.

Exhausted from carrying my secret, wiped out from planning the bat mitzvah, and realizing that I've officially entered phase two without a roadmap, I crash.

The kids and I hunker down at home, hopeful the power will return soon. I sink into the living room couch with a book Lynn lent me—a compilation of stories from now-adult children of parents who divorced because one of them identified as gay. The book's message is twofold: they all wish their parents had not stayed together for their sake, and they all believe that children should not be made to keep their parents' secrets. My head is a desk blotter littered with to-do lists. How do I tell the kids? When? How much do I share?

I'm preparing myself for potentially coming out to the world soon after coming out to them. I'm not ready; I only recently came out to myself, after all.

There's no sign of the power returning, so the kids and I head to my mom's. Once there I attempt to reach my support network, but my laptop won't connect to the Wi-Fi. My patience thins.

"Why don't you just use my desktop computer?" my stepfather asks.

My cheeks flush.

I remember being five years old and in the hospital for my second surgery to repair the cleft palate I was born with. Before the operation, two nurses came to give me an injection. Worried I would flinch, the larger of the two women sprawled over me in the bed while the other gave me the shot in my thigh. The weight of this heavyset woman across my tiny body, crushing me, made it hard to breathe. I feel this now.

To combat their boredom, the kids decide to play Life. I've never played before, so they explain the rules. I'm not focusing, distracted by the cumbersome thoughts in my head. The kids are moving my little car game piece around the board for me.

I hit the marriage square on the gameboard, and my daughter places a little blue man peg next to my pink driver. "Congratulations! You just got married!"

51

Lost to my own feelings and without the presence of mind to consider her experience, I say I don't want to be married; I want to live with my best friend and a dog in a Brooklyn brownstone. I at least have enough composure to keep my tone light.

She laughs and replaces the blue figure with a pink one, but soon changes them back, reminding me that I'm already married. It isn't long before she says she doesn't want to play anymore.

My fears are mushrooming, exacerbated by concerns of what my daughter is thinking.

The power remains out in our town and the schools stay closed. After two days at my mom's, the kids and I head south to visit Grace. The kids are excited about the spontaneous six-hour road trip, and I need to keep moving.

The drive there is uneventful, and we arrive in far better time than the last time we visited two months ago. The first thing I do is check my email.

My lifeline restored; I'm breathing again.

Two days later, we're on our way back home. I've spent the last couple months maintaining as much normalcy as possible, but now I'm aware that life will never be the same kind of normal again. I wrestle with this truth while using my snippets of solitude to seek out more support.

Back in July, Carren Strock emailed me about an online network of women who, like me, have had a late-in-life revelation causing them to question their life's path. Based in Philadelphia, this group was started by a woman who had this same experience in the 1970s. I didn't join right away; then, when I tried, it took a while to break through the security firewall—a barrier needed as protection from angry, sometimes violent husbands (discovering this truth of these women's experiences was like walking into a Wes Craven slasher film—terrifying). I made it in, though, and have since become an active member.

Reading posts and engaging in conversations with these women normalizes and validates my experience in a way I desperately need. Being a part of this underground railroad—women bonded by a common circumstance, helping one another—is like never believing angels wander the earth unseen, and then suddenly becoming one yourself.

Back in September, before the bat mitzvah, I attended LGBTQ events—functions ranging from hiking, biking, and trivia nights to lesbian singles events. I wasn't interested in a relationship but aspired to become more comfortable talking to women, considering my new truth—except I wasn't prepared to share my story yet, mostly because it was still being written. Still in its infancy, my self-awareness was like wet paint that needed to dry before judging the final color.

My first singles event was held in a crowded Manhattan bar. The packed midtown venue buzzed with women talking and milling about. Already feeling like a mole, I was unprepared when a woman asked, "What was your longest relationship?" The answer was twenty-plus years, with a man I was still married to—but I couldn't say this at a lesbian singles event. My hesitation, however, gave me away. The woman surmised I was married with children. "You're taboo," she warned me. "Women will run from you."

At another event, clusters of women standing about and the crowd near the bar spilling onto the dance floor made maneuvering around the room challenging. A woman asked me to dance. I declined. She took my hand, led me to the bar, and offered to buy me a drink. Again, I declined. The word *taboo* echoed in my head.

The generic conversation, mostly about our jobs, had us leaning in close to hear over the music. Then, without warning, she announced, "I get the feeling you live in the suburbs and have kids." She picked up her drink and returned to her friends across the room without saying another word.

I recalled how, long ago, Raia had said that women would seek me out. *Wrong*, I thought now. This initial foray into the Manhattan gay community had been apocalyptic. Rather than full of interesting women, my future looked bleak, barren. Now that I knew I couldn't continue to live the status quo that had defined my adult life, I pondered whether the punishment for pursuing an authentic life would be purgatory-like. Would I be perpetually suspended between two worlds? I imagined myself drifting in some permanent abyss. I channeled Nicolas Cage's character in *City of Angels*, who gives up eternity as an angel to experience love. He tastes intimacy and passion, briefly—and then loses it forever when Meg Ryan's character dies.

I knew I was better for knowing my truth; I had been working vigorously to accept it since Shira flashed the neon sign in front of me. But still, I wondered what or who awaited me on this life path. This journey was not for the faint of heart. No one could walk it for me, that I knew—but I longed to have someone who would walk alongside me.

At another New York Meetup event in late September, I met an older woman who identified as a lifelong lesbian. By coincidence she lived in my town, so we carpooled to events together. One afternoon, after we completed a charity bicycle ride at the Jersey shore, she insisted, "Go back. Don't try and live this lifestyle, it's too hard."

I don't know what prompted her comment, but it had the opposite of its intended effect: I became more determined than ever to make this work. This was not a lifestyle or a passing phase. The only life I'd ever known was at stake; I was putting everything on the line for authenticity. How dare she tell me to turn back when I was only just beginning?

 **Chapter Eight**

"It will take all your heart, it will take all your breath.
It will be short, it will not be simple."
—ADRIENNE RICH

Trees boast the last of autumn colors while street pole decorations and storefront window displays announce the start of the holiday season. I'm hustling through Manhattan like a native city dweller, navigating crowded sidewalks, weaving around street vendors selling books, hats, and cityscape photos. Curbside food carts scent the air with hotdogs and soft pretzels while honking cars and squeaking bus brakes drown the airwaves. Two-toned pigeons perch on square window A/C units after soaring around brick buildings. It's a kinetic city that barely registers as I concentrate on reaching my destination.

I'm meeting with Hallie, who runs a Meetup group for "late bloomers"—women who have come out later in life. She's also Jewish, and her children, slightly older than mine, attended the same sleepaway camp as my kids.

Over brunch, Hallie shares her coming-out story. Like Shira, she gives me hope that my husband and I can get through this as friends. She introduces me to two other late bloomers who also coparent with their ex-husbands.

Connecting with women who have walked the same path I now walk is like finding a treasure map. An attorney I met at one of the Manhattan events, also a late bloomer, advises me to protect myself before legally dissolving my marriage. She recommends separating our finances, getting my own credit card, and changing my beneficiaries, and suggests options such as a Memorandum of Understanding, divorce from bed and board, or in-home separation. I'm fixated on how and when to tell the kids, so I haven't thought of any of this; I welcome all advice about this scary step looming in my future.

My husband is house hunting, an endeavor he embarked upon soon after that night I told him about struggling with my sexuality. We agreed to an economical in-home separation to ease the transition for the kids, but he's anxious to move on. When he began looking, he was adamant that he never wanted me or the kids to leave our house. We've never discussed other options. I've shared my hope that he'll remain close enough for our kids to ride their bicycles to his house when they want to see him, and that he'll create a warm environment, so they feel they have two homes.

I'm committed to preserving our family, even as we ultimately divide into two houses. My husband's strength with the kids leans toward mechanical and athletic skills. He taught them to ride bicycles, spots them in martial arts, helps with science projects, and takes them to the schoolyard to practice hitting, catching, and throwing balls. He follows my lead when it comes to their emotional well-being. Along with my stronger communication skills, I have the advantage of learning from women who've traveled where we're now going.

Despite the groundwork we're laying to ensure a smooth transition as coparents—despite my husband's willingness in all of this—a simmering fear of being a single mom remains. That several people have commented, "Just wait until he meets someone, things will change," doesn't help. Grace reassures me that my husband would never abandon me. "He's not that kind of guy," she insists.

I don't think so either—but I can't shake this fear.

The designated late December timetable for telling the kids feels eons away. The pain of carrying this secret is unbearable. My skin feels two sizes too small, and agitation resides where calm once lived.

"How long do you hold on?" I ask Hannah.

"When it hurts too much to hold on, that's when you let go," she says.

I realize I'm not going to make it to December.

Aligning with my husband, I move the reveal date to the long Thanksgiving weekend and fast-track the information I need. At my request, Hallie shares her story of how she came out to her children. I'm shaking and crying as I read the email; my body aches like it's breaking apart. Do I have the strength to pull this off?

I stare out the sliding door into the backyard. All that remains as evidence of the young children who once played there is the wooden swing set. Gone are the garage-sale plastic houses, seesaw, and mini basketball hoop that littered the yard. Balls no longer hide in the grass, threatening the lawn mower. The brown wooden fence that kept those balls from reaching the street and the flower and bee cutouts that the kids used to peek out from are merely decoration now. The concrete patio is clear of colorful sidewalk chalk art, and the bottle of bubbles no longer sits on the step.

I purge my feelings to Grace: "Knowing I'm hurting my kids is searing. I imagine their life without me and wonder which hurt is worse. I hate feeling all this pain and still not having it feel real. I slip into my old life and feel sad. I'm tired of reaching out to strangers just to feel alive for a little while."

"Melissa," she prods me, "is your guilt due in part to that little desire of yours? The one where you live in a happy gay community with your dog?"

I've had a pebble in my shoe for years. Now that it's emerged, the fear that it's too late burns like an inferno deep inside of me. "My desire is to be with a woman," I admit. "I'm scared that I won't have the opportunity to meet anyone and explore this new life. For twenty-five years, I've been so lonely. I don't want to be alone anymore."

Thanksgiving is fast approaching. I search for words—ponder how much to tell them, and where and how to do it. This will be a watershed moment that I need to ringfence as much as possible.

"Be concise," Shira counsels. "They will likely stop listening after thirty seconds."

The weekend before Thanksgiving, we attend a camp-themed Shabbat at Cantor M's temple. I'm happy for the kids to meet the cantor. I'm hopeful she'll be a resource if they need one going forward. I can't predict how they'll absorb the news of the separation, let alone that I'm gay. I envision them bawling, screaming, "I hate you!"

I want to retreat from the noise in my head, but there's nowhere to go. I spend all my alone time crafting the words I will tell my children and dreading the day as it draws closer.

I send rapid-fire emails to my support network: *I don't have it in me to hurt my kids this way; releasing my burden puts it square on their shoulders. I don't want to be here.*

Thanksgiving arrives with all the dread I've been building up for days and weeks. I cooked the usual Thanksgiving dinner for my family of four, plus my mom and stepfather. I've been robotic, with nothing extra added to the day.

That evening, long after my folks have left and the clean-up is done, my husband walks into our bedroom to sleep for the first time in months. We've been alternating sleeping on the family room couch. It's nothing we've discussed, it just happened by default: whoever falls asleep there first stays there. Tonight, when he comes to the bedroom, I ask to be alone. For most of our marriage I've wished for him to connect emotionally with me, but tonight I'm grateful for his silence when he turns around to leave.

I'm memorizing the words I've written when I receive an email from Shira. She wishes me luck and says I'm birthing a new reality for all of us. "Model courage for them in the face of change and they will try to be courageous, albeit in their own ways and on their own timetable," she writes. "You are modeling for your children what it means to dare to be true to yourself, to be honest with the world. It's an invaluable lesson for them about integrity."

I carry her words like Linus carries his blanket. I've never been so frightened.

It's the day after Thanksgiving, Black Friday. I request a family meeting, trying to hide my fear. I'm approaching a doorway I can never return from—my green mile. Pain tears through my body like flying shrapnel.

I sit on the family room couch while my husband chooses the floor, by my feet. My daughter sits in the oversize chair to my left; my son stands nearby. I tell them I was asked a question years ago, and when I recently revisited the same question, my answer had changed.

I faintly hear my daughter ask what the question was, but I stay on course. Before continuing with the actual news, I say, "The things that don't change are: I am still the same person. Dad and I love you very much. We will always be a family, even if it looks a little different."

They ask about the question again. My heart races, my insides stab like barbed wire. I say the question: "Would I prefer to be in a relationship with a woman or a man?"

My voice quivering, I say, "As I think about my future, I now see myself in a relationship with a woman one day." This is harder than I imagined. I inhale, choke on my words, and add, "Because of this discovery, Dad and I can no longer stay husband and wife—but we will always be the best of friends. Some changes you'll see are that Dad will sleep in the extra bedroom, and eventually there will be a second house nearby." I stop talking.

My daughter moves from the chair to the couch next to me and puts her hand lovingly on my back. I'm crying. My son paces the floor. Despite my intentionally leaving words like gay, queer, or lesbian out of this conversation, my daughter's first questions are, "Is this why we went to meet Cantor M last week? Is she a lesbian too?"

My husband laughs out loud at the irony, and my son sits on the floor next to his dad while reaching his hand back to me, making a human chain. My heart explodes.

I nod. "Do you have any questions?"

My daughter asks, "Can we tell people?"

Recalling the book that said not to make the kids the keeper of your secrets, I answer, "This is now part of your story, and you can do whatever you need to do."

"Will you change your name?" she asks.

"No."

There's an awkward silence that my daughter intercepts by suggesting we watch a movie.

Out of the spotlight, I close my eyes and exhale.

When the movie ends, we move furniture from the primary bedroom, now "Mom's room," to the extra bedroom. My son helps his dad move a dresser, while I remove the large-framed wedding portrait that's hung over our bed for almost two decades and take down the Ketubah, our Jewish marriage certificate. The empty spaces are visible reminders of my life's transformation, but sadness floats like dust particles in the air.

My son requests to sleep with his dad, who will later tell me that he asks that night, "What if Mom changes her mind?"

"She won't, buddy," his dad tells him. "This is who she is."

One week later, I drive to my mom's house to tell her about the separation before she hears it from the kids.

I attended a support group in preparation for this conversation. The women welcomed me as if I were the new kid starting school mid-year. In a room of a dozen-plus women from different cultures and religions, several attendees talked about growing up hearing the same message—that they would burn in hell if they pursued a same-sex relationship. Others recounted being told that they just hadn't met "the right man" yet. One woman's family held an exorcism for her. They all spoke of a shattered sense of self and learning to suppress their feelings.

At my mom's house, I ask to speak with her privately. We head to the basement, leaving my stepfather behind in the kitchen.

As a young teen fresh from my parents' contentious divorce, I was unsettled when my stepfather entered the picture. We clashed on some things, but he was always supportive. A member of Mensa and a successful businessman, he was different from other men I knew. From him, I received an introduction to the Eastern philosophy to which he adheres, as well as Western philosophers he admires, like Henry David Thoreau. He taught me to concentrate on my breaths when I couldn't sleep—breathe in, breathe out. He immerses himself in things that bring him joy, like nature, or trying new activities he's curious about.

Young me was fascinated to watch him advance from idea to finished product, like learning to make stained glass, buying a boat and sailing the Atlantic Ocean, taking up photography in his late seventies (and subsequently winning first prize in an amateur photographer's contest), and playing tennis in his eighties. He made things happen.

He's liberal in his politics but tends to reject ideas that don't make sense to him. I don't know if he will understand my news. He's treated my husband like a son: he mentored him for years when my husband took a break from the physical work he'd been doing since high school, and they worked side by side until it became obvious that my husband wasn't well-suited to computer work and returned to his old job. There's also a twenty-three-year age difference between him and my mom, and I've witnessed some generational biases in him. This is why I worry that he might not be so understanding.

When my mom and I get to the basement, I'm reminded of the months my husband and I spent living in this large, fully furnished, apartment-style space while we transitioned from our newlywed rented condo to our current house. It has a separate bedroom, a full bathroom, and a kitchenette. The whole unit is dark—it has no windows—but I'm grateful for that now.

My mom and I sit on the large sectional couch where my young children spent hours watching Barney tapes and Disney movies. I take a deep breath.

When I was a kid I would watch my mom sleep, looking for the rise and fall of her chest that informed me she was breathing. Alive. Her mother died when she was nine, and the fear of losing my mom was ever-present. When I found the checkbook ledger entry for a PAP smear and learned it was a cancer test, I cried. After divorcing my father, she pursued a different life, one that didn't always include kids. At times, she seemed angry—expressed her karmic curse through clenched teeth, "I hope you have a daughter just like you," her finger wagging close to my face. I never wanted to give her reason to leave. Or be disappointed in me. At fifteen, I asked her to arrange for me to talk to someone. She didn't ask why. The following week, I swallowed some pills. Within seconds I called my neighbor, who drove me to the ER, then called my mom at work.

I was holding the throw-up bowl on my stomach when my mom entered the curtained exam room and asked, "Don't you love me?"

Hours later, standing by the curb just outside the hospital revolving doors, I told her to forget about my request for therapy.

She scowled. "Not after that stunt."

I shut down, resigned to bide my time until I could leave for college.

It wasn't until years later that I would understand the weight she carried as a single mother, longing for a life of her own.

I'm sitting on the edge of the sofa, staring at the patterned carpeting below my feet. I play with my hands, twisting my fingers together like bread ties. My mom adores my husband; I'm fearful of her reaction. I imagine her thundering, "How could you fuck this up?"

I'm undecided how much to tell her, so I start with the separation.

"I knew it!" she says, admitting she'd told one of her friends of her suspicions. "I just knew it. I could tell." Her vigorous response doesn't surprise me—she's competitive.

Softening her tone, she says, "Life is too short to be unhappy," but my relief is short-lived.

I don't know how to proceed.

She gets up from the couch and stands by the tile counter

in the micro kitchen, about ten feet away. I'm still fidgeting, looking down at my lap. She doesn't ask any questions. My mom is write-your-*New-York-Times*-Sunday-crossword-answers-in-ink smart, but asking questions isn't her style. My thoughts spool. Do I leave without telling her the rest? Do I want to go through this again? I'm motionless on the couch, my questions running loops in my brain. I want to tell her, but I don't know how. I push my feet deep into the carpet, anchoring myself as if afraid of falling, even though I'm sitting.

Without any queries from my mom to guide me, I steer the conversation with vague comments that finally prompt her to say, "Well, unless you're telling me you don't like men anymore."

Seizing my chance, I rush to confirm this statement—and she's quick to say it's okay.

"It is what it is," she says simply.

It almost feels too easy, but a weight's been lifted. Exhaling, I check the imaginary box next to "survive the third most difficult conversation of my life."

My mom offers to listen if I ever want to talk and, like my daughter, asks about telling people. I give her the same response I gave my daughter, with one addition: "I only ask you to consider why it's necessary to make this announcement." I remind her that even a short conversation, especially with family members, might invite unsolicited calls, and explain, "I'm still finding a place to land, wrestling with unanswered questions. I'm not ready to entertain curiosity or comments from anyone." The words stick in my throat as I speak.

"I understand," she says, and promises to respect my wishes. I wonder if she can tell how much I'm struggling.

She asks if we can run errands. Feeling lighter than when I arrived, I resort to cheesy humor to normalize the situation. "Go straight," she directs in the car, to which I respond, "I can't, Mom, I tried." She laughs.

At the phone store she selects a new case, a purple one. I smile and say, "Purple is very gay friendly." To which she responds, "So am I."

After the errands, I bring Mom home and thank her. I'm filled with gratitude for how she's shown up for me. I don't go back in the house. Like a medical resident who's eighteen hours into a twenty-four-hour shift—already depleted—I'm anxious about what's still to come.

It's not lost on me that on this exact day one year ago, Raia kissed me for the first time.

Once home, the kids are outside playing. I shift gears to finish the Memorandum of Understanding (MOU), one of the options recommended by the attorney I met in the city, which is designed to protect *both* our interests—mine and my husband's.

He's offered to sign the deed over to me in exchange for not seeking his annuity, and I've waived my legal claim to alimony in exchange for child support. Other than the annuity and the house, we don't have savings or assets to speak of. Our sole financial focus has been on the kids. Any discussions about the future have always pertained to them; they've never been about us as a couple post college-age. We set up special savings accounts and term life insurance policies—due to expire once the kids graduate from college—but have never discussed retirement. I haven't worked a full-time job since we were newly married. I have a scant few thousand dollars in my individual retirement account from my brief stint as a social worker. That program was cut from the New York City budget in 1995, leaving me unemployed and ultimately sending me back to school in search of a career with a more secure future. My children arrived soon after I started that career. I've always worked per diem around their schedules. Without benefits or a retirement plan, I'm faced with an uncertain future—the house is my only asset.

My husband and I have a clear division of logistical matters. I pay the monthly bills, and he manages the health insurance and the mortgage. I feel like a grade-schooler in college whenever I sit across from the banker refinancing the house in my name. I've never owned my own place. I've spent my adult years living with my husband, and he's always managed this charge. My folks loaned us money to buy our house. The property taxes are high. My new responsibilities taunt me like a schoolyard bully.

One hour ago, I was running errands with my mom. Now I'm standing in what was once our shared bedroom when my husband says, "You'll need health insurance."

I feel foolish about this oversight. I went from my parents' health insurance policy to his once we married. We agree that I'll stay on his policy for now, since we're in no rush to formally divorce. Obtaining my own insurance means increasing my work hours, and right now we both think the kids need consistency and stability more than ever—that kind of change could be too much.

It's a vital reprieve.

The MOU includes our verbal agreement to seek the amicable and cost-effective option of mediation when we ultimately divorce. Acquaintances I speak with tell me divorce is a nightmare. A woman from temple recommends avoiding lawyers and staying out of the court system. The numbers I hear for the average costs of traditional divorce shock me like a tree limb crashing through the roof of the house.

We review and notarize the final MOU. This step gives me hope for the future I've cultivated in my mind—one in which my husband and I amicably separate and coparent together seamlessly, and the kids grow up one day to say that the divorce barely impacted them.

 **Chapter Nine**

*"You may forget with whom you laughed, but you will
never forget with whom you wept."*
—KHALIL GIBRAN

I'm out of sorts, a stranger in my own life. My network
of friends and acquaintances within the community is
widening, yet I'm always deflated when I return home. Like
a spinning top, I need to keep moving. On my own, I remove
old carpeting, freshen up paint, and add curtains to windows
that previously had none, staying busy. I don't mind the kids
seeing me do chores once designated as "dad things."

It's mid-November when I reach out to a woman in the
Manhattan Coming Out Later-in-Life Meetup group who lives
in Connecticut with her husband and two young children and
can't attend the Manhattan events. We exchange messages,
sharing our stories, and she mentions a support group for late
bloomers near her that's being rebooted after a hiatus.

Mere days after coming out to my mom, I drive an hour
and a half to an LGBTQ center in Connecticut. It's the first
meeting of this revived group, and eight women, all mothers,
sit around a conference table in a jammed room that might
have once been a storage closet.

The prevalence of women who rejected their inner knowing
early on is stunning. One attendee recounts being nauseous
walking down the aisle at her wedding at the thought of denying

her truth. Others suppressed resurging feelings of their same-sex attraction by becoming immersed in school or home projects or having more babies—something tangible to tether them to the security of a heteronormative life. One woman admits she couldn't have sex with her husband without drinking two or more glasses of wine. Others say they cried during sex. A woman talks about the premarital therapist who counseled her and her future husband to ignore her feelings that she was probably gay and proceed with their life as planned. Women relay their parents' rebukes, from "You made your bed, now lie in it" to "Suck it up, for the children's sake." One woman says her mother gave her a book by Dr. Laura, who advises that women should have sex with their husband even if they don't want to because it's their duty and because men need it more than women. Another group member details her husband's reaction to her news of being gay. He said he would fuck the gay out of her. Then raped her.

These women are warriors. There's an authenticity in them that I have never detected in my New Jersey community. I will come to count this group among my most treasured sources of support and encouragement as we travel the next two-plus years together.

Shortly after attending that meeting in Connecticut, one of the two women I've been having private conversations with from the Philadelphia-based support network—she lives in New York—asks to meet in person.

Hope is slightly older than me, a mom who is struggling with her same-sex attraction. We meet at the same Starbucks where I met Hannah several months earlier.

When I arrive, she's there—an attractive blonde reading a Kindle.

She talks about not wanting to hurt her husband—shares, with a distinct sadness in her voice, that he's her best friend.

She describes her morning ritual of kissing him goodbye while adjusting his jacket collar, and I realize I never had such sweet moments with my husband. She tells of incorporating her same-sex attraction into their relationship, an arrangement he was initially enthusiastic about.

Other women I've met have talked about this as well. One woman told me her husband first recognized her best friend's attraction to her. He paid for a hotel room and encouraged them to experiment. I've learned this isn't uncommon. She later divorced her husband to marry that friend.

Listening to Hope, along with the confessional stories I've heard these last few months, is like discovering a time capsule of lock-and-key diaries, each holding the secrets and anguish of women maintaining the status quo before taking the leap toward living an authentic life. I've entered an alternate universe that a year ago I didn't know existed.

In my short time identifying as a gay woman, I've met women who have resorted to self-medicating and excessive drinking to numb the pain of their discovery; others have contemplated or attempted suicide. I now understand that my story, my inability to recognize my same-sex attraction until I was knee-deep and blinded by a flashing sign, could have been far worse.

 **Chapter Ten**

"The world breaks everyone and afterward many are
strong at the broken places."
—Ernest Hemingway

December marks the beginning of the winter solstice, when
the sun is at its lowest and shadows are longest. I keep a
winter sun–low profile around my town. I haven't spoken to
or seen much of anyone since the bat mitzvah. Building a new
community and watching for signs of distress in my kids are
my priorities. My husband is still searching for a house, and
there are times when we look like the family we've always been.

I'm sitting on my bed when a text from Joan, a woman I've
known since our sons were in nursery school together, appears
on my phone—*We need to talk*—and I fear the worst. The boys
were frequent playmates when they were small, and she and I
occasionally socialized together. I worry about the questions
my children might encounter and whether they'll know how
to handle the inquiries people will make.

I respond vaguely, then she calls. I watch the phone ring a
couple times before I pick it up and say, "Hello."

"Linda called me," she blurts out.

It seems my son told Linda's son that my husband and I
were separated. But I haven't been outed—not yet, anyway.
I confirm the separation and stutter something about privacy
while we adjust.

Joan ends the call with, "When things like this happen, you'll know who your friends are."

I never hear from her again.

The holidays arrive, but I'm like a ghost swathed in chains. I limit my errands around town to the bare necessities, performing my chores in the most perfunctory manner possible, and I dare not dawdle in places like the supermarket. I often don a baseball cap to avoid being recognized and targeted for casual chit-chat.

Attending temple has become awkward since the rabbi's sermon about the three worst sins in Judaism: murder, idolatry, and sexual immoralities. According to Jewish law, transgression of these cardinal sins is punishable by death. The rabbi detailed how adultery, along with bestiality and incest, was on par with murder. She spent an exorbitant amount of time discussing the destruction of family. I shifted in my seat, looking around at the other congregants. Was she talking to me?

In the weeks prior to this sermon, we'd informed her about our separation but said nothing else. She'd approached each of us separately, asked if the other was having an affair. I had neither confirmed nor denied, because the answer wasn't a simple, black-and-white response, and I wasn't ready to come out to her.

Her sermon lumped complicated issues into simplistic categories, with no modern interpretation or compassion for extenuating circumstances. I chafed at her words.

I want to explain the unexplainable. Mostly, I want to be vindicated—not for having an affair but for following the breadcrumb trail I saw as imperative to pursue. I want my quest for self-discovery to have meaning. This can't all be for naught. I search for any explanation that might provide a foundation upon which to build my case for these circumstances, those derived from my innermost desire to find myself.

My stepfather turns to Eastern philosophy and nineteenth-century intellects for wisdom; it's those teachings to which I attribute his understanding when my mom told him about me. She'll tell me later, "He only wanted you to be happy." Following his lead, I look elsewhere to counter the harsh message our rabbi rained down in the sanctuary that day—that adultery is unforgivable, akin to bestiality and murder, responsible for the destruction of the family, deserving of death. *Does my sin really warrant death?*

While initially the sermon unnerved me, as time has gone on it has fortified my belief that self-actualization is worth fighting for. Recalling the conviction shared by my earliest supporters—that kids are resilient enough to survive upheaval—I want to believe that adversity can become a source of empowerment. I hold tight to the prophecy that my kids will survive and even thrive, and reject the notion I am destroying my family. I choose instead to honor the fact that I'm modeling authenticity.

My daughter and I stroll through the Metropolitan Museum of Art, walking through wide corridors and exotic rooms displayed with paintings, armor, sculptures—samples of ancient and contemporary art from every corner of the world. Arriving in the Asian collection, we pause by the showcased antique artifacts inlaid with gold. The repaired ceramics are Kintsugi, the ancient Japanese art founded upon the notion of embracing flaws and imperfections. When broken pieces of pottery are repaired using precious metal, it creates a strong and unique piece of pottery. Its scars become visible for all to see. Kintsugi exemplifies Wabi-Sabi—an aesthetic philosophy, rooted in Buddhist thought, that holds that beauty is found in imperfection, celebrating things as they are, not how they should be. This discovery becomes the thread of a new language about myself. Stitching together a patchwork of discussions with enlightened people and wisdom from ancient rabbis, philosophers, authors, and religions, I construct a quilt of compassion for my broken parts.

At temple, my discomfort is punctuated by a high-ranking leader who has stopped talking to me. She's friends with my husband and has hosted my family at her house for holidays, but now walks by me in the halls of the synagogue without acknowledgment, ignoring me when I say hello.

The final straw is when the temple custodian, upon learning my husband and I are separated, asks me out on a date.

I limit my presence at temple, but the upcoming planning for my son's bar mitzvah and my daughter's confirmation, a ceremony for older teens affirming their commitment to Judaism, makes it a short-lived reprieve.

 # Chapter Eleven

"You'll never know who you are unless you shed who you pretend to be."
—Vironika Tugaleva

January is thought to be named after Janus, the Roman god of beginnings, endings, doorways, and transitions. Janus is depicted with two faces—one representing the past, one the future—and carrying a key for the metaphorical doors holding endless possibilities.

January is also my birth month. I'm now forty-five years old. I miss Raia and whatever she represented for me. My thoughts perseverate on *this time last year*. I thought the worst was over, but these feelings of missing her just ambushed me.

I no longer receive daily emails from Shira. I'm as frightened as a child separated from the protection of a parent's hand in the big city. I'm alone—questioning myself, questioning everything. I've been hiding behind my husband for years. He managed the mechanics of the house and cars; I wrote the checks. His reputation as a nice guy meant I could ride his coattails. People often reached out to me to tell me how nice he was or describe favors he had done for them. My dormant demons of low self-confidence wake up, ready to rumble. With nothing to hold on to, I'm drifting farther away from anything familiar. Out of fresh ideas, all I can do is write about my terror.

Hope's husband doesn't like that she and I spend time together. He's questioned if we're dating or if I'm encouraging her to pursue this life. Scenarios of him finding me and hurting me cross my mind. I can't explain to Hope that I'm fearful of him, so I retreat without offering an explanation.

My husband is dating. I don't want to be his wife, but I'm not ready to picture him with someone else.

He's standing by the sliding glass doors, having just hung new curtains in the family room, when he says, "I don't know who would want to be with me; I'm a façade, there's nothing inside me. I'm empty, I've always been empty."

"I'll gladly write a letter of reference for how great you are," I say, sitting on the old couch a few feet away. "Women will write me thank-you notes one day."

Suddenly he starts describing some hot bartender in Manhattan. As if I'm one of the guys from work. "Really I just want to get laid again," he says bluntly.

The last of the daylight dwindling through the glass door behind him, he puts his hands in his pants pockets and confides that he didn't know how to respond when a woman blatantly asked what was wrong with him—questioning his role in our separation, looking for flaws and faults. He shared that she wasn't the only one.

"Without my telling them about you, they don't understand why we're separated."

"Do what you have to," I say, my body tense. "I only ask that you tell my truth as a last resort for now, especially if you date anyone from around here."

A few nights later, he comes into my bedroom and says, "I don't know why I'm not fighting for you, for us."

A five-alarm siren rings in my head. I'm standing on another bridge—frightened about the unknown of my future life, yes, but more terrified of returning to the old one. I've heard about women who don't make it. Women who go back to their husbands and former lives, attempting to live as though they don't know their truth.

I can't let that be my story.

Six weeks later, in mid-March, my husband announces he's riding down to Florida to attend Daytona Bike Week. He only recently bought a motorcycle. Disturbing images of a paralyzing accident—and me, in turn, feeling obligated to be his caregiver for the remainder of our lives—repeats like a long bout of hiccups. I confide in Tess, another close confidant from the Philly support group.

"Make the week look like freedom," Tess reassures me. "As far as your fear about having to take care of 'him, the invalid'— of course you have that fear! Just as an escaped prisoner fears being recaptured. I won't let it happen. I will coach you through hiring a great aide. You have too much living to do!"

Dress-rehearsing tragedy is explained by Brené Brown as a fear of joy. To me, it feels like never having the opportunity to achieve joy. My concerns about staying legally married take on another dimension. The thread to the authentic life I envision—one filled with love, passion, and the companionship of a woman—is gossamer. It doesn't take much to imagine its delicate strands breaking.

Soon after my husband leaves for Florida, Tess's daily texts stop. One week later she discloses that she's been hospitalized after suffering a brain aneurysm. She's already had two surgeries. If her condition declines, I'll never know. Tess lives nine hundred miles away, and I don't know anyone in her immediate circle—none of them even know I exist.

Just as I wanted to take care of Raia when she was sick or hurt, I wish I were closer to help Tess. I call the hospital every few days to ask if she's still a patient there. I miss my friend.

I'm walking the city streets of Philadelphia amid the pink blooms of the cherry blossom trees of early spring, heading to a workshop hosted by the woman who started the online support group. Tess remains hospitalized, preventing her from attending as originally planned. We still haven't even met in person. Hope, however, is here—along with a roomful of other women of all ages who've traversed the country to attend—and we renew our friendship.

The couple dozen women seated in chairs arranged in circular fashion on the second floor of the brick Planned Parenthood building share their stories. Fighting back tears and with a brittle voice, a woman with long, dark hair speaks of her bad-tempered, alcoholic husband. She discloses that she had to fabricate a story to be here; she flinches when she imagines what would happen if he found out. Women describe condemnation from their parents. Some worry about losing their jobs if anyone found out; others fear losing their children. A pregnant woman shares that she's never acted on her same-sex attraction, but even without ever having so much as kissed another woman, she knows she's gay. She's married to a man and has a two-year-old son.

In a break-out group, one exercise is to write a letter to our future selves. My letter foretells becoming a single mom. I don't know if the worry has roots in seeing my mom morph into a single mother; watching her secretly accept money from my grandfather, sowing the seeds of financial insecurity in me; or the uncertainty of my husband's commitment after he left when I was pregnant with our son. Whatever its cause, this fear nags at me.

In the Philly gayborhood, some of the women and I walk the tree-lined avenues and alleys abutted by historic brick build-ings, reveling in the rainbow street signs, visiting Giovanni's Room (the country's oldest LGBTQ bookstore), and partaking in the nightlife. Although most of us have only just met, there's an instant connection, an understanding. Later, alone in my boutique hotel room, I reminisce over those times I spent in this town, for school and work conferences, immersing myself in the *The L Word* night after night.

The heartfelt emotions of these women, along with the empty chair intended for Tess, are stark reminders that this journey is not linear; a surfer's balance is required to ride these waves. But these women are also a bucket brigade of support, and we vow to stay in touch before parting ways.

I return home reinvigorated.

It's May when I drive to Provincetown—often dubbed "the ultimate gay destination"—again. Its reputation as a year-round port-of-call is supported by the Provincetown Business Guild, which plans themed weeks to attract visitors. It's my intent to visit during each of the several weeks explicitly dedicated to gay women.

This time, less than a year after my inaugural trip, there are no life-changing questions to answer, just experiences to dive into. I'm traveling with a friend, Em—a late bloomer and mom to young children—and it's singles weekend, with events specifically designed for women to meet other women. Em meets someone at a dance club the very first night and doesn't come back to the B&B. I am both relieved to have the extra time alone and acutely aware of my loneliness, which tugs at me like a hungry toddler.

I'm standing barefoot on the wide-planked, eighteenth-century pine floor in my second-floor room, undecided about whether to wear my flip-flops, exposing my sorbet-painted toenails, or my black high-top Converse for tonight's outing when a few of my friends from home call.

"I'm so jealous you're there, I can't wait until I can go," says one.

I flop onto the four-poster bed and admire the antique fireplace—this B&B is a gorgeous old captain's colonial—as I answer her questions about what's happening around town when another friend chimes in, "Don't wear those tanks you like to wear."

Just like that, I'm a tween-aged girl in Manhattan with my older cousin and her fiancé, who looked at my Pro-Keds and demanded, "Why don't you wear more stylish shoes?" Young me routinely changed aspects of my wardrobe. I played with colors, absorbed the styles of other people, and sampled anything that might feel like the me I searched to find.

All my life I've been told how much I resemble my mom; now, I often hear how much my daughter favors me. My two female bookends, one born in 1944 and the other in 1999, are both beautiful. The younger version of my mom was often compared to Jacqueline Kennedy, circa 1960-something, and I notice how quickly men's heads turn when my daughter walks by, yet I've never seen this beauty in myself. In the quarter-century I spent as one man's girlfriend, then fiancé, then wife, I never felt beautiful. With Raia, though, I finally knew desire and feeling desired. There's a newfound confidence that's accompanied my same-sex attraction.

I push my old anxieties aside, rejecting any recurrence of self-consciousness.

I end the call and head out the door.

Commercial Street bustles with colorful pedestrians, drag queens, street performers, restaurant barkers touting menus, pedi-cabs, dogs on skateboards, and bicyclists. Gay women crowd the clubs. I'm dubious of dating but open to meeting women for company. The line between dating and friendship is easily muddled, however.

I'm at the Pied, the DJ's playlist has the dancefloor busy while other women stand on the perimeter watching. I meet another late bloomer, a self-proclaimed Gay Girls Dating Coach. Offering pointers, she motions to the bar. "Look at how two women stand together. If they're facing one another, they're likely a couple or trying to connect." It's hard to discern those who are just friends and important to steer clear of talking to a woman who's already taken. These nuances were never an issue in the limited time I dated before going out with my husband; I've never been in the position of having to pursue anyone before. Unsure of how to proceed, I make only platonic connections.

Being in Provincetown is like sliding into a warm bubble bath after a long day. Rainbow flags adorn the buildings and houses. The air feels different; breathing is easier. I feel as if I'm Dorothy from *The Wizard of Oz*, questioning, "What is home: A place? A feeling?" *Whatever it is*, I think, *this is it.*

I ride my bicycle to the beach, stroll the brick-lined sidewalk of Commercial Street, sit on a metal bench outside town hall, people watching for hours. It's in these moments that the pieces of me fall into place.

Em and I are making the six-hour drive home. She tells me about the woman she's now dating and their plans to see each other again. I share stories about the people I met in the club and on the bike trail. I added a few numbers to my contact list, but I'm without dating plans. A flicker of envy at Em's changed relationship status prickles at me.

Just one week later, I return to Provincetown. It's Memorial Day weekend. Raia always talked about coming here on this weekend. I feel like an interloper and imagine what her reaction would be if we crossed paths. That said, I'm determined to make this my space too.

It's rainy, so I set aside my thoughts of biking and beach-combing. In the woman-owned bed-and-breakfast that's run by a same-sex couple, one of whom is also a late bloomer, I'm lingering over a croissant and chatting with two women from the Midwest who are visiting for the first time. One is a late bloomer with kids similar in age to mine. We exchange stories, and the connection is instant. They invite me to join them as they explore the town.

At the weekend's end, as I'm driving home and replaying the events of the last couple of days in my mind, I feel thankful that I never encountered Raia. I'm making friends—forging a place for myself in this town, in the gay community. I worried seeing her would be an emotional backslide, would taint the headway I'm making. Spending time with the couple I met has roused my imagination about what it would be like to be in a committed relationship with a woman.

My self-discovery has saddled me with a label I don't like—newbie. It means some women will see me as taboo; they won't trust that this isn't a phase. As a late bloomer, I can't share tales of being young and gay like those Raia shared with me. My solution is to collect as many stories as I can as fast as I can. I have a premonition that my freedom to do so will be short-lived.

Pride falls in June, to commemorate the Stonewall uprising. The New York City Pride Parade is on the last Sunday of the month, an event that draws millions of people. Now I'm one of them, here in Manhattan attending America's biggest Pride celebration, which happens to be practically in my backyard. The women from the Connecticut group meet me here and we share in this rite of passage, a first for all of us.

I stand wide-eyed and still, like a wooden carved bear, on the packed pavement near The Stonewall Inn, the historic site of the 1969 riots that launched the gay rights movement. The crowd on the sidewalk behind the police barriers is five people deep. Rainbow flags and balloon arches fill the airspace. Float after colorful float rolls by as people in every imaginable costume, from feathers to leather, dance their way down the black asphalt to music piping out from elaborate moving platforms. I see onlookers shedding tears and imagine that they are for the strides toward equality already made, with hope of more to come.

My tears are different. I've attended other marches for worthy causes, but this feels personal. I may be a newbie, but I belong here. I've found my community.

 **Chapter Twelve**

"Sometimes your only available transportation is a leap of faith."
—MARGARET SHEPARD

July—I'm fatigued by my friend's insistence that I "get over" Raia. One friend suggests a one-night stand, but I'm not interested. I wade into online dating.

Navigating through a web of profiles for a possible online conversation to determine the likelihood of advancing to the next level feels like playing an old arcade game. For privacy, I don't post any photos—quickly discovering that there's universal discomfort in taking a chance on someone sight unseen. When I post a picture, there's a noticeable change in responses.

The messages come from a mix of types, from earnest women wanting to meet The One to others only wanting sex to a few looking for a third to have sex with them and their boyfriend.

My short list of one-and-done dates include a British DJ on the rebound, and a healthcare worker who shows up for dinner having already downed an entire bottle of wine and spends the whole time telling tales of drunken escapades. Red flags everywhere. One woman, a math teacher who seems promising, meets me for dinner but has no further interest because of my newbie status. Another woman proclaims that as Jews, we're tied to our lineage of kings, and it's destiny that we met. From across the scrubby table, hands under her chin, she looks adoringly at me with wide eyes and a Cheshire-cat grin that makes me squirm uncomfortably in my chair.

Finally, I match with an attorney who sends seductive texts daily, declaring time is running out to meet her unshakable goal of being in a relationship by her fortieth birthday.

She's intense, and I'm intimidated. But after a few weeks of fervid emails, we agree to meet at a Barnes & Noble.

She arrives bearing a package of my favorite cookie, Oreo. *Well played.* We sit in the café and talk for a while, but as if there's a sudden change in the weather, I lose interest. She isn't Raia, there's no comfort, no connection. I tell her I need to get home. She accompanies me to my car, wanting to continue the conversation. She sidles into the passenger seat and tries kissing me.

I pull back. "I'm still getting over my catalyst," I stammer. I never hear from her again.

It's August. Another camp season is behind us. The kids and I are in gay- and family-friendly Rehoboth Beach, Delaware; I'm determined to create a new annual tradition of spending time alone with my kids in a destination spot we can all enjoy. We're at an LGBTQ-popular beach together for the first time, surrounded by same-sex couples. I don't know when I'll be ready, or when they'll be ready, to see me with a partner other than their dad—as a child of divorce, I know how awkward this is, and I want to be sensitive to my kids' new paradigm— but I at least want them to witness other same-sex families.

We set up our beach camp next to two women around my age and their one-year-old son. They share their story, as well as the challenges of being older first-time parents. Having left to explore the beach, my son comes running back to the blanket, announces he's going boogie boarding with Brenda, and, just like that, is off like a shot.

"Who's Brenda?" I say out loud to myself, already getting up to investigate.

I catch up with Brenda and my son and introduce myself. After reassuring myself that this forty-something woman is okay hanging out with my eleven-year-old son, that he's safe with her, I remind him to stay where I can see him and retreat back to our blanket.

Great, it figures my son would meet a woman before I do, I think, and laugh out loud at the irony. But mostly I'm just relieved he's comfortable in this environment.

A week after we return home from Delaware, Lori, the woman who ran the Manhattan Coming Out Later-in-Life Meetup group before Hallie took over, posts an online invitation: "It seems this group has not been active for a while. Let's meet at The Park for dinner." A week later, several of us are seated around a banquette in the rear section of a spacious two-story restaurant in Chelsea.

The first half-hour is awkward. We exchange names and occupations. One woman declines to share any information about herself, including her real name. The remaining guests represent a smattering of health professions—there's a psychologist, a physical therapist, a speech-language pathologist, a pharmacist, and so on. They're all educated, professional women ranging in age from their midforties to late fifties.

Between the large potted trees of the converted brick-floor taxi garage, I watch a tall, dark-haired woman with a Mediterranean complexion stride confidently toward our table. It's like a movie scene that suddenly shifts into slow motion. I can't take my eyes off her. She seems familiar, but as she approaches, I realize we've never met.

She slides onto the bench and introduces herself as Vivian. She catches up with the conversation effortlessly. Although there are two women seated between us, I spend the rest of the night trying to talk to her.

The group heads to a coffee shop after dinner. Along the way, Vivian and I walk together, and it feels as if we're the only ones there. Then she peels off and starts chatting with another woman. I'm a bit deflated. By the end of the night, however, she's back strolling alongside me and we're sharing pieces of our story again. She lives in New Jersey, about twenty minutes from my house.

Meeting a woman who lives so close to home feels like karma.

"If you ever want to get together for a drink," I say, offering my phone number. I hardly recognize myself as I make the bold move.

Three weeks later, Vivian texts, "Are you still interested in getting a drink?"

A pinball-like whoosh shoots through me.

It's late September. Vivian has just returned from an international business trip. We meet outside both of our immediate neighborhoods at a restaurant unfamiliar to us both. I'm unsure what to think of this meeting. Is it a date? Is it getting together to talk?

Vivian is a late bloomer of a different kind. She never married and doesn't have children. Raised Orthodox, she has endured a lifetime of messages from her church about the deviant nature of homosexuality. Her family reinforced the notion. She speaks of congregants she assumed to be gay disappearing from the church—one of the priests too. Vivian has spent the last decade suppressing her own truth.

She realized her true sexuality while living abroad for a year. When she returned home, however, she felt she couldn't risk the consequences of bucking the system. During that time, her dad had fallen ill and subsequently passed. He had been her rock, and his loss had left a void in her. Shortly after losing her dad, she underwent treatment—first for breast cancer, and soon after that skin cancer as well. Grief unraveled her. Feelings surfaced that she couldn't contain.

I'm not convinced that our drink date is an authentic date, but I will learn a few weeks from now that Vivian used this evening as an entry point into a seminal moment: coming out to her mother.

The day after our dinner, she drove her mother home from an appointment.

"I had a date last night," she shared as she drove.

Her mother responded with a delighted smile.

"Her name is Melissa."

Her mother's smile disappeared—and, after a pause, she asked, "Is that why you stopped dating men?"

"Yes," Vivian confirmed.

The conversation ended there, but the next day, her mother began a tirade of cruelty that would continue for years: "It would have been better to stab me," she would say. "I didn't want a lesbian for a daughter."

I remember Cantor M saying that coming out is a lifelong process. My comfort within the gay community will increase over time, but it won't be seamless. There'll be situations when I'll opt not to volunteer anything about my sexual orientation, despite openings to do so.

At work, I dread the Monday morning "how was your weekend?" exchange and limit my stories to those about the kids. Despite not feeling connected to the expression "coming out of the closet," my truth has pushed me deep into that proverbial dark space, worrying about fallout at my job. The identity I now claim remains divisive for some, is considered perverse by a few, and could put my personal well-being in danger.

I've become apprehensive asking male clients to bend their wrist for range-of-motion measurements, after several instances of them changing their voice to a high-pitched tone and mocking effeminate or gay men.

Not calling them out on this behavior is distressing. Am I becoming less authentic in my attempt to live more authentically? Now that I'm standing on the other side of the divide, I recognize heterosexuality as the default orientation it is. Assuming I share their views, people make comments or gestures without considering that I, or someone close to me, might be gay—that what they're doing or saying might be offensive. Managing my two worlds is a slippery slope.

 **Chapter Thirteen**

"Forever is composed of nows."
—EMILY DICKINSON

October: one year since my daughter's bat mitzvah and a couple of weeks since the drink date with Vivian. My husband and kids are visiting Grace. I'm at the movies in Montclair, a quaint LGBTQ-friendly town about thirty minutes from my house, with my Meetup friends. The film, *Concussion*, is about a gay woman in a passionless relationship who, after suffering a concussion, begins living a double life in which she has sexual encounters with other women that lead to greater self-awareness.

Vivian declined my invitation to join us for the movie, fearful of running into members of her church at the theater, but agreed to meet us afterward.

It's Friday night and there are seven of us at a long rectangular table in a popular restaurant. Vivian is sitting at the head of the table, I'm on her right. The woman sitting to her left is flirting with her. Attractive, sophisticated, well-traveled, and interesting, Vivian is bookended by two women who are focused solely on her.

After dinner, Vivian is already in her car and I'm about to say goodbye when she asks, "Would you like to come over for a little while?"

"Are you sure?" I ask. "It's getting late."

"I wouldn't have spent the day cleaning my house if I wasn't sure," she practically barks. Her fiery response gets my attention.

"I'd love to," I say, smiling.

Vivian lives in a second-floor condominium with a steep flight of stairs from the building's entrance to her unit's front door. Inside, I sit on the sage green couch, while she chooses the Dijon mustard–colored chair nearby. She's wrapped in a multi-shaded brown blanket, like a burrito. We talk about the movie (she watched it on her laptop before meeting us at the restaurant), her family, and sand dollars.

"I used to walk the OBX beach searching for them," I say, pointing out the sand-dollar charm on my silver necklace, but keeping my surprise at seeing a framed picture, along with a collection of the flattened invertebrates in her bathroom, to myself. If I were one to believe in signs (I'm not), I would have taken this as one. Sign or not, though, something about finding those sandy treasures, talisman for transformations, in her home intrigues me.

The conversation slows down. "I should go," I say, already heading toward the stairs.

She doesn't stop me.

I drive the twenty minutes back to my empty house. I didn't have any expectations, yet I feel disappointed. Once in my bedroom, I notice a text from Vivian: *Why did you run away?*

It's late, I write back, *I didn't want to make you uncomfortable.*

You weren't. Do you want to come back?

It's two in the morning, but I do want to go back. I didn't want to leave in the first place.

When I arrive, we talk a little more about family, until she announces, "I'm tired and going to bed." Standing up from the chair, she adds, "You're welcome to join me."

I nod and follow her to the bedroom.

"Do you want to borrow a pair of pajamas?"

The thought of changing in front of her, let alone wearing pajamas that aren't mine, doesn't sit well. I politely say no and slip into her bed still wearing my jeans and peace sign belt buckle. I position myself right at the edge.

Vivian hasn't been with anyone since living overseas ten years ago, and it's been well over a year since I've been with Raia. I welcome the fact that she doesn't have a closet full of ex-girlfriends and find comfort in knowing we're in similar places when it comes to relationships with women.

After a few minutes of lying in the dark, I break the silence. "Tell me what you want."

She hesitates before softly replying, "I'd like you to come closer."

I move nearer, and we hold hands. The softness of her hand in mine sends shivers through me. I reach for her leg, unsure how she'll react. She doesn't object. I sweep my hand along the length of her long legs as if smoothing the top layer of sand at the beach, grain by grain. I'm hypnotized.

She asks me to kiss her, but I admit that this feels too intimate.

"I understand," she says.

My belt buckle is pressing into her, so I toss the belt on the floor. Soon, we shed other pieces of clothing. We take turns exploring one another until, the morning light already peeking from behind the drapes, we fall asleep in each other's arms.

By the time we awake, the awkward moments have given way to weightlessness. Vivian makes us breakfast, and I join her at the dining room table. I think I could stay in this place forever.

One week later, I'm in Provincetown for Women's Week, the last of this season's themed weeks for women. I feel like a kid on a snow day. I pull into the gravel parking lot of the cottage park where I have a reservation.

Immediately, I'm drawn into a conversation with two women from Pennsylvania: Michele, a tattooed thirty-something with cropped hair, and her wife, Johann. I will soon learn that Michele is a published author, successful artist, and highly regarded expert in the medical sterile processing field and was diagnosed with end-stage ALS four years ago. Doctors predicted that she had five more years to live then. She's on oxygen now, and it's clearly a struggle for her to speak, but this doesn't stop her from engaging in conversation. Johann (a late bloomer like me; I'm quickly seeing that we are not anomalies) unpacks the car and joins in our chat periodically.

We say goodbye for now and depart to our respective cabins, where I ready my bicycle for the first ride of the weekend. Riding my bicycle in this town feels like food for my soul, a soul that has been starving for too long. Pedaling through the streets and navigating the nearby trails gives me the freedom I've been longing for. It's meditative, exhilarating, and gives me permission to release the restraints I only recently recognized were cleaved to me. Aided by the salt-drenched air, I shed a layer of skin with each visit here.

My friends from the Connecticut group are here this weekend, as are Hope and her girlfriend and the women I met here a few months ago. Seeing people I know in the clubs and on the street, breathing in the air of acceptance that's ingrained within this community, wraps me in a feeling of belonging that's eluded me all my life. I no longer feel like a stranger in this town or in my body.

Beautiful weather, dinner with friends, dancing, and bicycling make it hard to pack up and leave, if not for the distracting thoughts I have of Vivian. We had an hours-long phone conversation my first night here, well into the wee hours of the morning. We've seen each other one more time since the night I spent at her place a week ago, and though we only recently met, I can't stop thinking about her.

Vivian calls me as I'm driving home from Provincetown and invites me for dinner. I accept but struggle between indulging myself longer in this new life versus returning directly home to my old one. I feel guilty about being away from my kids. Reentry into reality after spending time in the gay community is like being smothered by a fire blanket.

Not at all prepared to merge my two worlds, I think about how I will walk the line between them—a line that feels like a tightrope with no safety net beneath it to catch my fall.

 **Chapter Fourteen**

"Take your broken heart, make it into art."
—CARRIE FISHER

I'm sitting on my bed, watching my husband empty his closet. The black funeral suit; the sports jacket and dress slacks he wears to temple. Short- and long-sleeve shirts; several ties, most of which I've bought for him over the years. When he's done, all that will remain is the shoebox full of birthday and anniversary cards I've given to him throughout our time together. Later, I'll see these clothes in the pages of our family scrapbooks and be reminded of what was and what would never be: that life I imagined for my kids, so vastly different from my own childhood. While my children will indeed live a life remarkably different from mine, and already have, their parents separating because one of them is gay is so far removed from what I envisioned that it still feels like a dream I'm due to wake up from at any moment.

A mound of my husband's clothing, with all the attached memories, is heaped at the foot of the bed. Soon the pile will be scooped up, heaved into the backseat of his car, and transported to his new house. My mind is running like a computer with too many open tabs, ranging from sadness and disbelief to the occasional thought of how to utilize the extra closet space he's just freed up.

He's closed on his new home and intends to sleep there starting tonight. I didn't expect him to physically move out of our house so soon. I imagined a more gradual process. Sitting on what was his side of the bed, I remember being twenty-six and moving into this house. I painted inside the closet—the only walls he'd let me paint. He customized the hanging bars for his wardrobe, built cubbies for shoes.

Watching him remove his clothes, I ask why he's doing it now, this afternoon.

"I don't want to do it in front of the kids," he explains.

They're not due home from school for a few hours.

What about in front of me?

Over these past eleven months, I've asked my husband to complete unfinished projects around the house. Concerned that once he moves out he won't make himself available to do them and knowing years from now I'll sell the house but need these tasks completed, I've tried to balance nudging him to get them done without antagonizing him.

This isn't my forever home. I fantasize about living in a community in which I could figuratively and literally hang a rainbow flag without being in the minority. Last June, before the NY Pride parade, I attended a Pride celebration in Asbury Park, an LGBTQ-friendly beach town in southern New Jersey where rainbow flags hang from the porches of updated Cape-style and Victorian houses. My dream is to exist in such an unprejudiced neighborhood. But who knows when something like that will be possible.

My husband's ability to accomplish any number of tasks, from pitching a tent to fixing anything that breaks, has always impressed me. Now I feel the impact of having lived in his shadow, depending on him. Envisioning being responsible for everything in the house, I've been short-tempered with the kids, and with him, lately. On the same day, the sliding garbage can track collapsed and it took me three tries to hang new pictures in my bedroom—and even then, they were still crooked. How am I supposed to hold this house together when I barely know a flathead from a Phillips-head screwdriver? I attempted to repair the kitchen garbage can and the kids said, "Wait until Dad comes home, he'll fix it." But I knew one day he wouldn't be coming home, and I didn't want my kids to see me failing.

To that end, I've spent these months of our in-home separation learning to perform the outside chores that have always been his responsibility. The first time I cut the grass, I wore work boots and a Mona Lisa smile. I was channeling Raia, who was as handy with a bag of tools as my husband. I planted my first tree (I look forward to watching it grow taller over the years, symbolic of my own growth). My friends inspired me to start a landscaping project. With every push of the shovel into the grass, I've edged closer to solidifying my place as head of the household, strong and confident. On my hands and knees, I've dug deep holes and excavated buried rocks—cool dirt staining my skin, sweat trickling into my eyes. I've planted carefully selected flowers and stood on my lawn each night watering the new garden, feeling every bit as if I gave birth to it myself. This nine-by-twenty plot of land is all mine, made by my own hands; it's visible proof that I'm capable.

We've had an eleven-month in-home separation, but still, this—him packing his clothes, him actually *leaving*—feels abrupt. I'm stiff as the starched collars of the button-downs at my feet, watching the repercussion of my discovery. My husband is moving out. My husband, with whom I've lived for over twenty years.

Can I make it on my own? No matter the degrees I've earned, exams I've taken, or difficult moments I've overcome, each hurdle of this journey tests my resolve like it's the first time. I have never been completely on my own. The intimidating responsibility I'm about to inherit—maintaining the house, being the kids' primary parent—and the sight of him removing his belongings jolts me like a live wire. For years, the nightly ritual was asking him, "Did you lock up?" It wasn't good night, or I love you, but *Am I safe?* I often envisioned an intruder coming into the house, and when I did, I felt secure in the knowledge that my husband would protect me.

Thinking of this, a reality unlike any other I've encountered throughout this sojourn emerges: *I'll have to protect myself from now on.*

How many more realities will I have to face before any of this feels real?

I can navigate my way around my house in complete darkness, I know it so well. My husband moving out is making me feel like the walls and stairs have been moved; I'm walking blindly through a space that was once so familiar. I clog my supporters' inboxes, pleading for help. I'm locked inside myself with feelings I don't understand, struck by the irony that he has his own place, with the freedom to come and go, when it was me who longed for that, not him. I worked so hard to reach this point of knowing within myself, and now that I'm here I'm entering a different unknown, as though I've mastered the new configuration of my rearranged house only to have the walls moved yet again. I'm told to let the process unfold one day at a time. I do my best—but still, this vertiginous feeling hurls me to the floor.

One of the persistent projects my husband left undone is gutter installation. He completed countless other projects, but the gutters remain untouched, despite my frequent requests. These types of advanced home improvement endeavors defined his wheelhouse; I know nothing about them.

After hearing me mention this particular problem one too many times, a friend said sharply, "He hasn't done it for nineteen years, Melissa, what makes you think he's going to do it now?" The gutters had become a thorn in my side, especially due to his procrastination. Per her suggestion, I got three bids, then handed them over to my husband, saying, "I need this done by August."

"I don't know what your rush is," he grumped. He finally hired a contractor to get the job done over the summer.

By then, I'd detected a pattern to his behavior, recalling his tendency to agree to do things and then not do them. He'd never denied his penchant for procrastination. It drove me crazy, but I was determined to keep the peace. I didn't want to need him, but I did; there was so much I didn't know.

As August wound to a close, we found ourselves together in the basement—a damp room that, if chocolate, would be considered bite-size, but is also the nerve center of my house. The electrical box, furnace, water heater, main water line, and laundry appliances are located there, along with two sump pumps to prevent flooding.

Over the hum of the dehumidifier, I admitted to him that I was scared. He rebuilt this house; he knew it inside out. I barely understood how it all worked.

"What if something happens that I can't fix?" I asked, heart in my throat.

"Call me," he said. "I'll be here."

I had no reason not to believe him. We still care for one another, and our children live in this house. Why wouldn't he do everything to ensure our safety and take care of simple fixes?

In these first couple of weeks after he moves out, he comes back every day. We have no formal schedule; he's welcome to spend as much time here as he wants. But I hadn't thought about what being separated would mean. I deemed his moving out a formality, not envisioning other changes between us or with the kids—grateful for how we've managed our in-home separation.

But we're about to enter a new phase.

I enter the garage from the house and see my son alone in the driveway a couple weeks after his dad's move.

"What are you up to?" I ask him.

"Dad's coming over to play catch," he says.

My son watches cars navigate up the street, disappointed every time they turn out not to be his dad.

I call my husband and ask his ETA.

"I'm not coming," he says.

I tell him our son has been waiting for him.

"What the fuck, Melissa?" he explodes. "When do I get to do things around here?"

I don't know what to say. I only know that our son has been waiting to play catch with his dad.

He shows up a half-hour later to toss a ball around on the front lawn. He's unapologetic and angry.

November arrives with the familiarity of a birthday. It's been a year since I came out to the kids. Obstacles include my daughter having occasional teenage meltdowns and my son slacking off with his schoolwork. He's failing one of his classes for the first time.

I seek outside help, as is my tendency when confronting challenges. After asking Lynn and Hannah for recommendations, I carefully vet therapists, assessing the candidates via email and through their websites to gauge their friendliness toward LGBTQ families. Between my own experience with subpar therapists and having heard disturbing stories about professionals' bias against divorce and same-sex relationships,

I'm aware there's a risk of doing more harm if we end up with the wrong person. The whole point is for the kids to have a supportive experience.

We still spend time together as a family, but my husband is dating someone—and I am seeing Vivian, though no one knows that.

A few weeks after his move, we're in Manhattan with the kids. In the city, my husband takes the lead since he knows his way around so well. We walk around midtown, take pictures, and have dinner at a restaurant he recommends. When the bill arrives, I don't know what to do. Am I supposed to offer money? What are the rules now that we're officially separated? It feels like nothing much has changed, yet somehow everything has changed.

We return to my house from the outing, and he proudly shares a message from his girlfriend: *You're a good dad.*

Watching him exchange text messages with another woman reminds me of what I'm giving up, even though I know there's no going back.

Having reached this one-year point, I decide to mark the moment by getting tattooed—a move often considered forbidden by Jews. The controversy originates from the belief that you can't be buried in a Jewish cemetery if you're tattooed, though this is not directly indicated in Jewish law. The aversion toward tattoos is also attributed to its connection with the Holocaust branding of concentration camp prisoners. My own family suffered losses during the Holocaust; I am no stranger to that pain. Still, my desire to symbolize my journey with a permanent token, visible only to me, is too strong to deny.

Sure as I am that I want this, I seek reassurance from Hope and Lynn that I've earned my stripes before taking the plunge. Funny how we can be so sure and so doubtful at the same time.

Feeling like a bear waking from hibernation and hungry for change, I contemplate what kind of tattoo would represent the last year. Parts of me have come alive in these twelve months, while others have died. I've been intimate with pain and fear but have also held on to hope. I've withdrawn from one community to find my place in another. Strangers have shown up for me.

My eyes are drawn to the kids' old board book: *Going on a Bear Hunt*, by Michael Rosen and Helen Oxenbury. Its theme is about overcoming challenges by going through them rather than going around them. The page about sloshing through the mud is especially poignant.

A computer search for symbols of courage produces pictures of lions. Lionesses' roles include mother, protector, and provider. They demonstrate strong maternal instincts, loyalty, and independence, and they work together communally. Tattoos of lionesses illustrate femininity, motherhood, and the courage it takes to be a woman. This resonates. The connection between lion prides and the adoption of the word "pride" by the LGBTQ movement rings of kismet as well.

Black Friday, exactly one year to the day since I came out to my kids, I'm at the tattoo parlor watching the ink form four muddy lion paw prints, representing my journey, being imprinted into my skin. Hannah once wrote to me in an email, "Walking in the mud leaves you muddy but it bears repeating that as long as you keep walking, ultimately you get to the other side." The first two paw prints are messy, dripping with mud, while the other two are lighter and cleaner, illustrating my steady departure from the mire. My tattoo reminds me of where I've been and the fact that I have the grit necessary to forge forward on my journey. It's symbolic, meaningful, and personal. I can't imagine when or how I'll tell my mom.

One more secret, but this one I wear with pride on my right hip.

By December, I've still not told anyone in my circle about Vivian. Shira has said more than once that it takes time to make this adjustment—emotionally, physically, and financially. "It takes about two years before things land when you divide one house into two; mostly the kids need to see that their parents are okay," she says. It can be detrimental for kids to see their parents in and out of relationships; I don't want to introduce the kids to a potential partner until I know she'll be around for the long haul.

I've spent nearly a quarter-century with one person. I need more time to adjust to my current circumstances and get to know myself more deeply—there's still so much to discover—and I worry that a serious relationship at this early stage might be an impediment to all that. Vivian and I see each other on an occasional weeknight for dinner, and on weekends when the kids are with their dad. I bring her lunch on days I leave work early. We haven't labeled our relationship, though neither of us is interested in seeing anyone else.

A later-in-life sexual awakening has been likened to having a second adolescence. With every new experience, you wonder how you lived without that thing in your life until now and are determined never to live without it again. I'm reminded of the day I found out I was pregnant with my daughter. Eve was having a bad day, so I purchased her favorite snacks when I bought the pregnancy test and brought everything to her house. I never liked peanut butter as a kid, so I don't know what possessed me to open the bag of peanut butter cups and try one—but when it melted in my mouth, I savored the texture and the sweetness, lingering in the moment.

Amazed, I asked Eve, "Does anyone else know about this?"

"No," she teased, "it'll be our secret."

Sex with Vivian is like biting into that first chocolate-covered peanut butter cup and wanting more.

One night, after being intimate, I hear Vivian whisper, "*Agapi mou.*" I file it away without asking her what it means. When I look it up later and see that it's Greek for "my love," I feel like a windsock on a gusty day. Not long after that night, these words come out of my mouth: "Please don't get attached to me. I'm new here and I don't know where I'm going yet." I don't know where this comes from. Vivian doesn't say anything, but a tear falls from her eye.

Another night, we're lying on top of the white quilt her grandmother hand knitted. Vivian kisses me. It's a kiss reminiscent of my first one with Raia—the one that opened hidden doorways I'd never known existed. Vivian's kisses are slow and tender; her long hair spills around my face. My sensations come alive, dancing and crackling like flames in a fireplace, but I'm statue-still, heeding the voice in my head that admonishes me, "Don't move, don't do anything that might change this."

Could I be falling for her? My confusion swells. I'm caught between my feelings for her and thinking that it's too soon. But for this brief instant, I take her in, attempting to eternalize the moment.

Despite my deepening feelings for Vivian, I maintain my privacy, even hiding the particulars of the relationship from Hope. She knows I'm dating someone, but not who it is— and she knows Vivian, being a member of the Coming Out Later-in-Life Meetup group that Hope and I now run. We've agreed on using a fake name when we discuss the woman I'm seeing: Gia.

The women from the Connecticut group are divided—half of us dating, the other half figuring things out. Although I'm dating Vivian, I still consider myself to be in the latter category, trying to decipher what it all means. Exposing our relationship will make it true, and right now nothing seems real; I'm in a parallel universe. I'm still adjusting to the fact that I'm gay, along with the upheaval that discovery has caused. My life feels like a game of Jenga: the whole structure could come crashing down at any moment, without warning.

Hope, Vivian (Gia), and I are standing outside the Manhattan venue of a holiday-time Meetup event Hope and I are hosting. There's been an unexpected glitch: the original venue is closed, and we'd had to switch gears quickly. We post a last-minute notice about the change of location, but turnout is low and the evening is harried, bristling with tension.

At the bar, Hope and I go to the restroom. I show her my tattoo. Hope compliments my ink, says she thinks it's sexy. When we return to the others, it's an effort not to out Vivian as Gia. I want to stand closer to her, to touch her.

She texts me, Meet me in the bathroom.

She and I retreat separately from our group, slip into a bathroom stall. The clandestine nature of our relationship, and this stolen moment, tantalizes me.

After a round of drinks at the old Irish bar we managed to find as a back-up venue, we're outside and it's cold. The air smells like snow. I cinch my jacket closed. Hope and I traveled into the city together, we're trying to remember where we parked the car. A woman is asking Vivian for a ride home, and another woman is asking about the next event. There are a lot of distractions. Vivian is wearing a knitted ear-warmer that's messing up her hair. Without thinking, I fix her mussed hair and ask, "Why are you wearing this silly thing, does it really keep you warm?"

Vivian retreats, revealing her annoyance at the intimate gesture and my question.

Hope comes to Vivian's defense—"Leave her alone!"

I didn't mean to cross a line. I know that Vivian is uncomfortable with public displays of affection. Members of her church frequent the city, so she worries not only about being seen but also about our personal safety. I need to think about things I never had to consider when I was with my husband;

I've lived for so long on the side of straight privilege, it's difficult to adjust.

I am struck in this moment, not for the first time, how different my life is now. Public outings with a partner will require more consideration, and much more caution. Since I'm Jewish, that is not an entirely foreign concept—I already have a somewhat guarded demeanor, a learned behavior from experiencing my share of Jewish jokes and comments over the years. But this is another level.

I remember a story I heard about a young woman who ignored a group of men catcalling her. One of the men took offense. If she couldn't accept a compliment, he told her, he'd see to it that she never received another one. He beat her, breaking numerous bones in her face.

Now I consider the triple offense, in some people's eyes, of being gay and female and Jewish. A trifecta. What reactions might I expect when I'm ready to hold hands with a woman as we walk down the street together?

The longer we stand outside the bar, the more introspective I become, immersed in my own thoughts. I contemplate how, despite frowning on labels, I seem to be collecting more of them. As a kid, I was labeled a tomboy. My father jokingly called me "son." Gender-based decisions were the norm, exemplified when my mom once said, "If you were a boy, you would have had a bar mitzvah." It didn't matter that my middle-school girl friends were having bat mitzvahs or that I wanted a Jewish education too. I was judged for my school and career choices, never asked about my feelings. Nothing seemed good enough, except getting married and having children. My adult labels have included *wife, mother, daughter, occupational therapist*—tags that identify me but have never truly encompassed me. It's like the person I am underneath those roles is invisible.

My conviction to no longer be defined by my roles or labels grows stronger. I'm adamant about being seen as a unique individual. If I followed a predetermined path and played the role of wife because it was expected, now I stand alongside other women on this cold December night who are extricating themselves from societal, familial, and cultural mandates. We are attempting to free ourselves to make personal choices based on who we see ourselves to be, not how others want us to be—that label trap that threatens the very essence of who we are.

Perhaps Vivian can shed the constraints of her church and family, Hope can extract herself from the demands of a controlling husband, and I can make choices reflective of my needs and longings rather than my assigned roles. My experience as a man's wife gives me a keener sense of the differences I'm stepping into. Existing on both sides of the heteronormative divide broadens my perspective, sparking an evolution in and around me.

I revisit the quandary of holding hands with a woman in public and being labeled, possibly put in harm's way. Whatever freedom I've gained with my new self-knowledge I've lost in comfort and security in expressing it. I've been detoured through an unexpected minefield.

The remaining women from the event leave, and I say goodbye to Vivian as though she were just another member of the group. I let go of my desire, my aching to be held, and walk with Hope to the car, bracing myself for the reentry back to reality. I wonder about a day when Vivian and I—or some other woman and I?—will walk off together holding hands with the same ease I once experienced with my husband.

Soon after, Vivian and I are back in Manhattan, frigid air smacking our faces, our winter coats, hats, and gloves insufficient against the wind. Trees wrapped in festive white lights line the streets; oversize silver snowflakes hang from lampposts. We're near Lincoln Center, a mere six miles from the West Village, yet it feels like we've entered another state.

Greenwich Village—birthplace of the fight for civil rights for the LGBTQ community—is a "come as you are" bohemian capital where rainbow flags fly year-round, not just in June. Upper Midtown, anchored by Lincoln Center and the Metropolitan Opera House, lacks the same air of acceptance.

We see *Blue is the Warmest Color*, a French romance about a teenage girl who falls for an older woman she meets in a lesbian bar. We hold hands under our coats in the Sixty-Third Street theater. As we walk around the area afterward, I feel people's eyes on us—and when I reach for her, Vivian is quick to shoo my hand away. She fears being seen, but she's also burdened by her shame and internalized homophobia.

It's been two months since Vivian met our group at the Montclair restaurant after seeing Concussion, and a couple from that evening is trying to set us up. Separately, they've invited us to a holiday-time dinner party at their house in New Jersey and suggested we come together. Vivian and I accept the invitation but commit to withholding the fact that we've been dating.

In the foyer of the beautifully decorated colonial-style house, we change our shoes for slippers, admire the sparkling Christmas tree alongside the staircase, and are introduced to the other guests. The dining room table is provisioned with sticky rice, assorted raw fish, nori, and cucumber slices. Our hosts teach everyone, step by step, how to make sushi rolls—and it's so much fun! Vivian drinks wine and laughs. I keep one eye on her, afraid she'll blow our cover if she becomes too disinhibited.

Since everyone else is coupled, Vivian and I become a team by default when someone suggests we play a game. The game involves answering personal questions—fantasies we harbor, who we want to be kissing on New Year's Eve. Some questions are provocative, others just amusing: Would you have a baby for your partner? If you had to wear only one item of clothing for your girlfriend, what would it be? Are you a thong or regular underwear kind of woman?

My cheeks blush, my nervous smile is affixed to my face as the others guess whose written answers belong to which team.

Driving home, we're confident we've gotten through without revealing that we're dating. Later, we'll learn we weren't as subtle as we thought: our friends will recall us smiling for "no reason" at the party, and the fact that at one point I intimately ran my hand across Vivian's stomach—something I didn't even realize I was doing, and from which she didn't pull away.

Vivian and I are driving to Pennsylvania, where we've been invited to a belated New Year's party. This will be our first overnight trip together, and our inaugural public showing. I told Michele and Johann about Vivian when we met in Provincetown in October, since they're outside my social circle and so geographically far away; here, we won't have to hide our relationship.

Arriving at the hotel, we pause in the lobby. Should we go to the front desk together? We wonder if it's safe. We check in but don't give any indication that we're a couple. It's like playing charades.

At the party we slip seamlessly into acting like two women who are allowed to touch in public without worrying about what anyone is thinking.

Michele and Johann's space is a refurbished brick building that was once a bowling alley. The hardwood floors are scuffed from its time as a recreation center. The floor-to-ceiling windows are spectacular. Michele is a consummate storyteller, and despite how difficult her ALS makes it for her to speak, she keeps us laughing at stories about when she, a lifelong butch lesbian who was as comfortable at the weight rack as she was with a toolbox, and Johann, a late bloomer who prefers nail polish, makeup, and handbags to sweating in the gym, were first getting to know one another.

In the morning, Michele and Johann join us for breakfast at the hotel before we head back to New Jersey. We stop on the way home for dinner at an Italian restaurant and debrief the weekend. We admit that managing the ins and outs of sharing a space and a bathroom was perplexing for both of us—we are still getting to know one another, and neither of us has ever spent a night away with a woman with whom we're intimate. But we also agree that the awkward moments pale in comparison to the glimpses of a future in which we will feel comfortable in our surroundings as gay women this weekend provided us.

This was the longest amount of time we've spent together. I think I could get used to spending my time with Vivian.

Not long after, I'm home when Vivian calls. I listen quietly as she tells me her best friend of twenty-five years is not adjusting well to Vivian dating. During their long friendship, they've attended family functions, celebrated holidays, traveled, and even lived together. Now, as Vivian struggles to find acceptance as a gay woman, she says, "I'm wondering if there's more to this relationship than I realized. It feels like a window is open, and I need to explore this." She pauses, "To make sure I didn't miss anything." She says she's sorry and ends the call as a sharp sensation pierces my chest.

I take my aching heart and drive into the city to cry to Hope and her girlfriend. I circle the streets, trying to find parking amid the mounds of dirty snow. I walk into the coffee shop, oblivious to the nutty, smoky aroma that I usually love, and plop into a seat at their table.

It's here that I reveal Gia is Vivian. They try consoling me, but I cannot be soothed; I leave soon after arriving. The two-block walk to my car, past piles of foul-smelling garbage and urine-soaked trees, leaves me wondering whether it's the cold or the sadness that is making me numb.

Images of Vivian and her bestie sitting at Vivian's dining room table—sharing a morning cup of coffee, a renewed friendship spiced with a newfound passion for one another—does laps in my brain as I drive back to New Jersey.

Vivian puts distance between us. I miss her gentleness, her humor, and the emotional connection I thought we were creating. Her occasional emails describe her struggle, her loss of self—an unraveling of her world stemming from her mother's rejection. She apologizes for hurting me.

I want to help her, hold her through the pain, be her soft place to land.

Within a couple weeks, Vivian calls to say she's positive she has no repressed romantic feelings for her friend, and she's learning to live without her mother's acceptance. The pull on my heartstrings confirms my deepening feelings.

A few days later, while I'm half-attentively flipping the pages of the local newspaper, an obituary gives me pause. I stare at the page with my former best friend's ex-husband's name on it. He's my age. Besides the shock of the announcement, I'm overrun by thoughts of Eve, the friend and "soulmate" for whom I pined after our friendship ended.

Eve's friendship was a first of its kind for me, one I'd always longed for but never experienced before her. She was the person who checked all my emotional-needs boxes. With her, I was heard, seen, and understood. She held space for what was meaningful for me. Our friendship was my sanctuary. We could have serious, intimate conversations as easily as ones where we laughed until we were breathless.

Of our friendship, my husband once said, "This is great—she takes care of your emotional needs so I don't have to, and I get the physical part."

My happiest time was when Eve and I were friends. When others implied more was brewing besides a close friendship, I rejected the insinuation even as I noticed a dependency upon her.

As Eve was starting her new career, I paused mine to be a stay-at-home mom. She was thriving, and I was lonely. She was dating, and I was envious of the excitement in her life. I pulled away after I miscarried in April 2001 by not telling her. She found out from her former sister in-law, who lived around the corner from me. When she reached out, I didn't respond. I shut her out.

Hurting Eve crushed me. I slipped into a depression. I missed her every day. The next time we spoke was five months later, the week of September 11, when she called to ask if my husband was all right. I said yes and told her we'd lost his brother—whom she knew, having spent holidays with us over the years. I told her that I'd just found out I was pregnant. She told me she was getting married that weekend. While I'd been pining for her, she had moved on.

I've never stopped missing Eve. I sent her a birthday card last year, but she didn't respond; I haven't reached out since. This death notice in the paper has torn open the scar.

I shut down after we parted ways thirteen years ago. Eve set the bar so high that I was sure I wouldn't meet anyone else with whom I had such a connection. I also never wanted to know that pain of loss again. But she's an integral part of my story, one I wish I'd handled differently. I acted on fear back then, shortchanging all of us.

I feel I must go to the funeral. Knowing I will see Eve when I pay my respects launches my thoughts like a game of fifty-two-card pickup. I'm reliving our short time together as best friends, am riddled with guilt for abandoning and hurting her.

She used to say she lived life on the edge of the fire, often not knowing if she was stepping into it or stepping away. I pushed us both into the fire.

Questions about the significance of our friendship inundate me. Was I blind to the true nature of this relationship? Was Eve my first love, and I didn't realize it? Like Vivian and her best friend, I ponder, *Was there more?* Were those comments by others another example of me missing what was obvious to everyone else? The idea of seeing Eve again like this—under trying circumstances and through the lens of a gay woman—feels daunting, and yet I know there is something to be learned here.

A massive crowd spills into the parking lot of the funeral home in my town. I take my place at the back of a line that seemingly has no end. I think about the times we talked about life; Eve always said, "No regrets." I know I have one. Michele and Johann told me, "One life, one chance. Don't leave this earth with unanswered questions if you can help it." There are questions in need of answers, a part of my story that craves clarity.

An hour passes before I reach the first viewing area. I break from the line, slide into a back pew of the main room, and find Eve among the sea of faces. She looks the same.

I wait a few minutes. Lost in a time warp. Gathering strength. I approach to offer my condolences. She hugs me. I'm solaced that our conversation is so easy. The deep connection we've always shared is still there—but there's no attraction the way I had with Raia or like I have with Vivian now. There's nothing more to figure out. The feelings I have for Eve are simple and genuine.

We stand in the funeral home, and it feels like we're sitting in my kitchen fifteen years ago: nothing has changed. If not for the words she casually drops in this moment—words that jolt me back to reality and drag me into a rip current of guilt and regret for the time we've lost—I might have let this moment slip away. But instead:

"Oh, I have breast cancer," Eve says.

I think of *Beaches*, a movie we both used to love and watched together once. I couldn't watch it ever again after we parted ways.

Now, suddenly, we're Bette Midler and Barbara Hershey.

When life imitates art, it can stop you cold in your tracks.

 ## Chapter Fifteen

"I took a deep breath and listened to the old brag of my heart. I am, I am, I am."
—SYLVIA PLATH

Unusual things are happening at work. I don't receive my annual parking pass, then I'm reprimanded for an incident regarding a poor patient-care decision that the office manager's son, an employee, was responsible for.

Two days later, I'm shutting down my computer, preparing to leave work. The office is quiet; most of the staff has already left. The office manager pokes her head into the therapy department and asks to speak with me in the conference room.

I pause at the door when I see that another employee is there, then join them at the large oval table.

"We're cutting expenses and won't be needing your services anymore," the office manager says.

I never saw this coming. I've been keeping my financial insecurity contained, but the ground beneath me just opened up. I'm tumbling through a widening crevice.

Tonight, when my husband picks up the kids for the weekend, I ask to speak with him privately.

We go to my bedroom, where I sit on the edge of the bed and he sits on the floor, leaning against the white double doors of the closet he emptied four months ago.

I try not to cry when I say, "I lost my job today. I'm so scared."

He listens but doesn't say much. Instead, he asks, "Would it be okay if the kids meet my girlfriend? She has a key and there have been some close encounters."

Really?

"Considering what's happened, can you wait a little longer?"

Only later will I discover that he gives out his keys like Halloween candy.

I text Vivian about my job. She immediately responds, "I'm coming over."

Just as my husband leaves with the kids, the house phone rings, startling me. I keep the landline for emergencies, but my mom is the only actual person who calls that number.

I answer the wall-mounted phone unthinkingly.

Raia. It's been eighteen months, but her raspy voice draws me right in.

"I've been calling your cell phone, but you weren't answering. I didn't know if you changed your number. I've been thinking about you. How have you been?" She's talking fast, not giving me time to respond.

She talks about the woman she's currently dating. I tell her about Vivian. I don't mention losing my job. Raia confesses how hard being together was.

"I know." I'm taken by how vulnerable she's being.

"I felt so guilty."

"I know." My voice is barely above a whisper.

"Why did you do it? Why did you go there? I mean, you were married and have kids."

She wants to understand, but I don't know how to explain to her the why of this journey, or whether the question itself is even a valid one. How do you explain attraction? How can you explain what a compulsion capable of upending your world feels like? Once I leaped into the knowing, my marriage was never going to be the same. You can't unknow what you know. I wasn't choosing another person; I was choosing myself. A later-in-life self-realization is beyond comprehension for anyone who hasn't experienced it firsthand.

"I've wanted to thank you for shining a light in a space I didn't know was so dark," I tell her. "You helped me find me."

I've momentarily forgotten about everything else that's transpired today.

We hang up and I hear knocking on my front door; reality comes rushing back in. Vivian is wide eyed and open mouthed, standing on the front porch holding two grocery bags full of food—her response to my news of my job loss.

I don't tell her about Raia's call. I need time to process; I tuck it away for the time being.

I turn my attention to Vivian—grateful she's here, wanting her comfort.

A few days later, my husband is back in my bedroom. He says he broke up with his girlfriend.

"She asked if I loved her, but I couldn't commit. I miss her."

He's sitting on the edge of the bed looking down at his feet. I sit next to him; he seems so sad. I hug him, but he doesn't respond.

Hugging him feels hollow; I wonder if it always did.

When he picks up the kids later that week, he says he's okay but reports the woman sent a series of drunk texts—one threatening, *I'm going to mail the crap you left at my house to your wife's house*, and another one jeering, *It's no wonder your wife is gay*. This was the woman with a key who he wanted to introduce to the kids?

"It takes time to really know a person," I tell him. "Be patient, this is still new."

His poorly veiled grin tells me he's already moved on.

"You've met someone else, haven't you?" I ask.

He confirms that he has.

I resist the urge to roll my eyes.

I use my unplanned hiatus to address a long-standing medical issue, tachycardia, which causes a rapid heartbeat, shortness of breath, and fatigue. The condition has plagued me since my early twenties. Prior to losing my job, I had a recent episode that landed me in the ER. A cardiac specialist has assured me that surgery will fix the worsening issue, and I'll never have to deal with it again. It makes sense to do it now, while I have health insurance and time to recover.

Two weeks pass. I'm in the hospital, resting. The surgery went well but left me feeling weak. My husband brings the kids to the hospital to visit. Within seconds of them leaving, Vivian appears in the doorway, surprising me. I can't imagine they didn't pass one another in the hall.

Vivian's been nervous about my elective procedure. She crawls into the tiny hospital bed, curls up beside me. I hadn't admitted to her that I, too, was anxious—but now, lying close together, my body softens, and I ease into hers.

The following week, I'm in Philadelphia for an annual work conference hosted by a prominent medical organization in my specialty. The event draws about one thousand occupational and physical therapists, features renowned experts who present on new research, and satisfies my profession's requirement for continuing education. Because of my job situation, I show up with an updated resume, ready to network about possible career opportunities.

Vivian is in Massachusetts, attending a yoga retreat for gay women. She calls me on my second day in Philly. The retreat was unlike anything she had ever done, she says—

she's lit up about it, firing on all cylinders and bursting with excitement.

"I need to see you," she says and drives four hours from Western Massachusetts to Philadelphia and spends the next two nights with me.

The Sacred Sexuality workshop Vivian attended provided a unique, intimate experience bonding with other gay women. Through discussion and exercises, the group explored sexuality and identity to foster self-acceptance. It provided her with the first meaningful antidote for those lifelong negative messages she's absorbed from her church and family.

I always opt for a single room while attending this symposium—enjoying the luxury of a quiet space. To my surprise, I like having Vivian here. Neglecting portions of my conference and skipping out on presentations, we spend as much time together as possible. We visit my favorite outdoor sculpture—*Freedom*, by Zenos Frudakis. The twenty-foot bronze composition depicts four figures moving from various stages of confinement to freedom. I once referred to it as "the coming-out sculpture," long before I knew I would be coming out myself.

We dine on sushi in the city, watch the sunset from the top floor of the hotel. Back in the room, we enjoy indulgent hotel sex. Our shared time is never wasted, and I never tire of her softness. Her touch casts a spell over me. She mesmerizes me with her barely-there caresses while capturing my full attention with her assertive alter-ego. What started as a simmer advances to a rolling boil.

Driving home from Philadelphia, each of us in our own cars, we stop for lunch at a roadside diner in New Jersey. We're in a booth, paying the bill, when my phone rings.

It's Raia. I still haven't told Vivian about her call a couple weeks ago; I didn't expect to hear from her again.

"I'll call back shortly," I stutter into the phone.

Vivian is quiet.

Once in our respective cars to finish the drive home, I return Raia's call. We talk for an hour as I drive. I'm perplexed when she asks why I haven't called since she reached out. After our conversation a few weeks ago, I was at peace—happy to know that she was well, and relieved that I'd finally told her what I'd longed wanted to say. I hadn't planned on resuming our friendship. Is that what she's seeking, or is there more?

Raia phones one more time over the next few days.

This time, I tell Vivian.

"I figured it was her who called at the diner," Vivian says. "I know how important she was to you. I wouldn't know you if it weren't for her."

I'm moved by her insight but withhold the fact that I've made plans to see Raia soon.

It's a forty-minute drive to Raia's house, a trip I haven't made in a long time. Everything comes rushing back—the early intrigue, the excitement, the pain.

Raia sits on the front step as I pull into her driveway. Her long, curly, caramel-brown hair and easy smile are the first things I notice. I remember how she once took my breath away.

We hug hello before retreating into the house and sink into her couch, immediately settling into a comfortable familiarity.

It's still easy talking with Raia—like driving down a scenic country road on a beautiful day with the sunroof open, music playing just a little bit loud. But the road has an end. There's nowhere to go from here. It was good while it lasted but it's run its course. Now I'm in a different car, on a different road, and although my destination may not be entirely clear, I know

I'm heading somewhere this time. It feels familiar being here with Raia, but this feeling isn't home. I still have a long way to go on my journey.

I tell Raia it's time and I leave. Driving home, I call Vivian.

 **Chapter Sixteen**

"Not until we are lost do we begin to understand ourselves."
—HENRY DAVID THOREAU

My life resembles shampoo instructions—*wash, rinse, repeat,* an endless loop of banality. I'm still out of work and out of sorts. I'm sitting at the gray Formica desk in my home office, a messy little room that's become a container for textbooks and binders from my years in post-graduate school, and a receptacle of backpacks, books, shoes, and anything else the kids drop on the herringbone wood floor—clarinets, glue guns, old vinyl records, tennis balls, LEGO creations, and more. A bulletin board runs the length of the desk, and another hangs on the opposite wall. Each are spattered with index cards displaying my favorite sayings. One, by Søren Kierkegaard, reads, "Life can only be understood backwards but must be lived forwards."

Painted a textured blue denim, one wall displays pictures of the kids, another my diplomas, each a demonstration of pride. On the narrow section of wall near the window hangs two framed originals by the kids.

This space is an accumulation of a life that no longer exists. I remember how my daughter used to press her nose against the glass door as she waited for Daddy to come home. I can play back my last twenty-five years, access all the memories, just by looking around this office.

April marks my son's twelfth birthday and Passover, one of Judaism's three pilgrimage festivals. My journey is not unlike the saga of the Jewish people—celebrated by incorporating both the bitter aspects and the sweet, each represented on the seder plate. The Passover story is the basic tenet of our faith. Passed from generation to generation, it's retold every year, a conduit for a shared memory but also an impetus for inner exploration. I peel back the layers of my own exodus and wonder where the answers lie—in my heart or in my mind?

The landscape is shifting. Should I pull up the tent poles? What's the advantage of staying in an expensive town that challenges my authenticity? How would leaving impact the kids? I imagine a different kind of life but ultimately hew to the remnants of the life I've created for them.

I sit at the desk writing, trying to process how my husband, to whom I now refer as DH, tongue-in-cheek for Darling Husband, and I are not in the amicable place I once imagined we might be—coparenting on the same page. The kids sleep at my house, since it's home base, which means that on the nights I go out, DH is there, influencing my choices and how late I stay out. When he calls and asks when I'll be home I feel like a teenager with a curfew, my estranged husband the gatekeeper.

In the morning, if I've gone out the night before, the kids inquire about my evening. I'm envious of DH's freedom to come and go as he pleases, answering to no one. The extra responsibility I carry as the sole parent they live with is heavy; the time they spend at his house is limited because of the twenty-five minutes it takes to get there, well outside of the school district.

Stress and exhaustion pile up like the laundry, as do the additional chores around the house. I continue looking for a new job.

I'm in Lynn's office pondering how the family man I once knew could morph into a person so unrecognizable. Now betwixt marriage partners and something else, I can't tell where we'll land anymore. I can't envision being divorced, yet any attempt to classify the man with whom I once expected to share my life leaves me confounded. Despite the passage of time since identifying my same-sex attraction, our in-home separation, his dating, and his moving out, I'm not adjusting to our relationship metamorphosis. The absence of the stability that I've sought since childhood has made the ground under my feet, formerly firm, feel like quicksand.

My childhood changed overnight when I saw my father— seated at our kitchen counter, his head resting in the crook of his elbow on the Formica peninsula, his other hand cradling the mustard yellow receiver of the corded phone that hung on the wall above, a puddle of tears below his mustached face—crying to a friend, "I love my family." This was the first time I'd seen him cry. Nothing was ever the same for my family again.

I heard my parents exchange obscenities. Witnessed objects being thrown across the room. I watched them quietly leave the house one night. Ten-year-old me wondered if anyone was coming back. My father never lived with us again after that night. Poor and often nonexistent communication comprised the entirety of their separation. I had no emotional reassurance.

Their divorce resulted in dicey situations for me. One of my mom's dates told me, "You're pretty. One day men will chase you with a mattress tied to their back and a club in their hand." Without my father to do repairs, strangers were hired. One handyman kissed me while I watched him fix the shower tiles—shoved his tongue in my mouth. I ran out of the bathroom as fast as I could, caught my mom as she was leaving to run an errand, and begged her to take me with her, without telling her what happened. She told me no—she didn't want to leave the man alone in the house. I hid in a closet under the stairs, shaking, as his footsteps tromped the floor over my head and his voice called out my name.

As for my father—after the divorce, I had an inconsistent relationship with him. He showed up for a weekly dinner and every-other-weekend sleepover, but there were periods when he went MIA for months at a time; later, those months extended to years. There was nobody to anchor me, to protect me.

When I ask my elderly clients, those married for decades, what their secret is, there are frou-frou answers about being one another's best friend and making each other laugh. One mildly cantankerous woman declares, "I was too damn lazy to get divorced." When I repeat that story to a woman on her forty-second wedding anniversary, she raises her hand and says, "Same."

How many people settle? Did my desire for him to protect me prevent me from realizing that I could protect myself? Did I dismiss my needs to maintain the status quo?

Lynn talks about the courage it takes to end a marriage, for any reason, because it means going from the known to the unknown without the safety net that marriage provides. "This is why so many people stay in bad marriages—because it's easier than change," she says.

Hope, Tess, and I plan to attend Women's Fest in Rehoboth Beach, agreeing that we all need a change of scenery. This will be the first time we've met in person since Tess's brain injury.

DH comes to the house to stay with the kids while I make the round-trip to pick Tess up from the airport.

He's relaxed on the family room couch—the same one I breastfed our babies on, catered to them when they were sick on, logged countless hours on watching old sitcoms and classic films, and on which I was perched when I told him of my struggle with my sexuality and, later, informed our kids of our separation. It's from this iconic piece of family history masked as furniture that he nonchalantly announces, "I can't stay long."

He knows I need him to stay with the kids while I pick up Tess; these plans have been in place for weeks. I remind him that I prefer the kids not be left alone, that I'll be home soon.

"I'm trying to get to know someone, and my stamina runs out by midnight," he says, an air of frustration in his voice.

A muted kaleidoscope of thoughts and emotions twists and turns in my mind. He's telling me he must get out of here so he can get laid.

Weeks ago, we sat in the living room—me on the sofa, him on the loveseat—and he talked about the woman he's been dating since my cardiac procedure in March, the one he met immediately after breaking up with the woman who sent those nasty, drunken texts. He shared how beautiful, funny, and smart his new girl-friend was, adding, "She's out of my league." I was relieved when he said she wouldn't introduce any man to her young son unless they had been dating for a year, assuming DH would follow suit, but I was still curious, so I looked her up online—only to dis-cover that she had a DWI arrest mere days before their first date, and several complaints have been posted in reviews of the place where she works, citing her bad temper. When I told DH what I uncovered, he excused her actions by alluding to extraordinary circumstances but agreed he'd never leave the kids alone with her.

As we talked he shared with me that his girlfriend was threatened by how much time he spends at my house.

"Does she know why we're separated?" I asked.

"Not at first," he said, "but when I told her, it didn't erase her fears. She's afraid you'll want me back—you know, because of the kids."

"She seems insecure," I said.

"It's not like I'm the most secure person either," he retorted before adding, "People tell me I'm still in love with you."

I froze, remembering the warnings that conditions would change once he started dating someone. I had brushed it off then, believing DH would weather these trying times and be the person I knew him to be: reliable, family-oriented, pressure-tested. He'd crashed before, yes—but he'd found his way back.

This is not the man I've always known, however, and the more capricious he becomes the more I feel compelled to examine our situation. Has he changed? Or have I been in denial all these years?

I consider how the next several hours might unfold. Will DH be uncomfortable meeting Tess? He doesn't know about Vivian; might he think Tess and I are dating? What if he leaves the kids on their own?

I'm thrilled that Tess, who will sleep in the extra bedroom, will meet the kids in the morning before I take them to school and then leave for Delaware. DH will be the parent in charge for the weekend starting Friday afternoon. Can I rely on him to follow through with that plan?

I walk out the door not knowing whether he'll still be here when I return.

During the forty-minute drive to Newark, my brain is still reeling from his comment about his "stamina."

When Tess and I arrive home, he is gone.

Can I continue trusting him with his responsibilities regarding the kids? Is this about letting go of my expectations of him, or being proactive about ensuring that my children are well cared for? They're my priority, but am I willing to forgo any time for myself because he's becoming less dependable? I'm teetering on the edge of a quagmire.

Despite my worries, I embrace the weekend. Hope, Tess, and I walk the beach, dance, and attend a concert by Chely Wright, the singer whose struggle with sexuality brought her to the brink of suicide but who is now happily married to a woman and raising twin boys. We coax Tess into participating in a speed-dating event. Cycling through emotional highs and lows, we find renewed solidarity in one another.

On Sunday, after dropping Tess at the airport, I catch up with the kids. I learn that DH left them totally alone Friday overnight, only returning Saturday morning to bring my daughter to track practice.

When I ask him about this later, his response is, "I was tired."

"Why didn't you sleep at the house, or take them back to yours?" I press.

He doesn't respond.

I can't undo what's been done, and I still need his help if I want to have any semblance of a social life, so I leave it alone—but I wonder how his inconsistency is affecting the kids. It's a chip in the windshield you hope doesn't spread.

Some weeks later, I run into Grace. We've fallen out of touch, but I know she's helped DH transition to his current house. It's happenstance that I see her pulling into my neighbor's driveway.

I gingerly walk the slate path to the sidewalk, watching as Grace crosses the street to meet me. There's no hug hello, and the air between us feels more like late fall than spring.

Grace is visiting Alice, who is like Gladys Kravitz from *Bewitched*. Our directly-across-the-street neighbor, Alice oversees the activity on the block, always poking around for information. Grace once found this idiosyncrasy funny and would tell me when Alice asked her questions about our family, like when Alice texted Grace after she moved away: *Did the Gibersons get a new car?*

I don't know, is there a new car on their driveway? Grace wrote back.

Yes, seems to be, Alice said.

Well, there you go, Grace responded. She laughed when she recounted the exchange to me.

Standing on the sidewalk, I ask Grace if she's told Alice about me.

"No," she says.

The skin on my forehead scrunches tight.

"People have been talking, they've asked me what's going on. I told them," she says in a *what was I going to do* tone.

I'm silent but my thoughts recall how often Grace told me, "We talk *to* people, not about them."

"You're gay, Melissa, so what? No one cares."

I take a step back, her sharp words like a sudden gust of wind. I don't respond.

Grace carried me through dark days, helped with the kids, got me through my daughter's bat mitzvah. I pointed my compass in her direction when I was crashing after Hurricane Sandy. Now, this once-beloved friend is talking to me like I'm a stranger who just hit her car in the parking lot.

Perhaps it's her way of saying being gay is no big deal, but making this discovery in my forties, while married with kids, *is* a big deal. I want to disclose it on my own terms.

We will never speak as friends again.

It's barely a week later, and I'm mowing the lawn when Sally drops off her son so the boys can play. Both her kids are friends with mine, and we've spent much time together over the years hiking, camping, and celebrating special occasions. I've always trusted her with my kids; for several years, she was their emergency contact at school.

I'm in ripped jeans and a baseball cap, dirty and grass-covered from mowing. I ready myself to wave hello and goodbye—but instead, Sally gets out of the car.

"Mind if I stay for a minute?" she asks. "To catch up."

We take a seat on the front porch.

"I miss my friend," Sally says.

As the first of our peers to separate, I'm feeling the stigma often attached to divorced women. "Even though I'm *that woman*?" I ask, only half-joking.

"What do you mean?"

I tell her about the phone call in December from Joan, whom she knows; I talk about the judgment I'm feeling from people who are aware DH and I are separated.

"You're still you, and I like you no matter what," she says.

My wheels are spinning. Does she know? I wonder if my daughter told Sally's daughter and if she, in turn, told Sally.

I burrow under my hat, avoiding eye contact. The soundtrack in my head might as well be playing the *Jeopardy* theme song. Under pressure, there's no time to process. I would give anything to excuse myself to change my shirt, brush my teeth, gather my thoughts, and exhale. She's opening the door, and I need to decide here and now what to do. I recall my old mantra: *Once you put it out there, you can't take it back.*

"Would it be true, you liking me no matter what, if I were gay?"

"Absolutely," Sally says without flinching. "Can I hug you?"

Her request is odd. We've never been physically affectionate friends, so my news doesn't seem hug-worthy. A litany of questions crosses my mind: Is she congratulating me on the discovery that's turned my world upside down? Is it meant to be a thanks-for-sharing hug? Is it intended as support, as if to say, "This must be difficult"?

Not knowing what else to do, I open my arms and accept the hug.

The disconnect between one person's experience and another's can create awkwardness, even with the best of intentions. Piggybacking each coming-out conversation is my underlying fear—of what their reaction might be and of bigger things, like, *What will my future look like? How will this impact the kids long term? Will I have enough money to retire? Who will I grow old with?* Living in your truth is wonderful, but starting over like this is the equivalent of erasing your life's chalkboard: everything you had and thought you knew is gone.

Needing to maintain two worlds, and finding the balance between them, is like river birling. Weary from parenting in the trenches without a reliable partner, and unable to immerse myself in the gay community, I find myself wondering what DH is doing with his free time and growing resentful because I have so little of it. My future life is a destination I don't know how to reach, and I'm a stranger in my old world.

Later, I will understand that I'm experiencing the stages of grief—and it's not a singular grief. In addition to losing my marriage, it includes my reckoning with the end of familiar patterns, another significant loss. A cycle of change and fear coexists with the usual life events still requiring my attention. I'm drifting in a boat that's taking in water.

I finish my outside chores, imagining a billboard on the roof of my house. People in my kids' community know my truth. I'm less concerned for my daughter and her circle of friends, but I worry about the boys my son spends time with— how they will react to the news that he has a gay mom.

It's not long before I'm at Sally's house, seeking help from her husband because my computer crashed. It's the first time I've seen him since I came out to his wife, and since my husband—his friend—and I separated. I'm antsy, because everything is on this computer—my lifeline, my means of reaching my scaffolding of support during my darkest times. All my career-related notes, letters to my kids, pictures, and the personal writing I've been doing to document my journey is interred in this mini-machine. Sally's husband is the only person I know who can help.

He agrees to back up my hard drive on a portable hard drive he has, inciting a cold sweat on my part. The depth of personal information stored in the bowels of my computer is profound—and now it will forever stay in his possession?

As we're waiting for the information to download to an external drive, a lengthy process, Sally's husband can't hide his childish grin. He's quiet, but I feel his eyes on me. It's unnerving being reduced to a product of his overactive imagination. I remember the time I struggled to slide the plastic wrap off a cucumber when they were over for dinner, and he watched me and giggled. His expression now is one I'd imagine on the face of a teen boy watching a sex scene in a movie.

A similar experience occurred recently with a family member: a poorly masked smirk crossed his face when I updated him about the changes in my life. I felt like I was riding the subway naked. What goes through a person's mind when they hear that a woman they've known for years is now gay? Maybe they question how a person could have failed to understand this essential piece of information about themselves. That's fair. But I struggle with the expediency with which their thoughts go directly to sex. I imagine them imagining me having sex with a woman. I assume they feel sympathy for DH, failing to comprehend how difficult this is for me, the one who "should have known." Maybe they surmise it's a phase, I'm hedonistic, or I did know and have been stringing DH along all this time.

I've seen this play out in my support group; women have shared how their friends have sided with their husband, the one whose life still resembles theirs.

I leave Sally's house, my dying laptop in my hands, all the information siphoned out of it now in her husband's hands. During the short drive home, a new fear germinates in my mind: If conditions spiral downward with DH, will my children blame me for setting this situation in motion? Will they sympathize with their dad because he was displaced? Will they care to know my story? My husband is fiscally irresponsible and has been accumulating debt—that's incontrovertibly true. But am I culpable for having created this circumstance?

Despite the early show of support on my front porch, Sally will later go on to defend my husband when I complain about his unpredictability. "He looks like he's doing a good job to me," she'll say.

After that conversation, she will become another once-friend who'll never speak to me again.

 **Chapter Seventeen**

"The longest journey is the journey inward."
—DAG HAMMARSKJÖLD

Mother's Day. We've aligned to take the kids hiking. We navigate the rock scramble and linger at the lake before hiking the dirt trail to an old stone castle. The uphill climb, uneven terrain, reflective water, and remains of a once-intact mansion all seem analogous to my life. Still, it's easy to be in the woods—a long-standing, ever-changing landscape ripe with symbolism. A rainstorm rearranges rocks, dry creeks transform into mini rapids, a downed tree becomes a new home for an animal.

Having shed the expectations of being a wife in a traditional family, I savor this quality time today with my children and DH—all four of us together. I always hoped we'd remain friends, and this day is proof of that possibility.

Perhaps wearing a Campaign for Human Rights T-shirt and matching hat is my attempt to distance myself from any heterosexual assumptions. When a stranger compliments my pro-LGBTQ attire, I contemplate whether the me who shuns labels is now looking to be labeled.

My daughter and I step over raised tree roots along the wooded trail, inhaling deep breaths of the earthy fresh fragrance. Twigs snap under our hiking boots. The shrill screech of a hawk between the tree branches above occasionally halts our steps. DH and our son are farther along, watching for the blue trail markers.

A man with a well-worn wooden walking stick veers right, toward the white trail.

"Look, it's Moses," I joke to my daughter.

"That's not Moses," she shoots back.

"Why not?"

"Because he has tattoos on his legs."

"They're the Ten Commandments," I tease. "He was afraid he might lose the tablets."

My daughter, typically good to banter with, looks at me, and—speaking as if I've never heard of the important fact she's about to tell me, a serious look on her face—says, "Jews don't get tattoos because then they can't be buried in a Jewish cemetery."

I'm glad I haven't told her about my tattoo.

We catch up with the boys, take pictures at the abandoned castle, tell jokes. It feels good to make a deposit in our friendship bank. My hope is renewed that we'll make this work—honoring the Black Friday promise we made about always being a family, even if we look a little different.

I've hoarded stories from women about their lives after separation—how they attend their kids' events, parent-teacher nights, school performances, college move-in days, and family weekends with their new partners and their ex-husbands and their current partners. The best of both worlds. I'm confident we will too. I want to give DH the benefit of the doubt. But lurking in the shadow of my optimism is the change I continue seeing in him. I shake it off again and again but it circles back, spiraling me into deep concern for our future, my future. It's like he's been cycling through a revolving door with each relationship he's engaged in since our split, each time emerging different from when he entered—less connected to us, to his family, to the man I knew as my husband and the father of my children.

I hope he's like my garden. Come winter, everything gets cut down until there's only dirt and you wonder if anything will grow again next year. But it does—the roots are there, and they're strong.

I cling to the belief that he's rooted in his family and will return, just as my yellow daffodils bloom again in March, and my lilies, irises, and roses after that.

Vivian gives me a Mother's Day card and gift. I wish she hadn't. Her wanting to celebrate my being a mom while I carry guilt for having hurt my children feels antiheroic. Anything pertaining to my kids is holy ground needing to be cordoned off. I spend the remainder of the night spinning scenarios in my mind. The next day, I write Vivian a letter.

On Monday, we meet midway between her house and mine. In the backseat of my car in a mostly empty parking lot, I ask the question I'm not supposed to ask. I don't want to put her on the spot, but I need to know what's happening in this relationship. In me.

"Do you love me?" I ask her.

Vivian hesitates before saying, "I think so. It's like the words keep bubbling up to my lips even though I don't say them."

My hands are clammy when I hand her the letter and say, "Please open this later." She quietly returns to her car and I start the engine in mine. Taking my time, I shift into drive and look through the passenger window; she's already reading it. My stomach sours and I slowly make my way out of the lot.

The letter is about time. I want to focus on the kids before they leave for sleepaway camp.

I will learn later that my words broke her heart. This will fill me with regret, but I won't know what I could have done differently.

Two weeks pass— the kids are with their dad for the weekend, and I've returned to Provincetown with Hope and Sparrow, another late bloomer from our group with whom I've become good friends. Sparrow is a couple of years ahead of Hope and me on this journey. She's a dark-haired, cargo-pants, leather-jacket-wearing woman a few inches shorter and a few years younger than me—a confident single mom who's both fierce and sweet.

Wrestling with my emotions while figuring out my needs feels like putting the scattered pieces of a puzzle together in a windstorm. Provincetown is restorative, my magic elixir.

We stroll through Beech Forest, take pictures, watch for warblers and woodpeckers in the birch and beech trees, and unpack the issue of love. I question whether I can trust myself not to hurt anyone again. My mind circles back to being in my twenty-year relationship with a man everyone said was great but didn't make me *feel* great. I was always impatient and wanting more—unable to identify what was missing but aware that there was a longing deep within me. *Do I even know what love is?*

Later, in my Provincetown cabin, I think about Raia, and how she's so different from Vivian. I ponder the characters from *Sex and the City* and wonder who would represent Vivian and Raia. They don't fit any of them, but surely Raia was my Mr. Big, the pendulum that swung opposite from my life with my husband. Have I been attempting to build a relationship too soon? Will I ever be ready? Perhaps I fell for Vivian when I wasn't expecting to, before I wanted it, and now I'm fighting myself about what I want and whether I've found that with Vivian.

She is my first real same-sex relationship. I upended my life for the opportunity to have it all— the dream, the passion, the connection. I want to exemplify Thoreau's words: "Go confidently in the direction of your dreams. Live the life you have imagined." Is Vivian that for me?

I'm reminded of shopping for my wedding dress. My mom and I stopped at a bridal boutique in a little gray house on a busy intersection, near her town. I liked the first gown I tried on—but it was too early to decide. My mom and I spent months visiting bridal shops in New Jersey, Manhattan, and Brooklyn. I lost count of how many dresses I sampled. We ended up back in the little gray house, the one where we started. I chose a silk shantung whose beauty was in its simplicity. I didn't realize until I was standing on the mini platform in front of the three-way mirror that this was the first gown I'd tried on all those months earlier. I'd been content with that first choice all along.

At dinner with Hope and Sparrow, I ask, "How do you *know*?"

That night we go dancing. I'm not interested in meeting anyone—in fact, I'm terrified of hurting Vivian. Yet I don't know how to be sure about her. I distrust myself. I want a sign that says, *Yes, this is it.*

Maybe there aren't always fireworks to accompany love—no smack in the head, no *aha!* event to announce its arrival. Maybe it's as Vivian said that day in my car when I gave her the letter—no bells and whistles or a neon sign, just the words bubbling up to my lips, informing me that I love her.

After the club, I say good night to Hope and Sparrow and return to my cabin alone. This weekend would have been my twenty-first wedding anniversary. I sit at the white and chrome kitchen table and compose an email to my husband. I apologize for hurting him. I thank him for his friendship. For our children.

I end the letter with, "My wish is to sit side by side one day and recount memories from our shared life and stories from our current lives, reveling in our children's accomplishments."

I send the email.

After I crawl into bed, I continue philosophizing about love. I'm a thinker—comparing, contrasting, exploring every nook and cranny of a situation. So it's not surprising that I find myself comparing my husband and Vivian. Throughout our marriage, I knew my husband loved me—but with Vivian, I *feel* her love. Her touch sends electric currents like mini lightning rods racing through my body. Energy from her fingertips lands on my skin, filling me with a sensation of warmth. Her gentle caress, her firm embrace, her scent—like freshly laundered clothes hanging on an outside line—envelop me. The way she looks at me with her soulful brown eyes melts me; her touch is an invitation to come home.

I recall our intimate times and feel the stab of imagining her not with me. These are the sensations of a love I haven't known before. I consider that there isn't a singular model of love, but a spectrum of love we experience at different times in our lives or with different people.

My reentry from Provincetown to New Jersey becomes a crash landing when I find my kids home alone. I call DH, and he admits to making plans for a dinner party.

"Why would you double book yourself? You knew I was out of town. You're the parent on duty, the one who was supposed to be minding the store."

He doesn't answer—his new M.O. His priorities are changing. I suggest counseling to help us learn how to coparent together—thinking that could be an olive branch, a solution to help bridge the gap as we transition from husband and wife to coparents.

But he snaps the branch: "I'll never go to therapy with you again."

The cracking sound of his renunciation reverberates within me. We're losing the threads that will allow us to weave this new relationship together. How do we proceed if he won't work with me and won't agree to get help? I'm looking for a sign, a cairn, but all I'm finding is a random scattering of the rocks he's throwing in my direction.

I'm transforming into a mama bear the way Bruce Banner became the Hulk—anger is taking over. I just want to protect my cubs.

May turns to June, and it's Pride month again. I'm heading to Fire Island for an annual charity event with Sparrow. The recipient is the Hetrick-Martin Institute (HMI), an organization providing alternative schooling, counseling, health services, and housing support for displaced kids. As a social worker, I once escorted a group of teenagers to HMI's Manhattan facility to learn about homophobia from their peers who were homeless after identifying as LGBTQ.

Basking in the warmth of the summer sun on the deck of the ferry, a quiver fishtails through me as we approach the dock, the rainbow flag fluttering in the breeze.

This is my first White Party event. Everywhere I look, there's a sea of women clad in white. Sparrow and I walk on the beach. She asks about my list of what I'm looking for in a potential partner.

I answer.

"Now tell me what you're willing to give up from that list," she says.

Vivian checks *all* the boxes on my list.

Sparrow is struggling with her girlfriend, also a late bloomer. "Sometimes I think we're just grooming them for their next relationship," she says.

Back at the event, I catch sight of a familiar redhead in the crowd. Suddenly it's two years ago, and I'm on this island for the first time, trying to figure out if I'm gay. I make my way through the lot, put my hand gently on her arm. "Toni?"

She looks at me with a subtle blend of recognition and curiosity. I remind her of the day with the football, and formally introduce myself. It's the first time she's heard my name. We chat briefly, then say goodbye. *Look how far I've come?* I think.

When I first noticed Toni two years ago, I detected an attraction, a clue to the question I'd charged myself with finding an answer to. When she gently squeezed my shoulder that day, her touch blazed through me—a sensation I'd first experienced with Raia. Toni's still attractive, but the charge is more tranquil now. Whatever feeling passed through me when we talked just now made me think of Vivian.

Perhaps Vivian's only flaw is that we met too soon. I want to sort through my emotions—but how long will she wait for me?

Driving home from Long Island, I call Vivian. She has respected my request for time. We've spoken, but not seen one another in weeks. She invites me to visit.

I drive two hours straight to get to her place. This time, we both sit on the couch. She compliments my all-white garb, and I tell her about the day. She has her hand on my leg. She likes to rest it there. There's not been a time when having her hand on my leg hasn't woken up all my senses, especially if I'm in ripped jeans and her fingers find my skin through the fringed tears.

All at once I'm at the foot of a waterfall, feeling its cool spray on my heated skin. Her fingers are like water sizzling on a hot griddle.

She takes my hand and leads me to the bedroom. We spend the next hour rediscovering one another until we're configured like quotation marks—skin on skin, me wrapped up in her arms as though she's my own weighted blanket, calming me from the outside in.

In my complete contentment I think, *I don't need to shop for any more wedding dresses.*

It's the last Sunday of June. Hope and I are in Manhattan for the Pride Parade. We pose for pictures with drag queens outside The Stonewall Inn as if they're old friends. Rainbow flags, marching bands, throngs of people flooding the streets— electricity fills the air. Though we are standing shoulder to shoulder with strangers, I feel oddly connected to everyone around me.

It's Vivian's first Pride; she's attending with her friends from the sexuality yoga retreat. While my core group of friends have long known about Vivian, I've not shared the news of my relationship with anyone in the Connecticut group. Marti, the woman who co-leads the group, was at the yoga retreat, and she and Vivian have become friendly. I knew she was going but didn't say anything. I didn't want to interfere with Vivian's desire to form friendships with other gay women— and, perhaps, wanted to preserve my privacy a bit longer.

Now our worlds are overlapping, the veil of secrecy slipping away. Maybe it's the effervescent season, maybe it's being surrounded by colorful declarations of love, but something makes me invoke Meister Eckhart: "And suddenly you know: It's time to start something new and trust the magic of new beginnings."

I've had one long-term relationship in my life; imagining myself in another, it's Vivian I see taking the journey with me.

 **Chapter Eighteen**

*"If all difficulties were known at the outset of a long
journey, most of us would never start out at all."*
—DAN RATHER

July—I'm working again. My new position is thirty hours
per week, per diem salary, no benefits, but flexibility for the
kids. The schedule is four weekdays, with a late-morning start
and an early-evening finish on three of the four. My "day off" is
for managing household chores, errands, and personal appointments. During the school year, I'll drive the kids to school every
day, and DH will pick them up on my late days.

I reach out to old friends to tell them I now identify as gay,
beginning with the two people I'm confident will be most supportive—they each say, "I can see that." It's perplexing having
others recognize something that eluded me for so long.

I'm meeting my oldest childhood friend for brunch. We
first met in middle school and were inseparable in high school.
Weekends were spent hanging out with friends, venturing into
Manhattan, and attending rock concerts. It was the eighties,
with its signature big hair and loud music. We lost touch in our
adult lives but recently reconnected. She's a devout Catholic,
happily married, a mother.

Now we sit at a bistro table on the second floor of a popular restaurant, but it might as well be the stage at Madison

Square Garden. With our plates of eggs and toast between us, the usual small talk behind us, I tell her my husband and I have separated. "I've come to realize I'm gay," I explain.

She starts crying.

"Are you sure?" she asks, as if I've announced a diagnosis for a terminal illness.

"Quite," I say.

There's a distinct sadness when she asks, "What about the kids?"

"They know, and they've never expressed an issue with my truth—only with realizing that we wouldn't all be living together anymore."

I didn't expect this reaction; I don't know what I expected, but it certainly wasn't tears.

"I've never believed staying together for the sake of the kids was a good idea," I tell her. "How does living a lie model anything other than hypocrisy? I would never counsel them to make such a choice in their own life."

I'm on a soapbox, defending my right to an authentic life. I continue, "I hope my children will ultimately see that I've modeled strength and courage and the importance of being true to oneself, even if the path there is littered with difficult circumstances."

Soon after we part, I write to her, again defending my right to pursue authenticity.

She responds, "You've been heard." But then she expresses her concerns for my family and surmises that the grief DH is experiencing explains his radical and unexpected change—though she calls his absence with the kids "a sin."

"The price of your decision may be great and is likely still unknown," she continues. "I want you to be happy, Melissa. I just wish it didn't require the rupture of your family."

And there it is: choosing to follow the path of my authentic self has caused the destruction of my family. How heavily these words land. Will this be my perpetual burden to carry?

I wonder if it will always be this hard as I read the final lines of her email: "Though I am uneasy about the choice you made, I care deeply for you. I would be very happy to meet and spend time with friends you've made during these past years. It would be a chance to catch up and get to know my oldest friend better than I do now, an opportunity I warmly welcome."

She will later make good on this offer by hosting me and Vivian at her house for a laughter-filled evening of food, drinks, and reminiscing. We will give each other grace.

Days before the kids return home from camp, I'm in the garage with DH. The two-car garage, the two attics, and the outdoor shed have always been his domain. He never liked when I infiltrated these spaces, and as a result, the clutter accumulated. Since our separation, I've reiterated my old request that we clean it up—for safety reasons, and to better utilize the space for the bicycles and sports gear.

Later, a buried can of spray paint will discharge—shooting purple paint into my eyes and requiring a trip to the ER—when I step on the pile of debris covering it. By then I will be way past the point of losing patience with his disorganization and procrastination.

Before that happens, though, we're in the garage, and he's asking about having the kids meet his girlfriend, the one he's been dating since March. He says, "I've already met her son."

I frown. "I thought she wanted to wait a year before anyone meets him."

"She moved up her timeline."

"I'm not comfortable having the conversation about dating with them," I say, "and you introducing them invites questions about me."

I worry the kids will fear they are no longer my priority if they think they are competing for my attention. And so much has transpired—me losing my job, my surgery, their two elder grandfathers having serious health issues, academic concerns, and bar mitzvah preparations. Both kids are in therapy. I don't want to deal with this right now.

"It's complicated," I say.

"I've been talking to people. They say the kids should see me happy, that people get divorced and start dating all the time." He's defensive.

"They should see you happy, period, not because you're with another person."

I question whether the people advising him know the intricacies of our story. His inner circle includes the rabbi and the temple leader who stopped speaking to me. Both have been married to their respective husbands for thirty years, and they each have parents who are still married. Their advice has not been shaped by a personal understanding of how it feels to be a child of divorce and parental separation. The conversation picks the scab of an old wound: the lack of support I've received from our temple. I'm resentful they've taken sides.

He's sorting the jumble of left-over construction material when his phone rings. He answers, and I hear a woman say, "Hi baby."

He smiles slyly and runs his hand through his hair—something he does when he's uncomfortable. He's not talking, other than a series of *mm-hmms*, until he grabs one of the garbage bags he's been tossing stuff into and walks it down the driveway to the curb. When he gets there, I hear him say, "Yeah, I can do that."

After lingering at the curb for a bit, he returns to the garage. He's on edge. He revisits the conversation about the kids meeting his girlfriend. "She has a lot of stuff in my house, especially in the kitchen, and the kids are going to wonder whose it is."

"I can't imagine they're paying much attention to your mini kitchen appliances and serving bowls," I say, unable to help myself. "Remember, in their mind, the four of us are a family; they're likely not ready to factor anybody else into this equation. I've been there, it's hard to see your parents with other people. And when I date, it'll be a woman, an entirely different concept to comprehend."

Raising his voice, he retorts, "I don't give a shit that you're gay, Melissa—my issue is how you went about it."

He and the kids don't know about Vivian. I'm in no rush to share this news with him, especially given his accusation from a few months back: "Being gay is all about sex, so don't lecture me about the kids seeing me with different women."

He's focused on what's transpired between us, not the kids. He won't acknowledge my explanations about being caught up in a spell-like trance, not understanding what any of it meant. I try comparing it to an emotional pandemonium not unlike his own ungluing after his brother died. Nothing connects.

We're so far out of sync with one another at this point that I wonder if we'll ever again be on the same page.

A week later, DH storms into the backyard huffing about almost losing his job.

"I'm just not making it," he says, his tone shifting to one of desperation.

He's referring to money. It's no secret that he's been running up debt. However, he delivers this news as though I'm responsible. Will I forever be blamed for *all* his troubles?

All the same, he's hurting. I take a deep breath.

"If I run to the store and pick up food, will you stay and have dinner with us?" I offer. "We can barbecue?"

He agrees, and the rest of the night is uneventful. It's even kind of nice.

A new school year arrives, along with DH's birthday. We take the kids to a restaurant to celebrate. There are jokes and it feels like any of the infinite number of times we've gone out to dinner before. We head to a department store after leaving the restaurant—boys in one car, girls in the other, for back-to-school clothes shopping.

Standing between the racks as the kids shop nearby, DH nonchalantly announces that our daughter will be meeting his girlfriend this weekend. There's been no discussion, just a matter-of-fact piece of information dropped into my lap, as if my feelings haven't already been made abundantly clear. What has been a great, celebratory evening becomes the pulled thread unraveling the entire blanket.

I'm taking my son to Connecticut for the weekend for a camp friend's bar mitzvah (while we're there, I'll learn that he's already been to DH's girlfriend's house—"Dad and I stop by his friend's house to bring her coffee, but I can tell they're not just friends," my son will disclose—but right now I have no idea that's the case), and my daughter will be with her dad. I'm hamstrung by the circumstances.

I remind him that my feelings haven't changed.

While I'm trying not to overreact, he says, "People said you wouldn't want to see me happy, that you would make my life miserable."

I remember a conversation we had before he moved out, in which I said, "I want you to be happy, to be with a woman who can be everything you need her to be."

He looked at me then and declared, "I *was* happy."

Conversations with DH will drastically change from this time forward. He will testily rehash old events while making uncharacteristic comments. Two years ago, during the brief time he went to therapy to deal with my sexuality, he told me, "It doesn't change anything to get angry." Suddenly, now, he's very angry.

We check out, the kids say good night to their dad, wish him one more happy birthday.

The kids are quiet in the car, and my mind wanders. I recall Shira saying that sometimes things must be completely torn down before they can be rebuilt. I'm powerless against the false messages DH is receiving, against the wrath those messages are spewing. I've lived this nightmare as a preteen myself, and I'm determined not to resurrect the experience for my kids—yet he keeps steering the boat farther out into a shark-infested sea.

As I turn into my driveway, I feel the weight of the emotionally exhausting evening bearing down on me. The garage door opens slowly, the headlights illuminating the disarray that's accumulated over two decades, like the disarray of my current world. Will either one ever get cleaned up?

I feel helpless to save my children from the approaching storm; we're tangled up in a Gordian knot, and I'm clueless how to extract any of us from it.

 **Chapter Nineteen**

"Put your ear down close to your soul and listen hard."
—Anne Sexton

Two years have passed since the bat mitzvah, and I still haven't picked up my daughter's photo album from the photographers. Coming out, looking for support, transitioning our living situation, DH moving out, and losing my job filled those years to exhaustion. Picking up the book wasn't on my radar.

Filled with dread at the thought of hosting another big reception, I'm now in the throes of planning my son's bar mitzvah. That this important life event may not be as celebratory for my son as it was for my daughter gnaws at me.

The kids and I are at the same apple orchard we've gone to since they were babies. A clear blue sky hovers above us and the trees burst with red and green apples. With our hands sticky from the juice of the sampled fruit, we walk carefully in the straw-like tall grass to avoid tripping on fallen apples and ask strangers to take our picture between the rows of trees. I take the traditional photo of the kids sitting on a tree branch.

We spend our weekends doing familiar activities, like Six Flags Great Adventure and antiquing, and add different adventures like walking across the Brooklyn Bridge, exploring Philadelphia exhibits, and attending our first professional hockey game. The kids meet and spend time with Eve and my new friends.

Our excursions awaken me to how much I relied on my husband. Planning was my wheelhouse, execution his. I'm stepping into my new role: doing it all. I miss the shared responsibility but revel in the quality time with my kids. I'm single-handedly trying to salvage their childhood. I preserve the moments with pictures and think about how I'll arrange them in future scrapbooks. Will there be a Part I and Part II collection of books? A before and after? I let this simmer before taking a page from Scarlett O'Hara: "I'll think about that tomorrow. Tomorrow is another day."

I pick Tess up from the airport and head straight to Hope's house in New York. We're going to Provincetown for the final woman-themed event of the year. Time to recharge my personal battery.

We drive through the night to the Cape, not wanting to waste a minute of Women's Week. It's too early to check into our B&B when we arrive, so we aim for the beach. Because of Provincetown's sickle shape, the sun rises over the bay and it has one of the few East Coast beaches in which the sun sets over the ocean. Along the way, a palette of reds and oranges paint the sky. The breathtaking colors mimic the mums and dahlias prevalent in this town.

It's cool and quiet at the beach. The air is damp and the seagulls fish for their breakfast. If you look far enough, you might catch a glimpse of a ship in the distance. Tess rests in the coarse sand, her knees bent, as if compacting herself before the vast ocean. She closes her eyes and lets the delicate sea breeze surround her, immersed in the whisper of the gentle waves, looking as tranquil as the glistening water before her.

The only other people on the beach are two men who are shore-fishing. I join Tess and Hope on the sand. The three of us sit at the water's edge, watching the undulating waves of the ocean, so reminiscent of the surging currents of each of our journeys. We spot the occasional gray seal passing by on its own journey as we savor this shared respite—a moment in which the silence is only occasionally interrupted by a squawking shorebird. We are three women, strangers to one another two years ago but now interconnected by our remarkably similar individual paths.

Provincetown is bustling with people. Vivian is here for her first time. She's sharing a house with her friends from the yoga retreat. We haven't made plans. I'm walking west on Commercial Street when I first see her. My stomach flutters like firefly wings.

I avoid labels like "girlfriend" and tell her, semi-joking, that we're still getting to know one another, even though this month marks one year that we've been in this stage.

It's Friday night and my friends and I are at the Pied, a waterfront club I frequent whenever I'm in Provincetown. It's unofficially tagged the lesbian bar, but even I know this is a misnomer, because there are always men in lesbian bars. When I visited the Pied on my first trip here two years ago, I stood alone at a high-top table near the bar watching the mostly vacant dance floor and enjoying the music. I was fixated on one of the handful of women dancing and looking for any noticeable changes inside me, still trying to determine whether I could be attracted to another woman besides Raia. I can't say if the woman who came over to me had seen me watching, but she approached and asked why I wasn't dancing. Caught off guard and abandoned by my quick wit, I sputtered, "I prefer to watch," which I rued the second the words left my lips.

Tonight, I'm sitting alone on a wooden bench near the pool

table when Vivian walks in. I'm swept away. She's wearing faded blue jeans and a black leather jacket. Her hair, sometimes unruly, is perfectly done, and her makeup enhances her already expressive eyes. She stands next to where I'm sitting and says, "Hi, is this seat taken?" as if we've never met before. I play along and say no, gesturing that she's welcome to sit.

She slides onto the bench. "Vivian," she says, reaching to shake my hand.

"Melissa."

She makes small talk, and I'm amused. I'm impressed at her ability to be so spontaneous and charming. She's highly educated, and usually comes across as quite cerebral. She says being serious grounds her. But there are times, like this one, when she surprises me with her humor.

It's late; Vivian's companions left earlier for a different bar, but she stayed behind with me and my friends. Refreshed by the cool air, the four of us gather in the narrow street outside before determining our next move. The bed-and-breakfast Tess, Hope, and I are staying at is a block away, whereas the house Vivian and her friends rented on the east end of town is almost a mile away. Standing on the illuminated street under the tilted wooden light posts, I ask Vivian if she wants to come back to my room. She says yes and takes my hand, and the four of us start walking.

Inside my second-floor room, Vivian takes off her jacket but nothing else. We lie together in the queen-size bed, completely dressed. I nestle up behind her, the outside spoon. I lightly brush away her long dark hair and kiss the back of her neck. Her fragrance is intoxicating—a crisp, clean scent, like climbing into a bed made with freshly laundered sheets. Her aura surrounds me like the mesmerizing fog that encases the harbor here in the morning.

Lying against her, I feel her body shudder and hear her softly crying.

"Are you okay?" I ask.

"Yes," she whispers.

"You're safe here," I say, hugging her tighter.

I imagine she feels the way I do; I've missed her too. I've missed sharing my silly stories with her, how her gentle touch wakes up every part of my body, the comfort of her hand in mine, how she lovingly takes my hand and guides it under her shirt until it's cradled around her breast when I'm lying behind her—a subtle invitation to ecstasy. I miss the way our legs tangle together when she's behind me and squeezes her knee between my two legs, making us an interlocking puzzle. I've missed all of her.

I gently make my way on top of her and touch her slowly, as if it's the first time. I don't know if it's her or if it's because being with a woman still feels like a novelty, but with Vivian it always feels like the first time, though not in an awkward way. She is enticing and exciting and soft and smooth, like a flower petal, and I can't get enough of her.

I gently take off her sweater and plant tender kisses on her skin, taking my time as I graze over her upper body—reacquainting myself with her contours, getting lost in her. My hands are meticulous as they glide across her belly and linger on her curves.

I believe I could stay in her arms forever. I've never known peace the way I do when she's wrapped around me, cocooning me, and all I feel is love.

As always seems to happen for me in Provincetown, this instant with Vivian feels like a Kairos moment—a "feed your soul, doesn't get better than this" flash of time, a trice that occurs only few and far between in which the universe pauses, takes a breath, and you succumb to the pleasure and peace of a truly serendipitous moment.

After we make love, we drift off entwined together. It's the most tranquil sleep I've had in a long time.

Women's Week ends, Tess heads home, and the weekend bubble shatters. The gap between DH and me is widening. I send texts and emails, appealing to his desire to be a good dad, hoping we still share a common concern for the kids' well-being, but get nothing back. At times I'm seething. Anger is said to be a secondary emotion. If so, I'm primarily feeling fear and sadness. And loss.

One night, I arrive home from work to find my son there. He should be at his bar mitzvah class. This schedule has always fallen on DH's watch. This isn't the first time he's dropped the ball.

"Dad had to work," my son says. "He was helping someone move a safe."

This means he was doing a favor, not working at his job. A glowing red charcoal heat smolders in me as I step into the backyard and call his cell. I pace the patio between the wrought iron table and the rusting barbecue.

When he picks up, I begin yelling.

He yells back, "Go fuck yourself. Maybe you should have thought of that when you were screwing around."

"I'm sorry," I scream, "I had no idea I was gay! I'll spend the rest of my life apologizing for hurting you, but we're here now, and the kids need us. They deserve better."

In a world where you're supposed to bend and not break, I've been broken. Filled to capacity, my dam bursts. Frustration pours out of me for everyone within earshot, including my neighbors and my kids.

DH says, "I'm sorry, I can do better. I *will* do better."

I believe him. I desperately want to end this vicious cycle.

The call ends. I head upstairs, collapse into a puddle on my bedroom floor, and cry until I'm empty.

DH's promise to "do better" is short-lived. He continues shirking his parental duties—neglecting the kids' doctor visits and offers minimal assistance with bar mitzvah matters. I start assuming responsibility for everything—making appointments around the kids' school day, activities, and my work schedule. *Will we ever recover from this seismic shift?*

It's dark and cold when I drive home from work these days. I keep my gloves on and the heat blowing to warm me. The kids are often home alone when I get there. DH provides takeout food and leaves. He tells them he's going to work but seldom communicates this to me.

Shortly after the fight about the missed bar mitzvah class, I arrive home, walk through the kitchen and into the family room, where my son is watching television. He jumps off the couch to greet me. I ask what he had for dinner.

He says in one breath, "Subs from the store and Dad even stayed for a little bit."

The following week, I come home early, just as my once-husband is getting ready to leave. I try talking to him about how much the kids are left alone.

"I'm here with them," he insists. "It kills me to leave them, not to say good night to them."

"You're always welcome to stay in the extra room," I say.

"I spend as much time with them as I can," he declares.

"I come home most nights and you're already gone," I press.

"I leave so I don't have to see *you*." The *you* drips with contempt. This man who once loved me now loathes me.

I shake my head. "Do you realize you just contradicted yourself?"

"I don't want to talk to you anymore," he murmurs, and leaves.

I'm a rubber-soled shoe whose treads are wearing flat. The added responsibilities, extra chores, and bar mitzvah planning add miles until I'm threadbare. These circular conversations don't help.

DH's unreliability means I always need to be at the house. I've instituted an alternate weekend schedule, wanting more consistency for all of us. Vivian and I only see each other on the weekends the kids are with their dad.

The kids don't know I'm dating anyone, but they have met Vivian: they know her as my friend—like they know Hope, Tess, and Sparrow. When Vivian comes over to play basketball with my son or has dinner with us, she's always extra cautious not to reveal our secret. She never pushes me for anything other than what I think is best for my kids. She doesn't want to be the cause of any more stress on them.

It's mid-February, and there aren't sufficient layers or socks thick enough to shake the chill from my bones. I'm driving home from work when intermittent flurries start falling. I pull over to the side of the road to call home, and the kids say they're alone.

I don't know what possesses me, but I can't contain my anger. I drive to the restaurant where I know DH's girlfriend works and spot his car in the parking lot. I send a text that I'm outside and would like to speak with him. He doesn't respond. I call his phone. No answer.

I call Tess—I need her to talk me off the ledge. She tries but can't. I'm too riled up.

He left the kids again, with no way of knowing when I would be home, on a night with inclement weather predicted. And now he isn't responding. What if this were an emergency?

I wait a couple more minutes. Crickets.

Screw this. I walk into the restaurant and ascend a long flight of thinly carpeted stairs. My heart beats with the speed of a woodpecker drilling into a tree.

He's sitting at a tiny table with his girlfriend to the left of the landing.

Over the railing I say, "I would like to speak with you, please." Without waiting, I turn around and go down the dank stairs.

He promptly joins me. Standing outside at the entrance, he thrusts his hands into his pockets, his shoulders hunched forward. My jittery legs are barely holding me up. Our frosty breath fills the space between us.

I go first: "I've been trying to reach you."

"My phone was in my pocket."

"What if the kids need you? You're the parent on duty."

His tone grows hard. "This is my Valentine's Day dinner!"

"That's no excuse to go MIA if they need you, or if I have a problem getting home to them." I'm nearly shouting but I can't help myself.

He's unmoved by my reasoning. I get angrier.

"You're becoming the same asshole you said your girl-friend's husband was," I snap.

Seconds later, his girlfriend comes down the stairs, walks between us, and heads to the bar—which apparently has a separate entrance from the restaurant. She says nothing, but the way she brushes past us, it's clear she's wanting to make her presence known. As does the owner of the restaurant, who asks DH if he's all right.

I've read about this guy: arrested for tossing a young man out of the bar and into the street, where he was injured by a passing car. His motivation for throwing the guy out was because the young man was presumed to be gay. This certainly wasn't going to be a supportive place for me.

After the restaurant owner's clear siding with DH, I leave. I'm worked up, and nothing good can come from trying to engage him further. It's not that he doesn't get it—he doesn't *want* to get it.

I arrive home just as the snow starts to fall with an urgency.

Some weeks later, two significant events occur. The first is that my daughter sustains a serious ankle injury from a fall during track practice. The second is my mom's increasing concern about my stepfather. He's had some mini strokes that have impacted his walking and balance; now, his doctors have determined that the brain injuries they've caused are leading to a slow-developing vascular dementia.

"I've seen the signs but didn't want to admit it," my mom tells me.

He requires more assistance by the week; she and I agree to hire someone to help him at the bar mitzvah with getting food and using the bathroom. When we share this plan with him, he rejects the person we suggest and instead invites William, his sixty-something-year-old son, to come help him.

William lives on the West Coast. He's had a good relationship with his dad. He has occasionally called my mom over the years for parenting advice about his son from a brief marriage to a woman years ago. When he arrives in town, he discloses his current relationship—with a younger man who, he says, doesn't work and "likes to play cards," by which he means gamble. It all sounds rather sketchy, and his awkward mannerisms make my mom and me uncomfortable. But he's here to help my stepfather, so there's not much to do but grit my teeth and bear it.

It's bar mitzvah day. I am the hostess du jour. Vivian, Hope, and my mom load up our cars with centerpieces, place cards, sign-in books, party favors, yarmulkes, prayer books, speeches, and my son's tallis. We'll need this caravan later to transport my son's camp friends back to our house for the sleepover I've promised tonight.

We set off to the temple, several towns away. There's no Plan B if we forget anything.

A notable difference between this event and my daughter's is the table of new and old friends, bridging the gap between my former life and current one. Besides Vivian and Hope, Eve and Sparrow are also here. In a burst of spontaneity, when Vivian and I find ourselves in an otherwise-empty hallway between the sanctuary and the temple library, I steal a quick kiss from her, momentarily unconcerned about who might see.

Managing all the logistics for this function has been like going into extra innings in the seventh game of the World Series. DH never provided a guest list, so I had no way of knowing if he was bringing his girlfriend. She isn't here, but Grace is, so I sit her and DH together. The only words she and I exchange are when we unintentionally stand next to one another in the lobby, outside the library doors.

"Thank you for making the trip," I say woodenly.

"Of course," she says, equally as stiffly.

Seeing us together and not knowing our story, my photographer insists we pose for a picture.

My son stands at the lectern in his blue suit and bowtie reading from the Torah. I'm thankful for waterproof mascara. Sitting in the wooden pews, my mind drifts. *Wasn't he just born?* He arrived into this world quickly, before they'd finished gathering my information or securing a hospital bracelet on my wrist. He arrived before my doctor did.

The rabbi gives me the nod, so I approach the bimah, the raised platform in the sanctuary, and deliver my speech on shaking legs. Continuing the train of thought in my head, I talk about how my son's birth was the fastest thing he's done— how he's taken his time ever since, excluding his speed on the baseball field or tennis court. What I don't say is that indelibly preserved in my brain is the sound of his dad exclaiming, "It's a boy!" I can't forget the raw emotion in his voice. I knew that meant a bar mitzvah would be in our future. And that future has arrived—in a far different shape than I imagined.

Later, at the party, the photographer says she got a great shot of my "husband" weeping during the video montage. DH doesn't say much, but midway through the event, he approaches me at the edge of the dancefloor and says, "You did a great job."

My body softens at the compliment, just as it did last night—when, sensing my nerves, he gently placed his hand on the small of my back as we stood together as a family during Shabbat services.

Among the chaos of this quickly declining situation are breaths when I see a semblance of the man I thought I knew so well, the man I hope is still there somewhere under this angry smokescreen.

On the Monday after the bar mitzvah, there's no hurricane, but there's another storm brewing that will last the better part of a year and cost over one hundred thousand dollars before it's done.

I land at my mom's house after she phones in a panic, telling me that William has announced he's taking his ninety-three-year-old dad back to California with him. He already purchased plane tickets and bought and shipped a motorized scooter to his house (apparently unaware that his dad lacks the capacity to operate one).

There's a heated kitchen table discussion, but my mom and I are adamant that her husband of thirty years isn't going anywhere. I take immediate action to prevent what feels to us like an attempt to adult-nap my stepfather—to protect both him and my mom. In no time, we are entangled in a legal battle of epic proportions.

Meanwhile—just after William's announcement, before I've even digested the bar mitzvah cake—another fire is sparked.

DH stands at the door of my bedroom in his dusty carpenter's jeans, chalky T-shirt, and steel-toed leather work boots, his smell of cut wood and coffee reminiscent of the long workdays once so familiar to me.

"Now that the bar mitzvah's over," he says, "I want a divorce."

I tell him I need time to get through this crisis with my mom first. But he won't listen to reason and becomes irritated.

"It'll be simple," he declares.

"It *isn't* simple," I say, frustrated. "I just need time to manage this issue."

"People told me I was stupid to give you the house," he snaps. "I'm going to fight for my half of it."

His face is hard, his words are heated. I don't recognize him. I'm standing two feet from him, stoic and still, but my heart whirs like a chainsaw, my legs tremble under me. I worry my daughter is hearing this exchange; she's in her room down the hall, reading. He seems overwhelmingly large to me, his six-foot-three frame looming in the doorway. He's filling up the space and spewing threats.

He storms off. Refusing to get piqued, I pile this ultimatum with the other empty threats he's made since this bully persona began emerging in March of last year. But still I wonder, *Will he take the house from us? What more will my children lose? How much can I endure?*

The last, perhaps only, time we had a conversation about divorce, we agreed it was unnecessary to go through the expensive process until either of us wanted to remarry. At the time, we were both frightened and, newly uncoupled, trying to find a way forward. I was absorbing my life changes, while—I imagine—he was barely keeping his own emotional head above water, planning for this unplanned next chapter in his life. I believe he wanted to be a good provider—but in the two years that have passed since then, we'd rarely found ourselves like-minded.

Ever since realizing that we might divorce, I've imagined that it would be an amicable one—that we'd do it ourselves or use mediation. But I never revisited what it would truly mean to go through with the divorce, because I didn't want to. That reality meant more change—the most obvious being getting my own health insurance, which would mean more hours at work and less availability for the kids.

I'm fighting to hold on to anything familiar. I'm a person who needs time to process. He knows this about me, and even so he came in hot, wielding his announcement as a weapon. I reacted by pushing it away. He had to have expected that. We know each other well—know exactly how to get a rise in one another. The fact that we are invested in the same ultimate outcome, these days, keeps getting lost in the how and when to make it happen.

I don't have the time or energy to put into DH's threats or demands right now, so I shrug them off and focus on attending to my mom. William has taken to showing up at the house unannounced, so I'm getting lots of fearful calls from her.

I'm worried about my job, because on more than a few occasions lately I've had to leave suddenly to help her deal with all manner of things—from shady lawyers to 911 calls to the police to psychiatric evaluations to home assessments to court appearances to warning all relevant financial institutions of potential fraud from William.

As my journey continues, this will become a major detour. My mom's world will shrink to a sequestered existence while my stepfather, one of the brightest men I've ever known, will decline further into the depths of dementia.

The very last thing on my mind is divorce.

 **Chapter Twenty**

> *"Ultimately, we have just one moral duty: to reclaim large areas of peace in ourselves."*
> —Etty Hillesum

I'm sitting cross-legged on the floral-print couch in the living room when I call for the kids. They plop onto the matching loveseat across from me. I'm leaning forward, my head in line with my feet. If I could fold more into myself, I would.

I tell them I'm dating Vivian. They know Vivian and seem to like her, but I trip over my words anyway. I take deep breaths, trying to stay present, but still I'm transported to my early teens, when my mom started dating my stepfather. There was no such conversation then, no invitation for me to express my feelings or ask questions. I was displaced—the third wheel to their twosome or left alone when they ventured off to do their own thing.

"You both are my biggest priority," I assure them. "This is your home; I never want you to be uncomfortable in it."

They don't seem surprised by my news, but they say very little. For all my emphasis on communication, they have taken to not sharing their feelings readily—which means I never know if any discomfort I detect is emanating from the kids, or from my self-imposed fear of creating more tension for them.

They wait the requisite minute before asking if they can return to what they were doing before I interrupted them. Alone on the couch, the old tug-of-war between the me who wants to be entirely present for her kids, and the me who wants a personal life of her own, reawakens.

As time passes, the kids develop their own relationship with Vivian. There will be times when I will be told, "Vivian and I are getting our nails done" or "Vivian and I are having a culture day," by which my daughter means they are going to the opera or a museum. When we travel in separate cars, my son will ask to ride shotgun with her. Vivian will get folded into our lives by way of sharing holidays and special occasions. Later, there will also be shared family outings and vacations with Vivian, but I'll still reserve time for just the three of us on a regular basis. The promise DH and I made on Black Friday is crumbling, but this one is between me and them. It feels sacred.

It's June, and Vivian and I are attending the annual Women's Pride Dance charity event on Fire Island. Among the hundreds of women, we see Lori, the woman who organized the Manhattan dinner where we met. She dubs herself a matchmaker and says, "If you decide to get married, I want to officiate at your wedding." We agree.

Through the crowd of women milling about, all dressed in classic white, I spot a woman—deep magenta hair, sleeveless white button down, accessorized in silver jewelry. Toni. Seeing her gives me a mental nudge to put another checkmark next to the passage of time.

Fire Island is a thirty-one-mile barrier island located off the south shore of Long Island. Dotted by seaside villages, two of its hamlets, Cherry Grove and Pine Island, are a magnet for the LGBTQ community. Cherry Grove has been designated "America's first gay and lesbian town," and it drew gay people seeking to express themselves freely long before Stonewall launched the civil rights movement for the LGBTQ community.

Being on this island makes you shed all the masks and expectations we get accustomed to in the suburbs; it's as if they all evaporate as you cross the bay. Part of the island's charm is the prohibition against cars, the wood-planked boardwalks that line the streets in lieu of concrete sidewalks, the natural dunes, and the water taxis that transport you from island to island. It's a mini utopia of diversity and acceptance.

Vivian and I are standing on the dock at sundown, awaiting the ferry. A man approaches.

"I hope you don't mind," he says, "but I took your picture."

He sends us the photo: Two women embracing, unencumbered, flanked by rainbow and American flags under a pink sky. A paradox of being connected and free.

Vivian and I are at my house when the news breaks announcing the Supreme Court's latest ruling: the Fourteenth Amendment requires all states to allow same-sex marriages, as well as to recognize same-sex marriages in other states. This decision also marks the second anniversary of the landmark *United States v. Windsor* case, in which Section 3 of the *Defense of Marriage Act (DOMA)* was struck down as unconstitutional.

Although I'm nowhere near ready to discuss marriage (I'm not even divorced yet), acceptance of same-sex relationships by the highest court in our land—knowing that we could marry if we so chose—is the ultimate in being seen.

After the years Vivian waited to come out, and her struggle with her mother's rejection, this news is as impactful as that first clean bill of health after undergoing cancer treatment. Each of us still has a foot in two worlds, but this verdict is validating. We both have lost so much in pursuit of our identity—but as we fall into one another, weeping, we know we have gained so much more. With no more secrets to protect, all that's left is to settle deeper into the life we've been working toward.

It's Pride weekend and the platform for the PATH train heading into Manhattan for the parade is teeming with folks decked out in rainbow everything, from socks, hats, and flags to face paint. We emerge from the underground station to a city pulsating as if under the spell of pixie dust. Two million people have come to celebrate this day in the wake of the Supreme Court outcome. It's like the closing ceremony of the Olympic events: thousands standing symbolically as one nation, fireworks lighting up the night sky, music playing. Witnessing it—participating in it—you know you're a part of something special.

A week later Vivian and I are in Provincetown for our first week-long vacation together. We rise early to chase the sunrise, spend lazy days at the shore, picnic on the beach under a setting sun, and hike through the enchanted Beech Forest. In one of the many art galleries, Vivian purchases a three-by-five seascape painting by a local artist. We stare at it feeling as though we're standing at the bay admiring the lighthouse and smelling the salt air. Our glorious week captured on canvas.

The romantic summer is a welcome change from the stress of my winter and early spring. But is it an illusion?

Once, my preteen daughter asked me to ride with her on an indoor roller coaster. With no loops or inclines in sight, I agreed. We circled the track a few times before the coaster eased to a near stop, and I prepared to exit—but then the car started inching backward, picking up speed as it went. Round and round we zipped, all in reverse. I was sure I'd be sick.

I think about that roller coaster often now, feeling trapped, like I'm waiting it out. I wonder how long it'll take to stop my world from reeling—how long it'll be till I regain control of my life.

 **Chapter Twenty-One**

"Maybe the journey isn't so much about becoming anything. Maybe it's about un-becoming everything that isn't really you, so you can become who you were meant to be in the first place."
—PAULO COELHO

Late August, four months since my son's bar mitzvah, and the day I've been dreading is here. I'm sitting alone on the second-to-top tread of the eight-step staircase overlooking my living room—taking a pause, contemplating time.

The steps overlook the hundred-year-old baby grand piano that's filled the corner of the living room since before the house had children to occupy its empty rooms. No one plays it. I dust it once a week—occasionally less, always when company is expected—but every December it comes alive like Frosty the Snowman donning his magic top hat. The grossly out-of-tune piano has always been the cornerstone of our Chanukah celebration, getting decorated with menorahs and books, dreidels, chocolate gelt, and the kids' old art projects from preschool. To the left of the piano, under the bay window, is where we stacked our piles of presents—boxes of all sizes decorated in different Chanukah-themed wrapping paper. I sit on these steps now and see years of memories play back in my mind as if I'm turning the pages of a scrapbook.

Soon, I'll be loading the car with luggage and setting the GPS. My son and I are taking my daughter to JFK airport, where she'll board a plane with thirty other kids as they embark on a four-month semester abroad in Israel. By this time tomorrow, my daughter will be living in a part of the world nearly as far removed from where I am as she could be—5,750 miles away. She just turned sixteen a few weeks ago. I would have welcomed this opportunity at her age, but now, at my age, as her mom, I'm terrified.

She sits next to me on the step, nudges me with her shoulder.

"You have to give me something, something of yours to have while you're away," I sputter.

"Okay." She rises and walks down the hall to her room. If she's nervous about the adventure she's about to undertake, she doesn't show it. She comes back quickly, as if she already knew what she would pick, and hands me a silver Tree of Life charm. I recognize it as one of her bat mitzvah gifts. I slide it on a necklace and promise not to remove it until she's home safe.

Prior to becoming a mom, I questioned my capacity to love deeply. I believed I lived my life never fully engaging. People have walked away from me; I've walked away from others. My most intense feelings have been with Eve, Raia, and Vivian, but oftentimes it's numbness I feel in times of impending separation. I've sometimes wondered if I'm emotionally callused.

What I'll eventually learn is that I'm a deeply feeling person whose body needs to protect itself from overwhelm—but I don't know this yet. All I know is that there's an ache deep within my chest as my daughter prepares to leave for four months. My job is to keep her safe. We have survived mishaps and big scares, including two trips to the emergency room within her first four years and a potential eye disease that would have rendered her blind. But now, I'm caught between my desire to give her the freedom to flex her wings, and my paralyzing fear of the one event from which I know I would never recover.

We arrive at the airport way too early, so we detour to the Billie Jean King National Tennis Center to walk around the gardens and watch the qualifying matches for the US Open. My stepfather made tennis fans out of all of us and it's a perfect afternoon with my kids—except for the fact that only two of us will be returning home to New Jersey.

In the terminal, I take pictures and steal extra hugs, as if banking them. I hold it together, but it takes every ounce of strength left in my exhausted body. I'm a Goodyear tire with a slow leak, starting to flatten.

The tire blows right as my son and I return to our parked car. Now, I'm an erupting geyser, just like I was the day my uncle died. My son is silently stalwart. He gently rubs my arm as I work to gather myself. I know these tears are about more than my daughter flying so far away that I won't be able to reach her if she needs me; they represent the accumulation of stress that's been mounting in me for the last several months and has finally reached a tipping point.

DH stopped all communication with me leading up to our daughter's departure. Over the course of eight hours, I sent three brief texts regarding the kids and logistics, including info about my daughter's prescription that she'd need before she left. He never responded. My mom even called him saying he needed to respond, but he didn't. He shut me out.

Twenty-four hours after sending the texts, and three days before she was set to leave, he walked into my house, stood at the top of the stairs of the basement—I was down there gathering laundry—and nonchalantly said, "I just saw your texts. If it's important you should call me."

I vaulted up the steps as he sat down at the kitchen table,

looking smug. I was all angst, and his latest unresponsiveness had been deafening. I would later find validation in author Jeff Brown's analysis of such behavior: ". . . silence can be violence when it's used in an effort to wound," Brown writes in his book *Hearticulations*. "It is one of the most potent ways to cause deep suffering."

Trembling with exasperation, I roared, "I've tried every way to reach you. I have called, texted, sent emails, and mailed handwritten letters. The only thing left to do is show up at your house to talk to you in person!"

His face turned red. "I'll get an order of protection against you," he raged. "You will be served."

"On what grounds?"

"For intruding on my life."

So rattled I couldn't see straight, I was shaking. I dropped the kitchen knife I was putting away; it fell point-down, narrowly missed my foot. As I bent down to pick it up I cried out, "Why don't you just kill me instead of torturing me as you do!"

He stormed out the back door. The kids were waiting in his car, thankfully. They'd already witnessed far too much over the last nine months.

I didn't recognize this fear. I'd only once or twice before reached this extreme level of overload, and while in the throes of it, all I knew was that I was slowly losing control. It was the soft, repetitive drip of a leaky faucet burrowing under your skin until you couldn't take it anymore. The chronic stress my body had been consuming had hijacked my brain, creating an overactive fear and anxiety circuit, setting my fight-or-flight response on a hair-trigger.

I called Hope—an SOS. I knew she'd understand. She'd been where I was now many times before. I was spent—mentally, emotionally, physically. I was an arid mountain canyon about to be pummeled by a flash flood. A Kevlar vest would have offered no protection from the spray of soul-crushing bullets I felt I was being pelted with.

After I hung up the phone with Hope, I crawled into my daughter's bed. Over the years, her empty bedroom had become my destination during my most downhearted times.

Thoughts of losing my daughter left me gasping for air like a punch in the gut. My daughter, who shows up in a way that soothes my wounded inner child. When she's okay, I'm okay and I never want to let her down. But now it was me who was not okay. In her space, I surrounded myself with her presence—my baby books mixed on the shelf with hers, a white cloud–painted ceiling, a picture of us in cowboy hats, souvenirs from our adventures, her artwork, the musical brown bear that played Brahms's lullaby when she was in her crib hanging on the bifold closet door. All evidence of the childhood I desperately wanted to give her now provided the comfort that eluded me as a child.

I curled into a fetal position and wept. I stayed there for hours, until Vivian showed up. I would find out later that Hope texted her a 911.

Vivian slipped into the twin-size bed, huddled in, and wrapped herself around me. No words were spoken. She just held me until torment released its ironclad grip.

My son and I are still in the parking lot at JFK. I know we need to leave, but I'm transfixed, bound by some force. My daughter is inside the terminal, getting acquainted with the other teens with whom she'll be immersed in Judaism for the next four months. I am here, apart from her.

Moving at a snail's pace, I start the car and inch my way out of the parking lot, then the airport, aware it's now me who's moving farther from my daughter. That understanding lands like a tree felled in the forest.

I remind myself she's where she's supposed to be. I'm not abandoning her. If I were alone, I'd stay there until her plane takes off, until there was no choice but to leave—but I'm not alone, and it wouldn't be fair to my son to stay. I couldn't have dreamed leaving her would be so hard. It helps knowing I'll see her in seven weeks, as my mom and I will be traveling to Israel as part of the program's Parents' Pilgrimage offering.

I pull into the garage. My son, unfazed, goes about his business, while I steal a minute of solitude in the car to reconcile what's poking at me—a nagging sensation, a knowing that things will never be the same again.

The next day, having arrived safely in Israel, my daughter posts a picture of a setting sun over the Judean Hills captioned with, "So I live here now."

I shake off the feelings parading through me and prepare to start my day—but one of DH's recent outbursts keeps thundering in my brain: "No, I'm not the same person anymore!" he yelled. "This is the time of my life I should have been smooth sailing into retirement, but instead I'm miserable, and you got everything you wanted!"

He barked at me that he hates his life, that I'm to blame for his suffering.

Unnerved by these changes in the man I once knew so well, I spiral into fear about leaving my son with him while I travel to Israel with my mom. I email the liaison arranging the trip, and she adds my son to the reservation.

I sigh, relieved at having dodged another stressor.

On the morning of Rosh Hashanah, my son and I ready ourselves for temple. I grab items as I think of them: a jacket for me, knowing the sanctuary can be cold; our tickets; his tallis. I toss them in the car and then walk the garbage to the curb, the last chore before we head out. My goal is to arrive early, for decent parking and so we can claim a seat near a door. Being at temple is awkward, but it's important to instill reverence, community, and connection to our Jewish roots in my child. I'm hoping for a meaningful experience for both of us.

As I walk back toward the garage, a man approaches me. He's in his early forties, wearing nondescript clothes. I've never seen him before. He walks across my front lawn to reach me at the top of the driveway.

He says my name and hands me an envelope. He says he's from the sheriff's department and adds, "Don't shoot the messenger."

I open the envelope.

I've been served divorce papers.

It's been five months since DH told me he wanted a divorce. He never revisited the subject, and I've chosen to ignore it, not wanting to face this reality and all its associated pain. My fantasy of a non-contentious divorce and a reconfigured family unit still hovers in my mind. Rather than recognize the unlikeliness of this or attempt to understand my feelings, I shove it away, as if I'm pushing a ping-pong ball that keeps rising to the surface back underwater.

The look on my face prompts the man to ask if I'm okay. I mechanically nod, saying nothing, and he walks across the lawn back to his car. How long has this stranger been parked there, watching my house, waiting for me to step outside? I feel violated.

For several years after this, every time I see a strange car parked on the street outside my house I will be filled with dread, and my already heightened fight, flight, or freeze cycle will get tripped into overactive drive, making my brain feel like the frenzy of letters that appears on a computer screen when a cat stands on the keyboard.

Right now, however, I know nothing of this—I can only feel shock. A closer look at the papers reveals that they were signed in June, over four months ago. Between then and now, he didn't bother to discuss our options, did nothing to try to spare the kids the ugliness of a hostile divorce. Is there anything left to salvage between us, or has his newfound hate for me superseded all aspects of our life together?

Images of our family falling off a cliff, landing hard, and getting pounded by the crashing waves until we're taken under by an unpredictable body of water becomes a recurring scene in my dreams. I awake breathless, crying the words, "I'm sorry!"

When I later unpack this issue, exploring my profound resistance to divorce and my agonizing reaction to the papers, it will become clear that I've responded in this way because everything associated with divorce is noxious to me. It represents danger, toxic and ugly, its trauma fingerprint branded into me at an early age. I've been avoiding a situation that my body deems perilous. In serving me papers, DH is forcing me to let go and allow us both to move on—but still I'm holding on.

Holding tight to not divorcing has been an assurance that I won't get hurt, that my children won't get more hurt, but of course that is an illusion. We cling to what we're afraid of losing. I'm supposed to shield the kids, and to me that means keeping our family intact. I have an instinctual fear of what happens when the father leaves: danger enters, chaos ensues.

I remember my first supporter, Hannah, saying that the time to let go is when it hurts too much to hold on. I never got there. For me, the thought of divorce has remained more painful than holding on.

With the arrival of these papers, I'm free-falling.

Temple is now the last place I want to be, but I've made myself go for my son. I've never arrived at services this late, however, and there's no parking. The security team directs us toward a side street I didn't know existed.

My panic has now ceded to a catatonic state. Like trying to listen though a wall with a glass, the world around me is muffled.

The side street is so far from the temple that it takes us another ten minutes to walk to the building. There are no seats left in the sanctuary, so we head to the spillover seating section in the library where the services are being shown via a large screen.

I'm physically here, but my mind is elsewhere.

When I was growing up, my family didn't belong to a temple, although we lived two blocks from a synagogue that I would occasionally sneak into to admire the stained-glass depictions of Judaic scenes. We were a self-proclaimed conservative Jewish family living in a largely Orthodox neighborhood, although the label of conservative was a stretch. Judaism fascinated me. I was surrounded by it everywhere, except within my own home.

I watched the men walk to and from Shul daily. Saturdays, I observed the resplendently hatted women pushing strollers on the sidewalk while their slightly older children skipped along. The men wished me "Good Shabbos" as they passed, and I returned the greeting in kind.

My intrigue with my observant neighbors never dwindled, and I recognized I was different from them. Still, this contributed to the seeding of what are now my firmly planted Jewish roots. Perhaps it was a romanticized version of Judaism, the tradition and history that called to me. Perhaps it was the cohesiveness I longed for in my own unstructured life. Maybe it was wanting to belong to a community. Either way, there was a pull toward it.

I try focusing my thoughts on the positive impact of Judaism in my life, but I can't hold steady—my mind migrates back to divorce. How will this likely contentious split impact our kids? They're the reason I joined this synagogue. My husband, a Protestant when we met and married, was supportive when I wanted to raise our children Jewish. We were married by a rabbi and stood under a chuppah to exchange vows.

I liked that the house we bought, years before our children were born, was a mile and a half from the local Jewish Community Center. I liked that the original owners, an older Jewish couple, left mezuzahs affixed to every doorpost, Judaic symbols throughout the house—it felt like a way to connect the kids to their heritage, give them a sense of belonging to something bigger than themselves. I wanted to plant seeds in them for that faith.

Now I feel alienated by the very place I've worked so hard to make my community.

Despite my pull toward Judaism, my Jewish identity is more about ancestry, traditions, and values than about religious observance. I seek wisdom offered by ancient as well as modern rabbis; the hymns are soothing and the writings thought-provoking. I don't seek guidance from a higher power, though at times I wish I did. Lately, I'm finding private contemplation more useful.

That said, I can't deny that my time here has been well-spent. I've participated in sisterhood and discussion groups. I've attended fundraisers, Shabbat and holiday services, and partaken in social-justice events. In past years, I sought the rabbi's counsel often and became an adult b'nai mitzvah. For so long, I've coveted permission to be the kind of Jew I choose to be. I've been looking for an instruction manual, not realizing I have to write it myself.

Sitting in the library, the Rosh Hashanah services a hum in the background, I can't help but recall my daughter's confirmation. The rabbi emphasized not making people feel invisible, the importance of being welcoming, as we were once strangers in a strange land. Her words landed hard, since by then her colleague had stopped speaking to me, and—not unlike her sermon about adultery—filled me with angst.

Not wanting to miss the opportunity, I requested a meeting to speak my mind.

I remember that conversation. We sat in her office on cushioned chairs, facing one another. I addressed her remarks about making people feel invisible. I referenced her associate—how she had cut off communication, was no longer offering even basic courtesies such as "hello," and in doing so was causing me to feel very invisible.

"Well," the rabbi responded, "she and your husband have a special relationship."

Her defense of a behavior she'd implored a dozen fifteen-year-olds not to engage in just a couple of days earlier left me speechless.

And then came her response when I asked what she knew about me: "I know you're a lesbian because you told me."

Coming out is a gut-wrenching process. I'd carefully chosen each person with whom to share my truth; she was not one of those deliberately culled people. And in none of those conversations with friends and family had I ever used the word "lesbian."

I snap back to the reason I'm in temple today: the holiday services. The assistant rabbi, Rabbi Ruth, is delivering the sermon, broadcast on a large monitor. I spoke with her after my son's bar mitzvah, too, a last-ditch effort to find clarity, possibly compassion, within these consecrated walls. Sitting in her office, I attempted to offload my residual frustration.

At that meeting, Rabbi Ruth chuckled when I vented about how DH's refusal to engage had left me shouldering all the responsibility. "You would have done it all yourself anyway," she said with a shrug.

From the people from whom I once sought support and understanding, I've received judgment. By the people I once considered friends, I've been ostracized. I imagine it's hard to envision the good-natured, helpful man they know my husband to be as capable of any abandonment of responsibility. There was a time it would have been impossible for me too. For him, there is plenty of grace—but for me, there is none. No benefit of the doubt. I have become an alien figure in this once familiar place.

This synagogue was once my antidote to having grown up feeling excluded, like the marginalized kids who float from table to table in the cafeteria. I believed this Jewish community would have our backs if we were in crisis. To discover the temple is no different, no better, than anyone else in my life who's choosing sides and harboring judgments toward me has been akin to the childhood disillusionment of realizing Santa and the Tooth Fairy aren't real. I'm losing faith in the place where I once sought that very thing.

There's a profound sadness inside of me over this loss. We all carry deep wounds within us, ones we're always trying to recover from. Is this ache that wound? This feeling that I don't belong? Or is my wound about abandonment?

Rabbi Ruth's Rosh Hashanah sermon regains my attention. She suggests not judging people but instead asking, "What's your story? What is the path you've traveled that brought you to these thoughts and feelings?"

No one in leadership at the temple has asked *me* that.

I must reexamine my place in this Jewish community. I have done this work before, but I'll have to start over. I'll customize my Judaism, just as I have reshaped my personal identity and sexuality. Reconstructing parts of my life has become a familiar pattern.

My son and I return home. Pulling into the driveway, I recall the events of the morning and shudder. I resist the emotions; my son has already witnessed too much.

I've wanted to do better than my parents, to shield my kids from the worst of the fallout between their dad and me, but I've failed on both counts. They'll bear the burden, and I the guilt, of expelling more emotion and information than they needed or wanted to know.

When I later cross another threshold of self-discovery, I'll learn how to better anticipate and manage my body's responses—but the impact my trauma reactions have had on my children will never be erased.

The tears don't come but the thoughts don't stop, either. I'm consumed by this aggressive gesture, delivered by a stranger at my home; the divorce papers become the incinerator of my hopes and dreams—a symbol of my unfulfilled promise to my children.

A few days later, when DH comes to drop off my son from the weekend, he casually walks into my house, seemingly unaware that I might have feelings about what's just transpired.

His mouth opens but he's speechless when I demand that he leave. "You are no longer welcome here," I say coldly. "If you cross this threshold again it will be trespassing, and I will call the police."

I'm back in the mud, unable to breathe, knowing I'm embarking on another messy journey. Tess says to be gentle with myself, but it's hard. Bleeding, I can only hope the path forward will be found in the words of a thirteenth-century Persian poet. Rumi writes, "The wound is the place where the light enters you."

The light will indeed find its way to me in the not-too-distant future—but I'll have to travel halfway across the world to meet it.

 ## Chapter Twenty-Two

"Every blade of grass has an angel bending over it saying, 'Grow, grow.'"
—THE TALMUD

I'm in the guest room, packing. It's mid-October, and we're preparing for the Parents' Pilgrimage to Israel. I stop counting socks and T-shirts and contemplate what books to bring. I think about Joan Didion, whose memoir is on the bed in the "to consider" pile for the journey. In *The Year of Magical Thinking* she writes, "Life changes fast. Life changes in the instant."

One month has passed since I was served divorce papers—since my life changed "in the instant." A week later, I sat in an attorney's office, still fuming. Getting served wasn't in the MOU, the document designed to maintain our amicable relationship. Unlike my mom's eldercare attorney, who was sensitive to the nuances of her unfolding drama, often saying, "You can't make this shit up," the divorce lawyer I sat across from listened to my story with an impassive expression on her face.

"Well," she said when I was done, "that's the man you married."

"No," I retorted, "they look alike, but any comparisons stop there."

This was the only meeting with my lawyer in which a clock wasn't ticking, charging me $425 an hour. I wrote a $5,000 retainer check to secure her services—what seemed like an obscene amount of money, but in the end would be a pittance. As sole owner of an aging house with high property taxes and kids just a couple of years away from college, the thought of accumulating debt triggered my financial insecurity, inviting images of hardship and poverty.

My mom offered to help with the costs.

I remembered being twelve years old and accidentally setting my pajamas on fire while lighting an incense stick. I ran to the bathroom in search of water while patting out the flame. As I sat in my attorney's conference room, the same urgency overtook me, like I was on fire and running.

My attorney was all objectivity; I was all emotion. There would be no padding for my open wounds, and the only validation she offered was, "Yeah, serving you without first informing you of his intent was a real asshole thing to do. I'm surprised his lawyer didn't advise him differently."

My attorney didn't recognize—or maybe just couldn't care, given the nature of her work—how intensely loaded the idea of ending my marriage is for me. Buried in the casket of that now-dead marriage are the hopes and dreams I've harbored of an intact family unit. Even though our roles and labels have shifted over the last few years, I still believed this version of us was possible until the day I was served with those papers. Its unraveling has left me wondering how this will change my children. Will their own paths be altered by their having to manage these difficult emotions?

I'm still seeing my therapist, Lynn. Our sessions are dominated by speculation about what is driving DH. I can't imagine he understands how much divorces cost—if he did, he wouldn't have started down this road. Shouldn't we be putting this money toward college expenses for the kids?

Compounding this angst are other obstacles. I discovered only recently that DH changed his address with the health insurance company, so all insurance-related mail goes to him—including the checks addressed to me that are intended to pay Lynn. He's withheld those checks. The post office has confirmed for me that his actions are a federal offense, but my only option is to show up at his house with a police officer to retrieve them. I haven't exercised this option.

Soon, the added burden of fighting for those checks will cause me to discontinue my sessions with Lynn.

Back in the guest room, I channel my energy into packing— liquid travel containers, passports, and a Chanukah present for my daughter—but it's not long before I'm distracted again.

Five days ago, when I returned to my bedroom to get dressed after making my lunch for work, I found my cellphone lit up with several voice mails from Vivian. In the first she said, "I've been in a car accident"—in the last one, "It's bad."

I rushed my son to school early and raced to the hospital, but not before passing what was left of Vivian's crumpled car. Alone in my car I screamed, *"No!"* as I veered around the residual pile of metal parts strewn over the street from the four-car crash.

After what I saw of the car, I didn't know what I'd find when I got to the hospital. In my panic, I parked in the wrong place, farthest from the entrance, before jumping out and running around the building to the emergency room.

Breathless by the time I found her room, I was flooded with relief when I saw her sitting up in the bed, still in the pajama bottoms she'd worn when she left my house earlier that morning. I wrapped myself around her, not wanting to let go.

She had been hit from behind by a drunk driver and pushed into the opposite lane. She was lucky to be alive and had somehow sustained nothing worse than a combined fracture and tendon injury to her little finger.

After bringing Vivian to my house, I hated leaving her, but I needed to sift her medication from the wreckage of her car—now housed in a junkyard that was closing soon. While rushing there, I called my office to arrange for Vivian to see a surgeon through my workplace.

I was entirely fueled by adrenaline at this point, so it shouldn't have been a surprise to find flashing lights in my rearview mirror when I glanced up. I stammered an explanation about the situation to the policeman, referring to Vivian as my "partner," not realizing I hadn't hung up or muted the phone call with my coworker. The officer took pity, gave me a warning, and told me to drive carefully.

As I drove away, I asked my coworker if she'd heard.

"Yes," she admitted, "I heard everything."

I hadn't thought about when or how I'd come out at work. It had never been a high priority; besides, circumstances continually changed. Now, the decision had been taken out of my control.

The next day, I walked into the medical practice with Vivian—the same office I've worked at for years, the same one where a coworker once asked why I'd stopped wearing my wedding band, and another asked why I'd removed my family picture from the windowsill. Showing up with my same-sex partner must have raised questions. I received grace.

Vivian's surgery took place the following day.

In the guest room, Sophie, our affectionate, soft gray cat with whisps of white in her fur, is anxious. She knows we're leaving. I'm distracted from my task, my thoughts scattered. Luckily, I'm a list-maker; I always rely heavily on multiple lists to ensure nothing is forgotten. For this trip, I will do so even more than usual.

So much has transpired in a month's time. I can't decide if it's a bad time—or the best time—to be taking this trip. Vivian is doing well. I'm torn about leaving her. I can't imagine any other scenario in which I would leave her so soon after such a traumatizing experience, but visiting my daughter feels essential. She's been great at sending pictures, but I need to see her in person.

I return to my packing—itinerary, chargers, emergency phone numbers.

More thoughts intrude: It's a ten-and-a-half-hour flight; I'm not a great flier. I haven't told my daughter that her brother is coming too. Since his flight was booked after she left, I decided to let it be a surprise.

My mom needs this trip as desperately as I do. Her world has shrunk since assuming hands-on care for my stepfather. With legal injunctions in place to deter William from doing anything shady, and a competent aide on call if needed, she has made peace with leaving my stepfather for the ten days we'll be gone and is looking forward to the respite our travels will offer.

The flight to Israel is long—*too long*. It gives me too much time to think. The flight itself is uneventful, but I let out a giant sigh of relief when we finally land.

We're navigating through the crowded airport, a brew of different languages whirring by. I'm comforted by the hanging Israeli flags, and relieved that many of the Hebrew signs are accompanied by English ones. We pass the world's largest mezuzah, affixed to a stone wall in the terminal, before arriving at passport control, and try not to lose sight of one another as we scan the luggage carousel.

Busy contemplating whether to change American money for shekels on our way to the bus, I hear an accented man calling, "Melissa," and see my cousin waving. He and his husband live in

Tel Aviv and have surprised us here. I'm excited to see them, but I'm still rattled by the events of the past month, and overwhelmed by the introductions to the other parents and program staff, by my uncertainty regarding where to go, and by my excitement at getting to see my daughter soon.

Emily Dickinson wrote, "Hope is the thing with feathers / That perches in the soul / And sings the tune without the words . . ." Any perceptible hope I held about DH and I reaching the other side of this journey as coparents was muted the second I was handed those divorce papers. In this month of tumult and the Jewish high holidays, I've sought wisdom in an interpretation of Yeiush (a Talmudic concept about hope and staving off despair) that suggests what is meaningful to us will be returned, even in unexpected ways, if we have hope. I want to believe this, but I wonder—what's left to be returned? We all have lost so much.

A medley of ancient and contemporary landscapes passes by the bus windows during the forty-minute ride to the hotel. I think of the time when, as I was sitting at our dining room table working on scrapbooks, my daughter came in with the most downtrodden look I had ever seen on her young face, delicately placed her sparkly blue Tinker Bell magic wand on the table, and, as if delivering a death announcement, solemnly said, "It doesn't work. I've tried everything, but it doesn't work."

I don't know what specific magic she was attempting to conjure up, but despite her best efforts and sanguinity, the magic wand she'd firmly believed would fulfill the promise of its name—would make magic—had let her down. It was her first head-on encounter with disillusionment. I had no words for this distraught little girl, whose only miscalculation was her fidelity in hope. She was crushed by the reality confronting her; there were no words that could soften the blow.

We hold on to hope like a talisman, but we're limited by reality. My once-iron grip on hope has loosened; I'm beginning to see that continuing to hold on would be detrimental. Is it time to let go, as Hannah once said, and stop delaying the inevitable?

The bus pulls into the kibbutz. Finding my daughter in the lobby of the hotel, I wrap my arms around her as if I'll never let go again. My willowy young woman, who inherited her grandma's brown eyes and mine, has a classic, Audrey Hepburn look. She's bright and quick-witted, an old soul with an appreciation for antiquity and a flair for fashion.

I've missed her so much it hurts.

I reluctantly release her; it's my mom's turn to hug her youngest granddaughter, who towers over her—five-ten to my mom's five-two. Then my son sneaks out from the room where he's been hiding.

I watch as the scene unfolds—my daughter's face agape as she reaches for her brother, near tears as they embrace. I think of all the mistakes I've made as a parent, but this I did right. My children truly love one another, and the sight of their mutual affection fills me with unbridled joy.

It's our second night in Israel. I'm attending a special meeting with Rabbi Rick Jacobs, president of the Union for Reform Judaism, the largest Jewish denomination in North America. He's speaking about this week's Torah portion, Lech L'cha, the same passage my daughter studied for her bat mitzvah three years ago. Just as was the case when my daughter stood on our temple's bimah and read her speech, his interpretation of this already-meaningful text feels tailor-made for me. Suddenly, I'm the only one in the room, and the only voice in my head is his.

I lean forward in my chair to get closer, to hear his words more clearly. I'm engrossed in the message about leaving the familiar and taking flight into the unknown. The Torah portion is about God telling Abram to "leave your land, your birthplace and your father's house and go to the land I will show you."

For three years I've embodied Newton's first law of motion—*an object in motion stays in motion*—careening down back roads as though my brakes have been cut. This image reminds me of the time in college when my freshman year roommate and I took a road trip to visit her brother at another college. It was winter in upstate New York, where snow starts falling in October. She was driving, the road was slick, and we were heading down a steep hill. We approached an intersection and she hollered, "Hold on, no brakes!"

That event has been no match for my last couple years, and now, sitting in this conference room on a kibbutz, ten miles outside of the Holy City of Jerusalem, my car has come to a full stop. I rest in this space—heeding the Zen proverb, "You can only see your reflection in still water."

Disentangling Judaic passages is a common undertaking, a Jewish Cat's Cradle, weaving one interpretation into another. In Hebrew, Lech L'cha is translated as, "Go forth." Rabbi Jacobs argues for a more accurate translation: "Go to yourself."

Lech L'cha is a journey, he asserts, one that travels to the root of the soul. I hear this as an exhortation to leave what we know and discover who we are.

I drape Rabbi Jacobs's interpretation of my already-favorite Torah portion around me like a prayer shawl, taking copious notes even as I luxuriate in the feeling.

Abram tuning in to the small-still voice of his conscience— what he called God, the voice imploring him to undertake a spiritual journey, find his purpose, and live life as his true self—resonates for me.

Like Abram, I commenced on a difficult journey—a quest to know myself better—that has given me a greater appreciation for the importance of living life fully. At one time or another, we all hear a call and engage in a personal, perhaps spiritual, journey. In the Torah, God changes Abram and his wife's names. In my case, my self-awareness changed.

Listening to this rabbi, my conviction to follow a path toward a more authentic life is strengthened, as is my rejection of the notion that the choices I've made have destroyed my family. My family has been altered, but not eviscerated. My children enjoy a loving relationship with one another, and the three of us are fortified by our adventures. Their relationship with their dad perseveres, and I'm happy for the compromise if the alternative is him not being present at all.

I pull an ember from the incinerator and plant a new, stubborn seed of hope.

In a part of the world closer to where Abram began his journey, relevance and inspiration surround me—an invisible thread of connection transcending space and time to those who came before. Walking the winding cobblestone streets of the sixteenth-century village Tzfat, one of the four holy cities in Israel, I remember to slow down. The narrow alleyways and galleries of the mountainside art colony evoke endurance. I touch the cool stone buildings accented with blue doors and balconies—passageways to a portal into the past.

I pause at the top of the Great Stairs of this hilltop city, views of the red rooftops and lush green hills below. A soft breeze, ripe with mysticism, brushes my cheeks. A tangerine glow overtakes the cloudy blue sky, casting a shadowy blanket across the fields. I've fallen through a crack in the universe and landed in another era. It awakens the old soul in me, tugs on those Judaic roots I'm sentimental for, and imbues me with a calm that I've been hungry for.

On busy Ben Yehuda Street, a pedestrian mall in Jerusalem, street performers fill the cobblestoned artery with music while the cafés tempt with hummus and falafel. My daughter and I buy matching silver rings inscribed in Hebrew—*Gam Zeh Ya'avor*, meaning, *This too shall pass*. The roots of this adage spread broadly; they include Persian Sufis such as Rumi, a Jewish folklore story about King Solomon, and even Abraham Lincoln, who included it in an 1859 speech he delivered prior to being elected president. My daughter recalls that I've quoted this phrase often over the years, and says it reminds her of me. This tangible connection to her brings me comfort since we'll be leaving in just a few days.

I walk through the courtyard toward the women's section of the Western Wall, the Kotel, considered the holiest place Jews can pray. Along the way there are women: black, brown, and white women. Young women with baby carriages and old women with canes. I maneuver around white plastic chairs, women holding their heads in their hands, others reading prayer books. I slip into an empty spot near the wall. I don't formally pray, but I'd be remiss if I didn't do something special in this sacred place. Wads of folded paper lie at my feet—prayers left by those who couldn't reach the wall, or which have fallen from the stuffed crevices. Alongside me are women in headscarves and skirts—some pleading with God, their hands in the air, others with their foreheads pressed against the stone wall that towers above them.

I leave my supplication, folded on a miniature piece of paper, tucked into a crack between the ancient boulders that were once a part of the Second Jewish Temple built by King Herod in 20 BCE. My version of a prayer is a petition that this situation into which I've been thrust will resolve itself in a peaceful way.

Weeks after our trip, the sparks of what I learned during my time in Israel still burn within me. I collect wisdom from the likes of Austrian poet Rainer Maria Rilke, who said, "The only journey is the one within," as well as Ramana Maharshi, considered one of the greatest Indian Hindu sages of the twentieth century, who taught, "Your own self-realization is the greatest service you can render the world."

The unfolding evolution of myself that began with a calling, then a desire for authenticity, is ongoing. Believing that change was the only certainty, when that inner voice called me to cross a threshold, landing me in a pool of mud, I failed to remember that beautiful things—like the resilient lotus flower—emerge from mud. The information that surfaced at age forty-four didn't exist when I was twenty-five, traveling a predetermined path. Knowledge elicits possibilities. Can we surrender the devil we know to forge a new path? Imagine if we stopped punishing people for their emotional growth, for developing at their own pace. What if we were more like phototropic flowers—growing toward the light, ever moving in the subtlest of ways? Suppose there was a universal understanding that the "fittest" in "survival of the fittest" doesn't mean the strongest or most dominant, but the most adaptive? Perhaps the glitch isn't in adapting to new information but in never making any changes at all.

In my post-Israel contemplative state, I muse on whether it's more about knowing when to crack things open than about holding it all together. In a world whose purest attachment may be to impermanence, where living things are in constant motion, why are we expected to remain stationary, judged for seeking change? Why is *being* more valued than *becoming*?

My son thrives these days—doing better than ever at school, attending his friends' bar mitzvahs, proudly sporting the Star of David necklace he purchased in Tel Aviv. I look at the pictures of us in Masada, and I'm right back there—climbing the steep, snaking, four-mile path overlooking the barren, tawny expanse leading to the ancient palace in the Judean desert alongside him.

With my mom, who has arrived by cable car at the cliff-top site built by Herod the Great around 30 BCE, we explore authentic archaeological terrain left untouched for over a thousand years. Before descending the rock plateau, a rare rain event and mini sandstorm create a thick fog, as if a dense white curtain has lowered around us. With visibility reduced to zero, we return to the Dead Sea by aerial tram. We disembark the bus at the lowest place on earth in time to witness a sudden waterfall in the desert rock wall and a rainbow in the clearing gray sky, as if the symbolism of the natural fortress itself—oppression vs. freedom—has been animated.

My time in Israel was like *Bein Hashemashot*, twilight. This is the time in between, when the day is ending, and the night has not yet begun. It is in this space where the seeds of change are planted—where possibility exists, and one can begin to make order out of chaos. As the boundaries of time dissolve, there is opportunity for a new connection.

Thanksgiving approaches, almost two years to the day since I had four muddy paws tattooed into my skin, representing my messy journey. From the same chair at the parlor, I watch the artist ink the Hebrew letters for Lech L'cha next to the existing tattoo. My new emblem is a tangible reminder to turn inward. When that small-still voice told me to cross the threshold, like Abram, I was changed. A journey into oneself is unlike any other.

My mettle will be tested often over the coming years, and each time it is, I'll look to my skin-soldered reminder of Lech L'cha. I will pause, reflect, and look inward. I will tirelessly work to make sense of what seems ungraspable. And I will heal.

I already sense the beginning of this anticipated healing. In medicine, wound healing occurs by mechanical means—sutures, glue, staples—or by leaving the wound to close on its own, from the inside out. The latter, which relies solely on the body's own healing mechanisms, takes a little longer but is a wonder to witness. I feel this now—the edges of my wounds slowly drawing together.

This widened understanding of my journey gives me fortitude to press on as I bridge the past with an inevitable future. I think about that fateful Rosh Hashanah day two months earlier, replaying my Jewish journey. I've been fighting for my stories, unwilling to archive or erase my children's foundational years. I don't want our family history to vanish. I want to tell the kids stories that include their dad. Our narrative is cemented, and at the same time the past is like its own open wound, needing to heal, to slowly draw itself together like my tattoo.

I've been scrapbooking since the kids were little but have been reluctant to pull those books out in these past couple years. They were never intended to be time capsules, but rather like Torahs—containers of stories that thrive on being told.

Our temple has a mini Torah, affectionately called the baby Torah. It was acquired from the back room of an antique store; the story goes that it was rescued during the Holocaust. The scroll was mildewed and in poor condition when the proprietor donated it to the temple. Experts declared, "It's a living thing, it must be used, any attempt to clean it will do more damage"— so, going forward, it came out on Shabbat services and b'nai mitzvahs. Over time, the edges of the scroll appeared cleaner, the parchment brighter, as if it were coming back to life.

I want my family's stories to be revived in this way— organically, through love and the attention paid to them.

 **Chapter Twenty-Three**

"When we are no longer able to change a situation,
we are challenged to change ourselves."
—VIKTOR FRANKL

March is the month named after Mars, the Roman god of war, but also of rage, passion, and destruction. This military god is second in importance only to Jupiter—in Roman mythology, the king of gods and also the god of sky and thunder. His Greek equivalent is Zeus.

Despite its association with destruction, March is also a month of renewal, rebirth, and new beginnings. This is evident in the longer days, blooming trees, flowers bursting with color that ushers out the gray of winter, and the sounds of birds filling the air once again.

My daughter has been home from Israel for two months. She's a junior in high school and we're planning for the next chapter in her young life.

Today, we pack up the car and embark on a road trip—something all three of us still enjoy. I love even just passing time in my car, driving or not. My earliest memories include taking refuge in tiny spaces. In the den of my childhood house, I hitched a blanket to the wood paneling with pencil stubs and draped it around the faux fireplace. In this two-by-two cocoon, I enjoyed privacy and security. Despite having a pint-size bedroom, I sought even smaller containment, often retreating to my narrow closet as though it was my own private dwelling. Cars are a natural fit for a minimalist person like me.

As I grew up and into adulthood, I more than once inherited hand-me-down cars, starting with my stepfather's, who stopped driving after his second or third mini stroke. His was a sturdy sedan, had low mileage, and was, most important, free. It lacked the studio-apartment feel of my previous car, an SUV, but it afforded me the insulation of a petite space when I needed it. My car has been my portable sanctuary where I sought time alone to quiet my world. And the open road is the perfect springboard for contemplation.

We're driving south on the New Jersey Turnpike, the kids doing their own thing while I'm consumed by the significance of this road trip. I took a similar college-visit trip with my father when I was my daughter's age. Every exit brings us closer to our destination and represents another milestone, an opportunity to recall the many we've accumulated. Lost in my thoughts, the radio is white noise while the kids listen to their playlists on their phones and post selfies on Snapchat. I alternate having the window open a crack and closing it when the whistling wind gets intolerable. The only other detectable sound is the crunch of the pretzel logs I'm snacking on.

Wasn't it just yesterday that my two-and-a-half-year-old said she didn't want to wait until she was three to start school, she wanted to start *now*? Her whole life has been about getting to this point. In middle school she announced that she wanted to be a marine biologist, researching universities with good programs. I suggested we get through eighth grade first.

She read the *New York Times* Science section at a young age and became gravely concerned about the possible destruction of the ocean ecosystem by giant jellyfish. She surfaced her worries about this at temple, submitting a question via a Hebrew school assignment. The rabbi, interest piqued, investigated biome eradication, and used what she discovered as a cornerstone of that year's Rosh Hashanah sermon. During it, she read the question—submitted anonymously by a "young person" in our congregation—aloud. I knew the author had to be my eleven-year-old daughter.

Our home was a playground for inquisitiveness. Every room contained heaps of books. DH spent hours working with both kids on prize-winning science fair projects and, at her request, built my daughter her own *mbira*, an African thumb piano.

Perhaps her enthusiasm for higher education began with the trips we took to prestigious universities—trips where we admired ivy-draped buildings and imagined who'd walked the red-bricked paths before us. It hadn't occurred to me during our excursions to Harvard and Princeton that she would envision herself one day studying in those hallowed halls, but of course she would—why not? And now her moment has arrived. We'll be touring different colleges, collecting data for what will be the biggest decision of her life thus far, one that will have a huge impact on who she becomes in this world.

The turnpike splits—cars-only on one side, both cars and trucks on the other. I typically opt for the cars-only lane. Today, though, I bear right and go to the trucks and cars lane. My GPS is outdated, can't report traffic snarls or adjust if the exit numbers have changed—and I rely heavily on my GPS. My sense of direction is so poor, in fact, that I often joke that I use it just to get out of my driveway.

I'm cruising along on my side of the divided highway; the cars in the cars-only lanes are at a standstill. I coast onward, feeling grateful for choosing the correct side. It won't change our lives, but I'm happy to keep moving. And not all sliding-door moments like this one are inconsequential; some split-second decisions can change everything. Countless times a day we make arbitrary decisions—booking a reservation, deciding when to leave a place—without considering the possible impact a different choice might make. Myriad decisions with infinite possible outcomes that we'll never know. What if I hadn't stayed to help my colleague the day I met Raia for the second time? What if I'd left for my softball game instead, and never looked into her eyes? What if, at some point during the hours-long traffic and subsequent struggle to find parking for the August meet-up dinner where I first met Vivian, I'd listened to the voice telling me to just give up, turn around, and go home?

It's hard to imagine my life now had I not met Vivian. In contrast to the oft-repeated joke about what lesbians bring to a second date—a U-Haul—Vivian and I have gone slow and steady. I feel her holding me even when we're miles apart. What we lack in quantity of time we make up for in quality. Whenever possible, we draw the blinds on one reality and relish in one of our own making. We socialize with friends, take road trips, and enjoy weekend escapades to New Hope, Lambertville, Philadelphia, and Provincetown. She's my warm cup of tea on a wintry day, my milk-with-Oreos treat, my perfect, dinner-ready-and-waiting-when-I-get-home day.

As I pass the accident on the turnpike that's clogging up the cars-only corridor, I consider where we'd be if DH had been able to show up as my coparent, as a dad fully immersed in the kids' day-to-day lives versus sitting on the periphery. He would be on this road trip with us. He would see the importance of this moment and have an opinion about this weighty decision. We would reminisce and acknowledge the emotional tug of a life going by quickly. We would be the family we promised the kids. We'd get two hotel rooms—boys in one, girls in the other—and we'd walk the campus together, enjoy meals, tell jokes, and, as a family, consider the pros and cons of each school.

This is what could have happened but didn't. I'm the family historian and sentimentalist, and this bypassed opportunity is another loss hijacking my emotions. I'm collecting losses like Indian Head pennies from my amateur numismatist days in middle school.

I continue driving southbound. The kids are sleeping now; the congested industrial areas are giving way to large swaths of land. Alongside DH, we've driven this road countless times on our way to any number of places: our annual trip to the OBX, several excursions to Florida, day trips to Philadelphia, week-end explorations of Washington DC. I couldn't have imagined during any of those travels that I'd be leading this next rite of passage on my own, without his support. A single mom.

I revisit whether DH is not showing up because he can't. His inability is evident to the kids now too, especially my daughter. How is this the same man who walked the halls at two in the morning with our crying month-old infant even though he had to wake at four to go to work?

Shortly before leaving for Israel, my daughter spoke to her dad about wanting to spend time with him alone. Her recounting of this conversation was the first time she'd uttered an expletive in my presence, and she used it while describing DH's girlfriend, adding that he's different when she's around. According to my daughter, they always plan things for the boys—my son and the girlfriend's son—and she opts to spend time alone in the makeshift room designated as hers.

In that talk with her dad, she asked him to see her, to hear her. A big deal: she spoke her truth to him.

She didn't receive the reaction she hoped for.

Still, I was proud of her. I recalled when she was five, acting out as five-year-olds do. I spoke to her kindergarten teacher about her behavior. She said my daughter was doing fine in school, suggested that maybe the upcoming holidays were hard, as they can be for Jewish children in largely non-Jewish communities.

When I picked her up from her half-day at school that afternoon, before making the one-minute drive home, I turned to her, strapped into her backseat booster, and begged, "Honey, I can't do this anymore. Please tell me what's going on."

"Everyone got new beds but me," she said, clear as a bell. "Even the guest room got a new bed."

She was right, and it hadn't occurred to me that such a simple thing could have been turning her world upside down. We drove straight to the bed store and bought her a new twin bed. My happy daughter was back after revealing this mystery and resolving the dilemma.

If only everything were so simple.

After the conversation with her dad, our daughter asked if she could stop sleeping at his place on his designated weekends. I reached out to him, implored him to pay attention to her. Inside, I reeled. He was modeling that men don't show up, teaching her what it feels like to be rejected, to not be seen. I told him she was brave for sharing her feelings with him.

He sneered, "She's a hormonal teenager."

Several months later, my daughter was staying with me full time. It was the night of her junior prom. She looked stunning in her black dress and soft curls spilling over her shoulders. We'd met her friend group at one of their houses for a photo shoot.

I was leaving, having taken my pictures, and she said she needed money in case they went out after the dance. I didn't have any cash, so I offered to bring some back for her.

"It's okay," she reassured me. "Dad's coming to take pictures, I can ask him."

I was happy he recognized how important this event was and credited my daughter's courage in sharing her feelings for spurring a change in him.

A half-hour later she called, her voice low. "Can you bring me a little money?"

My heart sank. "I thought Dad was coming."

"He isn't. He already went back to his place."

She was crestfallen. She didn't say it, but she didn't have to. It was in her voice. She'd expected him. He'd said he'd be there. She'd waited for him to show up.

We've all been waiting for him to show up.

Maya Angelou said, "When people show you who they are, believe them." Similarly, Michelle Obama once said, "The presidency doesn't change you; it reveals you." What if DH hasn't changed at all, but has simply been revealed? And might he say the same of me?

I carry residual guilt about the impact of my self-discovery, a sense of responsibility for striking the initial match that changed his life's trajectory. It's waned over these months and years, but still I feel the sting of the domino effect when I witness the kids being bowled over. I contemplate his experience often. Through no fault of his own, he had to leave the house he practically built, the home we created, and daily interaction with his kids to start a new life he didn't want. I can't imagine how painful that must have been—but now that pain is being passed on to our kids.

I'm often unmoored by how everything we built together came apart as easily as a LEGO tower. The weight of the feelings of remorse, sorrow, and even compassion can bury you alive at times. I fought against the breakdown of our family— tried to make amends and limit the losses. Now there's nothing left to salvage, and I'm just hell-bent on protecting the kids from further fallout. I'm constrained in my efforts, given that he has his own agenda and limitations—but my recognition of this fact doesn't curb my appetite for running interference for my kids. I look for buffers wherever possible. I've been planning for them since before they were born. Protecting them has been my life's work ever since they arrived in this world. It would be fantastical to imagine I could stop now.

We arrive at University of Maryland (UMD) in time for our tour. Shaking DH's absence from my thoughts, I walk with our group of prospective students and their parents through the expansive campus and wonder what their stories are.

Snapping out of my reverie, I refocus on the big task at hand: compiling the list of schools to which my daughter will apply. It's hard not to be flustered, seeing price tags on par with my annual salary.

My daughter falls for UMD. Its sprawling campus, active Greek life, and proximity to Washington DC all appeal to her. My son seems enamored watching the students on their skateboards. He just turned fourteen and is an avid skateboarder himself. I wonder if he's envisioning himself as a student at one of these large universities as well.

Over the next couple days, we visit American University and George Washington University. We explore Baltimore, take pictures at the harbor, and create lasting memories.

My son asks to visit a dive restaurant featured on the Food Network. We trek our way to the unassuming eatery, whose fifteen minutes of fame are owed to Guy Fieri doing a segment on their ghost pepper hot wings. Ghost peppers are the world's hottest chili pepper, and my daughter and I laugh until our bellies cramp when my son's eyes open wider than a blue-eyed lemur's as the chili pepper hits his tongue.

I can't help but think how much his dad would have enjoyed sharing this experience. His dad might even have known to ask for milk to wash down the hot wings—known that water only makes it burn more.

🌼 Chapter Twenty-Four

"What you do makes a difference, and you have to decide what kind of difference you want to make."
—JANE GOODALL

The next few months are more of the same, each month another road trip along the East Coast to look at more schools. I've limited the college search to within a "tank of gas" to avoid the added complication of booking airlines or shipping luggage. It gives me peace of mind to know that in the event of some future emergency, I'll be able to easily reach my daughter. Simplifying and planning are more imperative than ever these days.

August appears suddenly; it's a twenty-four-hour turn-around between wrapping up another season of camp, repacking the car, and pointing it northeast.

I want to share my beloved beach town with the kids and tour colleges in Boston on the way back.

We cross the Cape Cod Canal, stealing sneak peeks of the ponds and marshes visible from US Route 6 as I invoke Mary Oliver: "August of another summer, and once again I am drinking the sun and the lilies again are spread across the water."

Our couple days in Provincetown are like origami: I gently fold my kids into my reimagined life. We're on Race Point, the sun setting over the Atlantic, the aroma of a nearby bonfire mixing with the warm ocean breeze. Under a gray-blue sky pierced by a pink stripe, the kids entertain me with an Israeli dance they learned at camp. I snap pictures of them in the white lifeguard chair, and them on the sand, my daughter's head resting on my son's shoulder. This last picture will land on a wall next to a framed photo of them sitting side by side on the beach of our old vacation destination, the OBX—a then-and-now depiction of time passing. I wish I could bottle their happiness.

Over the next couple days, we savor lobster rolls, sushi, and ice cream—the whiff of fried clams carried by a gentle wind. It's Carnival week—the town's busiest time of the season, a week-long celebration of LGBTQ life. Rainbow flags are draped in abundance above bustling Commercial Street. Decked out in high heels, glittery gowns, body suits, or short skirts, drag queens with perfectly coiffed wigs and dramatic makeup hand out postcards for their evening shows.

One afternoon, I see my son, skateboard and helmet on the brick ground at his feet, sitting on a bench outside the green-and-yellow-painted town hall and talking to Freddie, a man with a gift for conversation who bears a resemblance to both Ru Paul and Michael Jordan. My daughter and I approach and join their discussion. Freddie says he once played Scar in an international performance of *The Lion King*. When we mention our college tour, he talks about Emerson College, his alma mater in Boston. "Cast a wide net," he tells my daughter.

Driving home from Provincetown, we tour Northeastern, Emerson, Brandeis, Boston College, and Boston University, covering a lot of ground in a short time.

We arrive home in time for my daughter's surgery for the ankle injury she sustained over a year ago when she fell during cross-country practice.

I've made all the arrangements for the surgery. It's embarrassing being unable to answer the surgical coordinator's questions about the insurance, informing her that it's her dad's policy but we don't communicate, especially since the surgery is in the orthopedic department where I work.

For more than eighteen years I wore a plain gold band on my left hand and kept the diamond engagement ring with diamond wedding band DH had bought for me in a box. When asked why I opted for the simple band and not the blingy set, I replied, "Because out in the world is a matching gold ring on my husband's hand, the one we exchanged on our wedding day, linking us together." I feel his absence at these times just as I felt the absence of that band when I removed it from my finger. I took for granted that he would always be here with me. Now, too often, I'm lost, unable to gain my footing on this uneven terrain, wondering what lies around the next blind turn. I can't imagine he isn't going to want to visit with our daughter after her surgery. I wrestle with how to manage this scenario, considering I've banned him from entering the house. He asked that I text him after the surgery but hasn't asked about seeing her, and I don't want to make his needs my responsibility.

After much debate, I decide to make an exception to the ban and allow him to visit when she's recuperating.

Surgery day, I'm an outward beacon of calm, despite being nervous. We woke early to arrive at the surgical center on time. It's only been a week since we left Provincetown, two weeks since the kids were in camp, three weeks since my daughter's seventeenth birthday.

Nurturing my kids when they're sick or injured is easy, a freebie in my mom portfolio. I make every color of Jell-O, dress the couch in "boo-boo" sheets—ones they long ago outgrew but still bring time-honored comfort when they're not feeling well—and cater to their every food request. It's my chance to compensate for my penchant for talking more than any adolescent wants their mom to talk, for showing more emotion than they're comfortable with; it helps me feel I am making up for falling short in all the ways I fear I have. When they're sick, I'm Florence Nightingale–meets–Alice from the *Brady Bunch*; it's like there's a back-up generator inside me that kicks on when they need extra TLC.

I bring my daughter home the afternoon of the same-day procedure, relieved that it has gone well. Homemade chicken soup and fresh-baked chocolate-chip cookies aromatize the house while she rests on the family room couch, her casted foot elevated on pillows, *I Love Lucy* on the television, and Sophie the cat nestled in beside her. Tuesday has always been the designated day the kids have dinner with their dad. He'll be at the house to pick up my son soon. Anticipating his text asking to come inside to see our daughter, I contemplate which entrance would be better: the mud room, which means he'll go through the kitchen he installed a lifetime ago, or the family room sliding doors, where my daughter is convalescing.

Suddenly, my son bounds through the kitchen and into the family room and hands my daughter a pint-size flowerpot-arrangement of fruit before breathlessly saying, "Bye! Going to dinner with Dad now."

I wonder how many more times I'll land on the wrong side of giving DH the benefit of the doubt. I can't tell if I'm more disappointed in myself for trying to anticipate what he might do, or in him for not making the effort to see his daughter.

Thomas Merton—author, prophet, monk, and later priest—urges letting go of specific outcomes, emphasizes valuing the process more than the results. Václav Havel—Czech statesman, Gandhi Peace Prize recipient, one-time prisoner, and later president—echoes liberating outcomes in exchange for whether something makes sense, regardless of how it turns out.

I turn the Rubik's Cube over in my mind but still I cannot make sense of it. I wonder, *Will I always be trying to?*

A week later, it's the first day of school. My daughter, now a senior—on crutches, with a bulky white cast on her right foot—and my high school freshman son indulge me for a picture, both smiling, their thumbs pointing up. My son announces he wants to join the wrestling team.

I've long been against contact sports, considering the kinds of injuries I see in my line of work—fractures, spinal cord injuries. I struggle with the burden of these decisions, am torn between staying true to my gut and appeasing the kids, who've been dealt a crappy hand.

By coincidence, a patient who happens to be a high school wrestling coach comes into my office the day after my son makes his excited declaration. A former wrestler himself, and passionate about his sport, he espouses the benefits of wrestling—how it's both an individual and team sport, how good it will be for my son's confidence. He's convincing; I agree to let my son join the team.

My son attends the pre-season workouts while I order hundreds of dollars' worth of wrestling attire: special shoes, head gear, mouth guards, school-sponsored personalized clothing. I hear about horrors I never knew before and cringe—germ-ridden mats, skin infections, cauliflower ear, potential eating disorders from pressure to maintain their weight.

Am I really letting my fourteen-year-old do this? I ask myself. But I've said yes, and I stick to it.

The months between the start of school and my son's first wrestling match are busy as usual, which helps keep me from fixating on my worries. More college shopping brings my daughter and me across the border to Montreal to look at McGill University. The downtown campus, with its easy access to shopping, museums, and galleries, and the diverse student population check all her boxes, making this her first-choice school.

My kids are thriving. Everything is good.

My son's first match comes on a rainy Wednesday at the end of November, when the days are getting shorter. It's already dark when I leave the office.

As I'm driving home from work in heavy traffic my phone rings, but I don't recognize the number, so I ignore it. Soon, it rings again. Again, I ignore it.

The third time the same number rings through, I answer. A man's voice on the other end says my name as a question.

"Speaking."

"This is Coach Tom," he says. "There's been an accident, and we'd like you to meet us at the hospital. We'll be arriving by ambulance."

I set the relic GPS and find my way to the medical center, my stomach in knots, reliving the day when I rushed to get to Vivian after her car crash. My heart beats like a jackhammer, and again, I don't know what to expect when I get there.

I find the emergency room at the same time the ambulance arrives. Groaning from a stretcher, my son's right knee is twisted seventy degrees from where it belongs. A major dislocation. I worry he'll need surgery.

My daughter is still in physical therapy for her ankle. I've been in physical therapy for my back, which has been out of alignment and unstable. My calendar is already filled with medical, physical therapy, attorney, and temple appointments; I can't imagine where I'll find time to attend to another serious injury.

I don't know a worse feeling than watching your child in pain, powerless to stop it. I don't know how this injury, this latest disappointment, will impact him, how he'll cope. My kids' load is my load, and I want to keep my hands under their backs as they learn to float in the water, but I know I need to let go and let them become buoyant on their own.

We're in the corridor close to the nurses' station. I'm stroking my son's thick hair, kissing his sweaty forehead, oblivious to the bustling of people and beeping monitors. Within a few minutes, the emergency room doctor materializes at the side of the hospital bed. Without warning, he grabs my son's kneecap in his hands and manipulates it into place with a quick jerk.

My son lets out a scream and a "*Fuck!*" before his head slams back into the pillow. He breathlessly utters, "I'm sorry, Mom." I'm not sure if he's apologizing for the expletive or for getting hurt.

I look up—and there's his dad. I haven't seen DH since we split the camp visiting day to allow each of us time alone with the kids back in July. The stress of the situation and the stress evoked by his very presence sends my anxiety skyrocketing. I shouldn't be surprised to see him; the coach mentioned that when I didn't answer his first call, he called DH. But I've been so focused on my son that no other thoughts have been registering.

The doctor grabs my son's knee again and forcefully adjusts it a second time, sending my son into another round of shouting expletives for which he once again immediately apologizes.

My son gets moved to a room while we wait for his discharge papers. DH and I follow his stretcher as if we are strangers in a subway station. Adrenalized, I call my office, hoping to catch someone still there and schedule an appointment with the orthopedic doctor for the next day.

My son is given a leg brace. I decline the crutches; we already have a pair at home. As his pain medication kicks in, I start thinking about the accruing expenses—about how I'll have to deal with everything on my own.

We receive the papers. As we're leaving the hospital room, DH reaches for my son's duffel bag.

I seize the bag. "If you want to reach for something, try reaching into your pocket and paying for the medical expenses that have been piling up," I bark.

We walk to the car in silence, my son being pushed in a wheelchair by one of the staff.

As I pull the car around, I contemplate the possibility of another kid needing surgery, having to take time off from work, and having two convalescing children at the same time. I hop out to help my son into the car, and as soon as he's inside with the door closed, I turn back to DH and hiss, "You've become a deadbeat dad."

One year into the divorce process, we've been at a standstill for months. The next day, however, his attorney sends a seething letter, jump-starting negotiations for a settlement agreement again.

Before I can deal with the letter, I have to escort my injured son to the orthopedist to have his swollen knee drained, then to undergo thorough diagnostics to determine the extent of the injury. I'm relieved to learn he won't need surgery; the recommendation is physical therapy, crutches, no sports, and a lot of patience. This knee injury may become his Achilles heel, however.

At home, I box up the still-new wrestling shoes and head gear. I return what I can, marking the end of the shortest stint in a sport and a betrayal of my own values.

My son is upset at my decision, thinking he can regroup and get back to wrestling. At a therapy session I'm asked to join, his therapist tells him, "When it comes to parents who are different—one who's easy-going, bordering on apathetic, and one who's overly concerned—you always want the one who cares too much, who cares enough to say no."

Over the next several months, Vivian, the kids, and I celebrate my daughter getting accepted into McGill University. We go to Broadway shows and travel to Chicago, where the kids attend a Jewish youth conference, and meet Vivian's cousins.

We've grown more comfortable in our public appearances as a same-sex couple. However, we're asked too often, "Are you sisters?"

"Partners," we reply.

"Business partners?"

"No, life partners."

It's been a Mount Everest kind of year, and as I look ahead at the events still to come, including prom, graduation, and college preparations, I see a range of other daunting mountains in my immediate future. I'm already geared up to start climbing—but not by choice. It's simply my reality.

🌸 Chapter Twenty-Five

> "*Days pass and the years vanish and we walk sightless among miracles.*"
> —CHAIM STERN

I'm glad to bid farewell to winter, and to 2016, with its injuries, recoveries, abundance of time spent in physical therapy, psychotherapy, unfinished divorce business, and navigating logistics so my daughter can attend an international university. Our lives have become a treadmill running at 7.0 without a giant red stop button. I read Anne Morrow Lindbergh's *Gift from the Sea* and perseverate on the line, "There are so few empty pages in my engagement pad, or empty hours in the day, or empty rooms in my life in which to stand alone and find myself."

Two major changes in the first half of this year begin to sink in: that my daughter obtains her driver's license, and the reality that she's off to college soon. May and June arrive quickly, and we're checking other noteworthy boxes: AP exams, prom, and graduation. The days are filled with dress shopping, manicures, hair and makeup sessions, photo shoots, and unexpected emotions.

I'm dressing for the graduation ceremony. It's hard to believe it's been thirty years since I stood in my daughter's place. These rites of passage are like shuffling Mahjong tiles before the deal. I remember my graduation lacking that family moment, and now here we are again.

I fast-forward to the first day of graduate school—sitting in an ordinary classroom, eager to learn about child development. Instead, the professor talked about grief. My minimal understanding of grief back then was relational to death, of which I'd experienced very little to that point—but the instructor that day introduced grief as a different kind of loss, one I'm only now beginning to comprehend. She spoke about parents progressing through pregnancy carrying hopes, dreams, and expectations for their child and life they anticipate, imagining holidays, vacations, varied activities, and life achievements. She spoke about the deep grief experienced when those things do not come to pass.

Seldom are we given the tools for mourning the loss of intangible expectations. Misunderstood or minimized grief can leave us feeling isolated while a lack of empathy or being denied expressions of thoughts and feelings results in invisible grief. Life presents perpetual reminders of what is lost. For me, it's a high school graduation ceremony.

My unfulfilled dream of providing my kids with a sense of family, even after divorce, surfaces as evidence of what's unattainable. It's ironic how the word *loss* conjures up a void, an empty space, like a lost tooth or luggage, yet loss can be heavy. We carry lost hope and dreams with us for years, if not forever. Loss may imply emptiness, but it's by no means weightless.

In that graduate school classroom, I was introduced to a world I'd never thought about before. Disenfranchised grief was a curious concept for me then, but now it's ever-present on my mind as I grieve the life we won't have. Significant events leave me longing for closure, which I imagine as a box where you pack up your hurt and leave unfulfilled dreams behind. I conceptualize closure as the relief you feel once the splinter poking you from under your skin is removed. Ideally, closure fosters understanding—but when there's no conclusion, the unanswered questions linger, the shards of wood continue to jab at you.

We all have relationships we can't resolve or change. There are no hard-and-fast rules for attaining closure. For an oft-mentioned word, it seems rather elusive.

My daughter's high school graduation takes place on the football field at school. Vivian attends; she, my mom, my son, and I find seats on the aluminum stadium benches. Not wanting to be the subject of people's gossip, I'm on high alert. Scanning the seats, I see Joan and her husband among other parents of my daughter's friends. I bob and weave to avoid conversation. I wonder where DH is, how he'll manage the post-ceremony congratulations. I monitor my surroundings vigilantly, intent on avoiding surprise run-ins.

Once the graduating class has been officiated, I wend my way down the metal bleachers and see DH heading off school grounds. He has a distinct walk I would recognize anywhere—hands in his pockets, shoulders forward and slightly rounded, as if he could curl up into himself like a South American three-banded armadillo. He was here, but he's not coming to the field to congratulate her in person or grab a photo together. I stop and stare like it's the closing scene of a sad movie. I watch him walk off alone along a dirt path toward a side street. Is his pride worth the price he's paid?

I consider the price I've paid too. I wonder if it's time to detox from the guilt and accept that, just as I veered off the path to carve a new one for myself, he's walking his own path now too. I can speculate all I want about what drives him, but I can't really know. All I know is that my children are on the field, and that's where I want to be.

Late Bloomer

I find my daughter on the crowded football field, still in her navy blue cap and gown. Juggling pride, joy, love, and sadness, I absorb the significance of the occasion. *Am I ready?*

I'm not sure.

Nevertheless, my daughter tosses her graduation cap in the air, à la Mary Tyler Moore, as I snap picture after picture.

 **Chapter Twenty-Six**

"We are, each of us, our own prisoner. We are locked up in our own story."

—MAXINE KUMIN

In the 2010 scrapbook picture, my shirtless son is eight years old, the outline of his ribs so clear you can count each one. His sneakered feet are planted in the grass; his extended left arm holds the bow while his flexed right hand pulls the string back toward his ear. One eye closed, he's concentrating on his target before releasing the arrow in forward motion. Sometimes going back necessitates moving forward.

It's August, and the kids and I are heading to the OBX, our once-beloved family vacation spot. Our second year there marked the beginning of my daughter's formal education, kindergarten. It seems fitting to return there now that she's ended those mandatory academia years and is ready to embark on her undergraduate studies. We haven't been back since our last family vacation, right before the bat mitzvah.

We're driving south on the New Jersey Turnpike. Each stop along the way of this trip will offer opportunities to gain a different perspective on the past and create fresh memories.

I approach the exit for Philadelphia and remember attending the support group for late bloomers, where I met Norah. Norah was insightful, younger than me, with two boys and the most supportive husband I'd encountered throughout my journey. Having fallen in love with a woman, she was attempting to extricate herself from one life while building a bridge into another without disturbing the pillars already in place. Our common struggle was preserving the image of the family we'd worked so hard to create. We both desired to keep our framed pictures intact, to ensure that our kids could forever replay their stories through photos on the pages of scrapbooks or displayed throughout the house.

This was how I matched my longing with what I thought was our reality. My vision of creating a childhood vastly different from my own was successful—until it was no longer sustainable. What impact will everything that has come to pass since have on my kids?

As I pass the exit, I imagine myself standing among the shattered glass of those framed pictures. This trip to North Carolina is one way to sweep up the shards and reclaim my memories.

The kids and I drive south on US 13, a highway that crosses Delaware, Maryland, and Virginia before entering North Carolina. We stop for pancakes and eggs at our favorite breakfast nook at the border of Delaware and Maryland before continuing. I call out each state sign we pass, enjoying showing the kids geography in real time. Passing folks sitting on their front porches is like driving through a Norman Rockwell painting. From the backseat I hear my son shout, "Georgia! Delaware!" He's playing our traditional road trip thirteen-colony state game. I smile at the things that haven't changed. We reach Nassawadox, Virginia, a rural town named for the Nuswattocks Parish established in the 1600s.

I discovered this town, perched between the Atlantic Ocean and the Chesapeake Bay, on one of our early trips. There's a farm on the main road that grows cotton. We stopped to capture a picture of me, a born-and-raised concrete jungle New York City girl, kneeling among the green and brown plants sprouting white tufts, my smile as big as the cotton field itself. For years, the picture hung on the bulletin board in my home office, with the tiny ball of cotton I'd picked pinned to it. Later, I handwrote an index card sign: *When was the last time you did something for the first time?*

Years later, I would daydream about this question as I relived the first time Raia kissed me and in doing so birthed revolutionary sensations and broke a trance I'd too long been trapped in. Every risk I took later in life awoke dormant parts of me, surging my battery from red to fully charged.

On this trip, the kids and I stop at the edge of the same cotton field, breathe in the earthy scent and take a new picture of the parcel of land that from a distance appears dusted in snow. We cross the Chesapeake Bay Bridge–Tunnel, a seventeen-and-a-half-mile complex connecting Virginia's mainland with the shore, landing in Virginia Beach. We stop here as we often did en route to our destination. Fishing lines over the wooden pier form triangles that mimic sailboats in the bay. There are buckets of bait near the benches, gulls soaring overhead, the scent of fish hovering in the air. The rhythmic sound of water crashing into the concrete pilings is soothing. The view of the bridges separated by spans of water, under which the tunnels run, reminds me that everything sitting on the surface has a counterpart underneath, tucked out of view.

Forty miles from our destination, we arrive at the home of retired monster truck Grave Digger. I envision the scrapbook page, the photo of my five-year-old son standing next to a tire bigger than him and compare it to the picture I take now: my fifteen-year-old young man standing on the grass in his white socks, black sweats, and tie-dye T-shirt, Grave Digger looming behind him.

We drive over the Wright Memorial Bridge to our long-awaited view of the Outer Banks and Albemarle Sound, marking our official arrival on the island. Boaters, jet skiers, and drifting parasails above the saltwater jog my memory to that last summer we crossed this bridge. It's a full-circle moment between then and now. So much has changed.

Throughout that previous summer, I was trying to reconnect with my husband even as I was starting to explore LGBTQ-friendly places, attempting to sort out my emotions and understand the pull I was feeling to that other world. That mission started after we dropped the kids at camp in Western Massachusetts and headed to the riverfront shores of New Hampshire for time alone—atypical for us.

I, still in the outskirts of my confusion, was laboring to figure things out. He, seeing the detectable change in me, was suspicious.

We walked around Portsmouth's historic seaport, visiting boutique shops and eating at outdoor restaurants with river views. All the while I searched for feelings that might rekindle any passion, hoping to quell the questions that had me reaching out to strangers, reading books in hiding, and traveling hundreds of miles to gather evidence for or against a change in my sexual orientation.

The self-trial underway wouldn't have been complete if I hadn't searched for answers in my husband, the man with whom I'd expected to spend my life. He knew I was struggling but hadn't asked for more information, likely grappling with his own fears.

His was the face etched in my mind; he is still the man who continually appears in my dreams all these years later. Yet we were strangers in that Portsmouth hotel room. We hadn't been intimate in weeks. He hadn't seen me without clothes on for months because of the burns I'd gotten from the candle incident with Raia.

Lying in bed, he huddled against me in an uncharacteristic spoon configuration. We weren't cuddlers; it felt odd.

"Would you touch me?" I whispered.

"Are you sure?"

"Yes."

He could always satisfy me physically when we had sex; the problem was that I drifted emotionally. And no more was there this time than had ever been before. We had a shared interest in activities and an attraction that was now just familiarity, but emotionally, we were incompatible. I needed more, and he had no more to give. I was lost, and he could feel it.

I've learned since then that attempting sexual reconnection is not uncommon for women wrestling with their truth and trying to balance between two lives. Hope once told me about the last family vacation she and her husband went on together.

He wanted to have sex; she agreed, reluctantly.

"I felt ripped apart, like it was an assault," she told me. "I cried the whole time because it was evident this wasn't who I am anymore."

A woman from the Connecticut group talked about sleeping in bed with her husband after she had come out. They couldn't afford to actually split into two households. While she'd been trying to figure things out, he'd had an affair. Soon afterward, lying in bed together, she rolled over and initiated sex. She knew she was gay, but he was her husband.

It must have been confusing to my husband when our sex life improved after I met Raia. He benefited from my exuberance over my new "friendship." But during sex, I imagined her. This was another common thread I heard in my support groups—all of them fantasized about a woman during sex with their husbands.

Hope insisted, "I couldn't *not* fantasize about a woman while having sex with my husband."

By the time we went on that Portsmouth vacation, I no longer wanted to be intimate with my husband, though I'm the one who initiated it that night; sex with him made me feel sullied in what should have been sacred space—it had started to feel like a personal affront. After being with a woman and experiencing unfettered intimacy, I wasn't willing to sacrifice the emotional connection for the physical release. Sex with my husband seemed wrong in a way it never did with Raia.

The morning after we had sex in New Hampshire, Raia texted me. She was sitting vigil in a hospital, sixty miles away, where her mom had just undergone surgery. I told my husband I wanted to see her—be there for my friend. He agreed.

He dropped me off at the hospital and drove around town while Raia and I walked outside together. We eventually landed on a bench in a tucked-away grassy area not far from the road. I saw my husband drive by several times, unmistakable in our white SUV with black rooftop cargo carrier—my two worlds in a split-screen. If he suspected anything, he didn't say. Not that day.

Raia and I returned to the hospital to check on her mom. I waited on the first floor, in a sitting area obscured behind some stairs. She was only gone five minutes, but as I sat there, my husband walked toward me. He needed to use the restroom, he explained.

My time with her was a bubble, and he was a pin. He could tell I was angry and left before she returned. When she got back, I said goodbye and my husband and I returned home, never addressing the incident.

But here's the part I never told anyone: A short time after that trip he confronted me, blocking the doorway, getting in my face. "Are you having an affair with Raia?" he demanded. I was unprepared for his accusation. I slid past him and ran out of the house shoeless. The affair was over, but the unanswered questions and confusion dominated my every thought. My world and my sense of self were coming apart as I struggled to hold everything together.

When we reconnected, I confessed I had crossed a line but offered no details and said nothing about my confusion. I drew a boundary, and he stayed on his side of it. He could have pushed for more, but he didn't. He hugged me tight, pleading, "I don't care what you do, just don't ever leave me." Immersed in the unrelenting fog of my own uncertainty, I didn't have the capacity to consider how traumatizing the experience must have been for him.

The Outer Banks is a two-hundred-mile string of barrier islands jutting out into the Atlantic Ocean. When we cross into them, nostalgia overcomes me. In a snap of spontaneity, I decide to drive past the house where we stayed every year for almost a decade, wanting a glimpse of the A-frame oceanfront property.

As I cruise along Lighthouse Drive, noticing the old familiar as well as the recently refurbished beach houses, I slow down before making an unexpected full stop. There's a forty-something-year-old man in the driveway of "our" house, stretching as though he's about to go for a run. I pull into the long driveway and explain how we rented this home for years, and he invites us to look around.

We cross the threshold of the front door, passing the carved wood fisherman that greeted us all those years. The house looks as we remember it.

My kids find the American-themed bulletin board hanging in the foyer, outside the bedroom where my mom and stepfather slept, and the two photographs of them that I slipped behind the red ribbon long ago. They pose by the bulletin boards, pointing to the photos, and I take a quick picture of them.

The gourmet kitchen has a large center island, and we can practically smell the linguine with fresh white clam sauce and mixed shellfish their grandpa used to prepare. He was an excellent cook before the dementia.

I recall how, on our last family vacation here, my daughter shared a dream that her dad and me were getting a divorce.

I didn't insist against it, just told her she was safe and loved. Whatever she was picking up between us was translating into her dreams, portending what was to come.

When my husband and I stood in this kitchen for the last time, I was unsettled—one foot in my new world, one foot in the old. "What if I'm wrong?" I asked him.

Tapping his callused hand on his chest, his thick fingers spread wide like a paper fan in a hot auditorium, he pleaded, "Then come back to me, I'm right here."

In the oceanfront kitchen, I glance at the red and blue serving dishes featuring illustrated crustaceans on display above the mini accent windows, each adorned with a hanging white ceramic angel. I take mental snapshots, fast-forwarding through the precious memories associated with these decorations as if leafing through a flip book.

The kids return from their mini exploration of the house; we thank the gracious guests who are staying in what will always feel like our little utopia; and we head to our hotel one town away.

I'm riding my bicycle in pitch blackness, blinded by the occasional headlight of a car driving in the other direction. The kids are asleep in the hotel as I pedal the fifteen miles to the northern beach, where the Corolla wild horses roam. A pink shadow pushes up on an indigo sky as foamy water splashes against strategically placed wooden posts upon which seabirds rest. Alone on the beach, I reflect on being here twelve years ago, days before my daughter started kindergarten, and again now, a week from her beginning college. From between the tall, grassy reeds I watch the sun climb, changing the sky's rosy hue to a glowing yellow-orange, feeling the rebirth of the day and one in me.

I return to the hotel, where, over the week that follows, the kids and I soak up the coastal life with beach days and sunset nights. Our new memories reflect fun-filled dinners, jet-skiing, and photos of us at the Currituck Beach lighthouse, with my goofy kids pretending to push one another into the crab-filled water where my son caught his first fish when he was two years old.

On the last morning, we load up the car, point it north to head home, and prepare for the next transition in our lives.

Chapter Twenty-Seven

"We can do hard things."
—Glennon Doyle

September. My daughter and I are in Montreal, where she'll attend McGill University. We've been talking about and planning for college since she was a toddler watching *Barney*. Along with a college savings account, DH and I purchased term life insurance years ago to cover college expenses and the mortgage if one of us meets an untimely death, requiring the surviving parent to stop working. I also opened a credit card whose rewards have deposited bits of money into the college savings plan with every statement payment.

It's all been about this moment—but just like every momentous occasion of the past several years, it's nothing like what I imagined it would be. My daughter and I unpack the car we stuffed, with nary any room to spare. We set up her dorm room before heading to local stores to purchase accessory items—hangers, wall tack, a drying rack, and so on—quickly learning along the way not to respond to *bonjour* with the same greeting or the conversation will continue in French.

We explore Montreal: brunch in the gayborhood, a hike up the gravel path and steep stairs of Mount Royal —a small mountain in the city with spectacular views of the island—and visit the historic district of Old Montreal, admiring its seventeenth-century buildings and cobblestoned Rue Saint-Paul. We shop the Rue Sainte-Catherine corridor, passing homeless people camped against buildings, weaving through construction and heavily trafficked sidewalks that feel no different from the Manhattan streets to which we're accustomed. We land at a restaurant with patio-style dining and, the drinking age here being eighteen, toast to my daughter's new chapter with Cosmopolitans while conversations in French and English flow around us.

I'm in the hotel, dressed in my workout clothes, ready to go to the gym before packing up. I put in my earbuds. Trace Adkins sings "You're Gonna Miss This."

The floodgates open: I flop on the bed and sob. I'm crying for my pride in my daughter, for knowing I will miss her, for the exhaustion of the nonstop pace I've been running at, and for the passage of time, which keeps sneaking up on me.

I'm crying tears of anger, too—anger that I'm here, launching my daughter into this much-anticipated next phase of her life, without her dad.

I pull myself together, abandon the plan to exercise, and gather my belongings, including the bracelet engraved with our beloved *Winnie the Pooh* mantra—"You're braver than you believe, stronger than you seem, and smarter than you think"—and the decorated box of books I've been saving since my daughter was a baby, and head to the dorm. When she isn't looking, I leave the wrapped shoebox on her desk.

I'm a house of cards dreading the exhale when I say, "You got this," and wonder if I do too. Before I drive away, I flash her the sign for *I love you* with my right hand. I taught them sign language when they were babies, starting with *more please*, if they wanted more food. Over time, they also learned the signs for *please, thank you, you're welcome,* and *sorry.* When they attended playdates or parties, I would subtly sign them prompts to thank their hosts so as not to embarrass them with verbal reminders. As they went off to school, I did the same by signing *I love you* from across the room.

This sign, a raised index and little finger along with an extended thumb, became our special, silent farewell long ago. Standing in front of her dorm building now, my daughter flashes the sign back to me. She's eighteen, taller than me, radiating the beauty of the young woman she is, but all I see is my five-year-old daughter—tan from our OBX vacation, a colorful beaded braid in her hair—awkwardly configuring her fingers into the same sign as I leave her on her first day of kindergarten.

I drive forty minutes to the border crossing, the music from my playlist soothing me.

At the border, I hand the young officer my passport.

"What was your business in Canada?"

"I just dropped my daughter off at university," I sputter, and begin spewing like an open fire hydrant—chest heaving, nose running, bawling.

The border patrol officer returns my passport. "Drive safely."

After I cross into the United States, I pull over to dry my eyes, blow my nose, and open the package of conciliatory Oreo cookies that will get me down the New York State Thruway.

I look at my phone and see my daughter has left a message: *I found the box of books and now I'm crying. Thank you for everything you've done to make this happen. I love you so much.* And just like that Kenny Chesney is singing "Don't Blink," filling my head with questions.

Have I done enough? Told her everything I wanted her to know? Given her the tools and confidence to find answers to her questions?

I've been preparing her for this moment since before she

was two. She was eager to get here, always independent and determined. At twenty months old she jumped out of her crib, thirsty for freedom. She's been ready all along.

Am I?

After two years in the legal labyrinth, November thirteenth becomes my own seminal day. I recognize the date because of the iconic voiceover from the 1970s television show *The Odd Couple*: "On November 13th, Felix Unger was asked to remove himself from his place of residence. That request came from his wife." This led to this date becoming known as Odd Couple Day.

I am in the courthouse; I've lost count how many times I've been here. After hours of final negotiations, we arrive at a settlement. With the judge's raised stamp on the final contract, we are officially divorced.

It's unorthodox, but I ask to speak; this feels like my eleventh-hour opportunity to address the unanswered accusations, to wipe this slate clean. My last chance to be heard.

My harangue goes too long; I can't help myself. I refute every last erroneous charge leveled against me—my earning potential, the professionals I vetted to help our children, and, most egregious of all, that he didn't tell me of his intentions to initiate these very divorce proceedings before serving me with papers. He says nothing.

My now official ex-husband and I wait alone in an under-size room while the attorneys complete the paperwork for what seems like hours. Our shared purgatory.

"The irony is that several of the women I know who went through this same experience returned to their husbands and their lives," I say aloud.

I don't know why I say this, other than to try to hurt him in the throes of my own hurt. Perhaps to suggest he should have tried harder to make it work, even though I never considered that an option.

Again, he says nothing.

We sit in awkward silence in this compact fishbowl room with tall glass windows on three of the four walls, offering views into the two adjoining fishbowl rooms and the corridor. My heartbeat is reminiscent of my tachycardic days. My labored breathing fills my lungs with stale air. I think of leaving but feel glued to the seat, doomed to suffer this castigation.

There's nothing in this empty, sterile room but time to think. I wrestle with the emotional separation from who we were as a family of four, the sacred picture of everything I always thought I wanted.

I can't cry here, in front of him, so I use the photos on my phone to transport me elsewhere. Montreal in October, when my son and I visited my daughter—pictures of us atop Mount Royal at night, the lights of the city twinkling in the background. I scroll to September, when Vivian, my son, and I took an impromptu weekend trip to Provincetown. I smile at the live shot of my son standing on the pier in a nor'easter, his T-shirt blowing in the wind, while we waited for our fresh fish and chips.

Vivian and I have vacationed in Provincetown throughout the year for the last couple of years, experiencing all its seasons and moods, from its extroverted summers to its solitary winters. We love it when the streets are swelled with tourists and when it hosts only us and our shadows. We've put miles on our bicycles, chased sunrises and sunsets, gone gallery strolling, hiking, beachcombing, and whale watching, and enjoyed shows, tea dances, and the nightlife.

We've fallen in love with this historic town where the Pilgrims first landed in 1620, and we've fallen in love with one another there. It's where we explore, recover, and renew. We recently decided to try to buy a place there, to have a teeny footprint in the town that feels more like home each time we visit. We're solidifying this next step in our relationship by committing to a shared space that we can call ours.

In 1967, psychiatrists Thomas Holmes and Richard Rahe attempted to determine whether stressful events cause illness. They measured forty-three life events. The higher the score, the more stress it carried and the more likely the patient would become ill. Dubbed the Holmes and Rahe Stress Scale, their results revealed the correlation between stress and illness. The top three life events deemed most stressful were death of a partner or spouse, divorce, and marital separation, which was weighted only two points more than imprisonment. Curiously, the death of a child was not included in the original scale.

The skies are overcast when I drive home from the courthouse with the papers designating my newest label: divorcée.

The rest of my day is busy with errands, including several more appointments for both me and my son. A 7.3 magnitude earthquake struck the border of Iraq–Iran today, killing hundreds. It's also World Kindness Day, intended to teach children the value of being nice. Nothing stops simply because I'm now divorced. This high-ranking life event doesn't garner the same support as a death or serious illness or injury does. It doesn't get celebrated as engagements, weddings, and birth announcements do. It's not a Hallmark moment. I only have the fifteen-minute car ride to absorb the impact of its finality before readying myself for the rest of this ordinary Monday.

The car is quiet. My body is heavy. For years I've been circling this grief—for the loss of our shared history, the security I once held believing DH had my back, the things we enjoyed and did well together. Grief isn't linear or time sensitive, and it's certainly not logical. But on this cloudy Monday, it lands hard on me.

This grief is my ongoing work, the penumbra accompanying me wherever I go. I wonder how I will reach resolution—if one day I'll look at the ground and realize the shadow has broken free.

I don't know this yet, but the final severing will only happen when I finally break my habit of giving DH the benefit of the doubt. He's shown who he is, only ever to my own detriment. He orchestrated the divorce, and yet I'll soon discover that he won't comply with the agreement bearing his signature. In what will be the last text I send to him, I'll throw a Hail Mary, asking him for the accrued money owed for our kids' medical expenses.

I need an accounting of the money for the deductible reimbursement, he'll respond. *Please send me copies of the receipts.*

Hope can be a seductive trap. I will honor his request in good faith, mailing the manila envelope with the receipts and a letter outlining the expenses to his current address.

He'll never respond.

As the weeks pass, memories play relentlessly in my head. Not all landings are smooth, and I wonder if I'll know when I get there or if I'll perpetually drift, lost between the dream I clutched with white-knuckled hands and the reality of its painful demise. I vacillate between the Judaic decree of maintaining hope at all costs and the Buddhist concept that continually hoping for better prevents living fully in the present.

One of the memories I replay is when DH, Grace, and I were sitting at my dining room table shortly before she moved, and I asked DH, "Do you ever regret marrying me?"

"Sometimes," he admitted.

We cross into the new year and my latest label is an itch on my back that's just out of reach. I'm reminded of it every time

I check the box on medical forms, forcing me to contemplate what being divorced means, and what marriage meant. Our marriage not crossing the "till death do us part" finish line doesn't qualify it as a failure in my mind.

The failure was not making the transition from spouses to coparents, and in not doing so, breaking our promise to the kids. Herein lies my greatest wound. Later, when I'm farther down the road to healing, I'll tell my therapist, "I didn't marry a schmuck." The secret I'll keep deep in my heart is that I miss the friend I once had in my ex-husband.

Maybe I'm destined to land at a place where it's okay not to be okay. My own personal paradox. An imperfection branded into my life.

As much as DH has let me down, I let him down too. Maybe forgiveness isn't erasing accountability or excusing wrongdoing but a personal journey. Maybe it isn't emotional absolution for the person who's hurt you but absolution for yourself. Maybe it isn't the "if onlys" but, rather, the "what is."

 **Chapter Twenty-Eight**

"To love is to risk not being loved in return. To hope is to risk pain. To try is to risk failure, but risks must be taken, because the greatest hazard in life is to risk nothing."
—Leo Buscaglia (Dr. Love)

On June 21, 1857, Henry David Thoreau journaled that he had called upon Provincetown native Nathaniel Atwood—fisherman, legislator, and lecturer—at his home on Long Point. Nathaniel's father, John Atwood, built the first house on the sandy peninsula, approximately one and a half miles across the harbor from the west end of Provincetown, which for three decades was a thriving fishing village. Between 1818 and the late 1850s, dozens of houses, a lighthouse, a post office, a general store, a bakery, a saltworks, and a school occupied this fingerling strip of sand. When the fishing was no longer fertile, the residents floated their houses on scows across the harbor to the mainland. Nothing remains on this desolate spit of land today but the lighthouse with a nearby oil house.

Nathaniel's parents are interred in Provincetown's oldest burial ground, Winthrop Cemetery. Nathaniel's brother, John Jr., relocated his house from Long Point down the street from the cemetery. Today—June 8, 2018, 161 years after Thoreau and Atwood met—a studio sits on a piece of land equidistant between the graveyard and John Jr.'s Cape-style house. Vivian and I are laying claim to this dwelling, marking another portentous chapter in our relationship.

We're closing today on our three-hundred-square-foot condo with wide-planked hardwood floors, an outdoor patio, and a gorgeous garden in the town that's had a profound impact on me, and on us. Our shared sanctuary will be where we go to recharge. Vivian and I will spend many days and nights in this pint-size flat talking, loving, working through challenges, retelling our stories, and writing new ones. We'll turn to this place for solitude as well as togetherness. It's where we'll laugh and cry, hurt and heal.

I will spend time alone with each of my children here. My daughter will discover the beauty of this coastal town during an extended stay. It will be home base for me and my son as we go deep sea fishing and biking, explore the lighthouse, and venture to other Cape Cod islands for photoshoots, scootering, and mini adventures.

Having our own *sukkat shalom*—shelter of peace—in Provincetown stirs my soul. This nirvana awakens my dormant feelings—the way my emotional connection to Eve did, the way my physical awakening with Raia did. In different ways, those women and this place unearthed a little more of me. Provincetown has become my muse. Being here feels like those unique times I experienced with Raia and now with Vivian. Connected and embraced. Alive.

Provincetown's calling has been anything but subtle. It started as a rumble but grew increasingly and inexorably louder. She wakes every sleeping fiber deep within me. She's both my playground to explore and the warm blanket swaddling me, rendering me safe and secure.

I'm sitting on the bay beach—basking in the sun and taking deep breaths of the salt air. Ducks swim between the wood posts of an old boat launch; gulls rest on the flat tops. A man paddle boards while another kayaks toward the lighthouse across the bay. The smell of fried fish escapes from a nearby restaurant. An artist paints the scene from his easel and dogs run in and out of the water, chasing balls. I remember my first time here and how much I didn't know about myself. What was once escaping now feels like coming home. Overlooking the harbor, I read *Time and the Town*, by Mary Heaton Vorse. She writes about "falling in love at first sight" with Provincetown: "I knew that here was home, that I wanted to live here always." I look out at the water she once peered at and understand.

Leaving the water, I ride my bicycle through the narrow streets, admiring the unique light that has inspired writers, artists, and photographers since the late 1800s. Well-known names such as Tennessee Williams, Eugene O'Neill, Norman Rockwell, Jackson Pollack, Stanley Kunitz, Elise Asher, Charles Hawthorne, Susan Glaspell, John Waters, and Michael Cunningham, among others, have taken up residence here, permanent or temporary, in past decades.

I detour through the cemetery on my way back to the studio and find Norman Mailer's tombstone, which reads, "Norman Mailer is buried in a place he came to love." On the beach, walking in town, or exploring the burial grounds, I feel the presence of kindred spirits. It's in this wonderland where I'll flourish and where, like Mary Heaton Vorse, I'll long to make my home.

Before summer gives way to fall, the kids and I initiate the college-shopping tour for my son. In Canada, we tour the University of Toronto, where we watch black squirrels dart about on the sprawling green campus and admire the views of the CN Tower poking a baby blue sky amid billowy white clouds. We explore the brick-lined streets and industrial buildings of the Distillery District and marvel at Casa Lomo's colorful gardens. We pose for pictures with the roaring Niagara Falls behind us before returning to New Jersey.

Once home, we shift gears to prepare for my son's junior semester in Israel, the same trip his sister went on three years ago. This time I'm better prepared. As Julius Caesar is credited as saying, "Experience is the teacher of all things." We pack, pick up school materials, submit paperwork, and have the prerequisite goodbye dinner and photoshoot with Grandma more efficiently this second time around.

Before leaving for JFK, I retrieve the necklace strung with the Tree of Life charm I wore when my daughter was overseas, add one of my son's favorite guitar picks to it, and adorn my neck with the chain, not to be removed until he returns home safely. This time, I'm accompanied to the airport by Vivian and my daughter. By the time my son lands in Israel, my daughter and I will be back in Montreal, starting her second year of university. I'm staring down the barrel of a trial run with an empty nest.

Labor Day. My son is in Israel and my daughter has moved into her Montreal flat. I'm driving down the New York State Thruway, lost in thought but not emotionally distraught as I was one year ago. I recently turned fifty, and I mull over my relationship with time. *What is it about time that keeps tugging at me? Is it wistful longing for a life I wasn't wholly satisfied with when I had it? Is it fear of what's to come, or fear that what I want will elude me?*

With the kids in various states of launching, I contemplate what's next. Surely there will be fewer physical demands in my role of mom in these coming years. How many more thresholds will I cross?

The next four months will provide ample time for Vivian and me to sample living together as a couple. I've asked her if we can spend these months together as a dress rehearsal for what feels inevitable. As I drive down the New York corridor toward this next chapter, it's as though I've seen a double rainbow after a storm. I'm looking forward to a future that I've fought hard for, and while not unscathed, Vivian and I remain committed to walking our paths together.

 ## Chapter Twenty-Nine

"In the end, we'll all become stories."
—MARGARET ATWOOD

Journeys aren't simple, and they aren't singular events. They are cords of twine braided together, strands of our story overlapping until they can't be teased apart anymore. Often, you don't necessarily realize you're on one until you're well on your way. Other times it's a choice we make—we Lech L'cha as if it's a verb, we choose to go forth, but we don't always know where we're heading. These journeys require us to travel light, to let go of expectations, to release our binding ties and replace them with trust and faith in what we can't yet see, to forge forward toward the series of blind curves ahead. Some journeys, like grief, don't make sense; they're simply a path we must walk to arrive someplace else.

My journeys, like stacking cups, fit one inside the other— each part making up the larger whole, completing me as I move along; each cup is necessary or the rest won't fit properly. My journey as a mom, a woman, a Jew, and a gay woman is a sophisticated scavenger hunt; I unearth pieces of my puzzle along the way.

Vivian and I scramble on this harried October morning. Last-minute changes to our flight to Israel include departing from JFK instead of Newark, as planned, for the Parents' Pilgrimage. It's our first overseas trip together.

We arrive at the airport to find a jam-packed line snaking from one end of the check-in counter to the opposite side of the room. *We'll never make our flight* crosses my mind more than once. We land at the back of the queue, where a man looks at me straight-faced and says, "Welcome to the line." I'll soon realize he's one of the dads from my son's program. Learning that gives me the first sense of ease I've felt all day.

The late modifications to our tickets also mean that Vivian and I have to sit separately on the plane. I'm sandwiched between two gentlemen, adding to my discomfort of flying. On my right is an Orthodox man and I'm fearful of falling asleep, lest my drifting head land on his shoulder. On my left is a priest who spends much of the flight talking about his annual pilgrimage and how he always requests a seat away from his group for quiet (leading me to wonder if he realizes he's being anything but quiet).

I'm relieved when we finally land after an uncomfortable ten-plus hours, and I can reconnect with Vivian. It's her first time in Israel, and I'm excited to share it with her.

When we arrive at the kibbutz, I disembark the bus among a frenzy of unloading luggage, parents reuniting with their kids, and staff trying to help. Over the din I hear, "Melissa!"

My head snaps up. I hear it again, and through the crowd I see my son rushing toward me.

Seconds later I'm in the arms of my young man, soaking up the bear hug. I ask if we're on a first-name basis now, and he just laughs. "If I called *Mom*, all the moms would have turned around, and I only wanted to see you," he explains.

This moment is a salve soothing those old worries about whether he'll hate me for having disrupted his childhood. If the trip ended here, it would be enough. Lately my son, who used to love to talk, has begun pulling in, as many teenage boys do. He holds his emotional cards close to his chest, and I'm never sure what's percolating in his busy mind. The separation impacted the kids differently. He's closer to his dad—perhaps a gender thing, maybe they're more compatible. But standing in another part of the world and seeing him in this context, all I feel is awe for my beautiful boy and the person he's becoming—a sensation I drink in.

We've already explored Jerusalem and Tel Aviv, immersing ourselves in both the old and modern aspects of Israel. Today, a flash flood necessitates an itinerary change, and I'm not unhappy about it. Instead of visiting Masada and the Dead Sea, we return to Tzfat, the mystical village above the Sea of Galilee that enamored me three years ago.

Our group slips into an ancient hillside cave and stands in a circle atop the loose gray gravel, surrounded by extinguished candles, damp, earthy air, and untold history. We close our eyes and listen to the guide's echoing voice: "Judaism sees the body as a vessel, and our worth is in the contents. Look into people's souls, know them on a deeper level."

We take a collective deep breath as she softly strums her guitar and sings the morning blessing, *Elohai Neshama* ("breathing the soul alive"), and I feel the deepest recesses of my body fill with the very breath of understanding. In this shelter, I embrace the meaning of the word *Kabbalah* and am open to receiving knowledge. Torah says the living soul is what is seen and what is unseen, and in this transcendent chamber I absorb it all.

Vivian and I walk the cobbled streets of the artists' quarter. I spot a gold-framed painting of two women with an inscription of the Hebrew word *ahava*—love. It's the last thing I would have expected to see in a relic town untouched for centuries.

The artist, an Orthodox woman, explains that whenever she tries painting a man and a woman, it always comes out as two women. She talks about her oldest daughter, one of her seven children, who is studying to be a doctor and recently came out to her. The artist says she already knew, reminding me of all the people who saw it in me long before I did.

She tells us about the dilemma if her religious husband ever found out. "He's an old man," she says with a shrug. "He should live with his old beliefs and not be upset." The love and acceptance for her daughter alongside wanting to protect her husband from a reality he wouldn't understand strikes a chord. I wonder what Vivian feels. Her mother, after all, is no closer to accepting us than she was four years ago, and Vivian struggles to exist between two worlds.

Vivian clings tightly to the familiarity of her family, even after realizing the closeness she thought defined them was a cloak for her mother's narcissism—a fact evidenced more and more since Vivian came out. Vivian holds on to hope, looks for any sign of movement from her mother; in the absence of that movement, she attempts to release the dream of her mother showing up in a way she needs and wants.

This commonality we share—holding on to hope as we wait for people in our lives to show up in the way we desire—isn't lost on me as we stand in this grotto-like gallery five thousand miles from home, sharing stories with a stranger. We fall in love with the artist's heart, with the gold-and-burnt-orange painting depicting two women, and the representation of a love resembling our own.

The artist's parting words to us are, "Have a great life together."

After Israel, we head to Greece, where it's Vivian's turn to introduce me to her family's roots. It's a CliffsNotes version of Athens—a family dinner, a day on the island of Hydra, and then, before we know it, it's time to return home.

This time, Vivian and I sit together, and despite being long, it's a far more relaxing flight.

As the plane touches down and we start to taxi, I offer up silent thanks: *Baruch Hashem—thank God*. My mind drifts to the souvenirs stowed away in our luggage. Like a kid on her birthday, I'm eager to unwrap everything. I'm most excited about the bronze sculpture we purchased in Plaka, the pedestrian village at the base of the Acropolis. It depicts a nude woman—legs bent, back arched, arms stretched out behind her, head falling back, consumed by rapture. It embodies beauty, sensuality, confidence, and an enviable disinhibition. I fell in love with it the second I saw it and am already envisioning it on our bookshelf in Provincetown.

The plane stops, the cabin lights flash on, and we gather our belongings. I unbuckle my seat belt and turn on my phone. There's a voicemail from my mom.

In a quiet place, I listen to her somber voice. "Melissa, it's Mom. We're at the hospital, he had another stroke. They say he may not make it through the night. We're saying goodbye and heading home, it'll be a long night."

Twenty-four hours ago I was on an idyllic Greek island; now I'm winding my way through Newark airport—suffering through customs, navigating to luggage return—and trying to wrap my brain around the possibility that my stepfather might die tonight.

It's late and we're exhausted, so Vivian and I reluctantly agree to head home and go to the hospital first thing in the morning, hoping that he'll wait for us.

Not only does my stepfather survive the night, but he also demonstrates coherent moments when we visit the next morning, making me forget he's been held in the clutches of dementia for the last couple years. I suppose we've *all* been in the grips of his dementia—no one more than my mom, who's carried the load of caring for him in every way. When he no longer remembered the rest of our names, it was my mom's name he never forgot, calling her throughout the day.

Theirs is a love story of a different kind: a second marriage for both, a two-decade age difference between them, her always supporting his dreams. They amassed many tales of their adventures sailing from the Bahamas to Nova Scotia under the tutelage of a sea captain with a taste for alcohol. They visited ports, entertained friends, and fished off the stern, making sashimi from their catches.

Since we've been aware of the dementia, my stepfather has often forgotten where he's been but has never forgotten his quest to be a professional singer. We've relished his stories of competing alongside Frank Sinatra, appearing on the same ticket as *Gone with the Wind*'s Hattie McDaniel, and rooming with Mel Tormé, not least because their recounting has brought life back to a man being drained by a siphoning disease.

Notwithstanding his distinctive history, of course, the most heartwarming feature of this multidimensional man is his adoration for my mom.

The man who once resembled the bearded Pernell Roberts in *Trapper John, MD*, is now thinner than I've ever seen him. I remember a couple months ago when we gathered around the dining room table for a birthday celebration. Before heading to bed, he paused in his wheelchair—my mom at his side, as always—and proclaimed, "I want to thank you nice people for coming to visit but the most important person in this room is standing next to me: my beautiful wife, who I love very much." A predawn kind of quiet filled the room as tears filled our eyes. The one memory his dementia couldn't erase was his deep love for the woman who had become his lifeline.

Witnessing yet another flash of clarity as we sit here with him in the hospital room, I wonder if the recent stroke obliterated the dementia, as if flipping a switch.

Prohibited from eating solid foods, he will soon trial viscous liquids to determine his swallowing safety. In his slurred speech, he begs to go home.

I look into his blue eyes and say, "You need to get stronger first."

He reaches for my hand, and I abidingly place my fingers into his palm. He squeezes them tightly. I agree that he *is* strong, but the muscles in his throat must get stronger. He lets go of my fingers.

My mom is already struggling with bed and wheelchair transfers, hygiene, and dressing, and the stroke can only bring new challenges. She's called 911 so often after he's fallen that they know her by name. I've been worried about the toll the level of care she's been providing has taken on her—physically, mentally, emotionally. She's had no time to grieve for her independent husband as he's transitioned into a man entirely dependent upon her. After these last many years, I understand grieving for a person who has changed. Months ago, I reassured her it was okay if she couldn't do it anymore, if she needed to find an assistive care facility. She said, "I can't do that to him." Now, though, she may not have a choice.

A week passes, and he continues doing well. He transfers to a subacute facility. I visit him when I can; my mom goes every day. His legs are contracted; he's in pain when the staff turn him. He's bedbound. It's clear he won't return home. My mom is tired and lonely, yet every day, in every way, she shows up for him.

A few weeks later, it's Thanksgiving. My daughter comes home even though she'll miss classes since it's not a Canadian holiday. It's me, Vivian, my daughter, and my mom for a simple

Thanksgiving dinner. I feel the absence of my son, still in Israel, and my stepfather.

After an early dinner, my mom goes to the nursing home while Vivian and I prepare for the long weekend. Our plan was to go to Provincetown, and we stick to it; conditions seem stable enough that we can take a breath from the nonstop upheaval that's infiltrated our lives since we landed at Newark airport last month.

My stepfather is unhappy in his facility, often asking when he can go home, once uttering, "This place is killing me." Last week, he spent most of his time sleeping, not even waking to eat. But my daughter plans to join her grandma for visits to him, and to catch up with old friends while she's home, and she encourages us to go.

Saturday night, Vivian and I have hot toddies on the beachfront patio at the Canteen in Provincetown, a cafeteria-style eatery on Commercial Street, before heading to another restaurant nearby for dinner.

We're in between our French onion soup and main course when the phone rings, startling me. It's my mom. Perhaps it's the hot toddy I had before dinner, but my mind doesn't do its usual round robin of bad news she could be calling to deliver.

I press my finger in my left ear to hear her better.

"He passed," she informs me.

Despite all that's occurred, I never expected to hear those words. Did I really believe he'd go on forever, or at least closer to the age of one hundred and twenty, as he said he would?

"What?" I say, as if I heard her wrong.

She says it again. I'm without words.

She tells me how when she went to visit him earlier, he woke up for a little while. She fed him the mush, and he ate it. It was the first time he'd eaten in days. He was lucid and spoke more clearly than he had in a long time. He looked at her and said, "I love you." She returned the sentiment and left feeling happy.

"A couple hours later," she recounts, "they called and said he'd passed."

She wants to have the funeral as soon as possible, perhaps Monday, but doesn't know who to call. "I'll take care of it," I say, though I'm numb and not processing. I need to make the funeral arrangements and tell my kids their grandpa has died.

Once we're back at the studio, I call my daughter. Before we hang up, I ask her to wait till I can tell her brother before telling anyone else.

I email the principal of the school, who says my son will be accessible at four in the morning my time. I set my alarm, even though I know I won't sleep. Next, I call Hannah. She agrees to officiate the funeral. Her ultra-orthodox Jewish upbringing notwithstanding, she's an ordained interfaith minister.

After we hang up, I sit and wait.

Once 4:00 a.m. finally arrives, I take a deep breath and call my son.

"Hi Mom."

"Hi honey," I say, choking back tears. "I need to tell you something. Grandpa died tonight."

I detect the sadness in my son's voice but realize he's trying to console me. My younger child is trying to take care of me from a desert in Israel halfway around the globe.

"He had a long life; he had a great life," he says. "It was his time." He's sixteen years old and doling out such sage words.

While I don't disagree, I'll spend much time reconciling whether it was truly his time and what that means over the next few weeks.

I stare out the passenger window driving down I95, spellbound by the stick-figure trees, providing glimpses of houses typically hidden behind fully blossomed woods in springtime and summer. We're heading home to prepare for the funeral. How strange, the way life can stop and pick up speed at the same time. I'm exceedingly conscious of the time; there's so much to do.

On Sunday afternoon, I'm sitting at my dining room table, in the chair my stepfather sat in on holidays, trying to drown out the chatter of the others who are visiting my mom and write a eulogy for my stepfather. I calculate that he lived 35,465 days and invoke my son's sentiment when I write, *That's a lot of time. That's a lot of life.* I find words and stories to depict the man who entered my life when I was twelve and became a pillar of support, an influencer, and an occasional adversary in the ensuing years. I consider that before he was about to leave her forever, he showed up for my mom one last time.

Our stories matter. Our emotional houses are built with timbers that strengthen us, windows through which we peer onto the world, walls we lean on or hide behind, and the ghosts of those with whom our lives have intersected—but it's our stories that fill the empty rooms, giving them life. They're not always pretty but they're uniquely ours, and they shape us as we travel along our life's journey.

My son comes home from Israel in January. One of the first things we do is go to the cemetery so he can pay his respects to his grandpa.

He gets reacclimated to school, and we plan what colleges to visit over the next few months. Starting in February, he and I spend our weekends venturing off to Delaware, Virginia, Pittsburgh, Ohio, and Vermont. We do this on my designated weekends with him and in between his tennis matches. He's the team captain, has excelled to the State level of competition, and I'm immensely proud. With the help of occasional physical therapy tune-ups, his knee injury hasn't prevented him from succeeding in this sport.

I'm conscious that my son's leaving will usher me into a future as an empty nester, and I begin to prepare myself for that new phase. This endeavor starts with applying a fresh coat of paint to a couple of rooms in the second most important house that's built me.

These walls have not been painted since the kids were toddlers. There isn't a room in this house that doesn't have my ex-husband's fingerprint on it. His signature is everywhere—in the paint, the floors, the crown molding, and the built-in cabinetry that serves as the focal point of the family room. A simple project becomes a major remake, one I couldn't have predicted would be so physically and emotionally taxing. Every preparation is infiltrated by ghosts and memories. Every wall, every room has its own story, and I relive them all. I pull up the carpeting in my daughter's room, where I sat waiting for her to crawl into my lap asking for a story about my childhood when she was upset, upon which she hosted tea parties for her American Girl Dolls and Sophie the cat.

I do the same in my son's room, the room that served as both their nurseries. It was on this forest green carpet where the kids spent hours building cities and towns with blocks. I replace their twin-size beds, the ones I crawled into to read them books. They're both taller than me, and it's time for bigger beds. I give away the baby furniture, the desk that turned into a changing station when they were infants. I throw out the crib they slept in. I purge drawers, closets, and cabinets and stand on the sidewalk twice a week, feeling the bittersweet pang of knowing those stuffed black garbage bags on the curb are filled with pieces of my family's history. I paint over the kitchen cabinets that my ex-husband installed and cover the ceramic floor he laid down.

I carry the weight of my emotions, often taken off guard by their intensity, until I lose it on the poor, unsuspecting painter who's become like Eldin from *Murphy Brown*. His persistence in talking about "my husband," who he's aware did all the work in the house, becomes too much. He's ever in motion, pacing, moving, and talking nonstop, so much so that it's dizzying and hard to keep up with him. He continually contemplates out loud why my "husband" did this or that—at times condemning him, other times praising his handiwork. It's a finger poking around in an open wound, and I imagine an apparition of DH following us around the house answering the painter's questions. Like *The Ghost and Mrs. Muir*, he's become ubiquitous.

During a weak spell, I succumb to the pressure and unleash it: "You skillfully transform the visual landscape," I practically shout, "but these rooms contain a million memories, and I'm working hard to find peace in them."

He never brings up my husband again.

I find myself worming inside the crawl space—a dirty, cramped subterranean passageway beneath the kitchen, family, and dining rooms that I've never been inside of. I encounter decaying mice carcasses informing me of a separate world in the underbelly of my home. On the far end of the musty tunnel, I spot a pink string—strategically placed, but for what reason I'll never know. Only my ex-husband knows the story behind the string; it's now just one more ghost living within the walls of my home.

I'm exorcising the spirits of our shared house, creating a space that feels more like my own—one I can share with Vivian one day.

The painter paints the shutters, front door, and fence that my ex installed and the porch he built from scratch. I replace the ceiling fans and recessed lighting. I donate the kitchen table where we ate family dinners and find pleasure sitting on the new furniture and looking at the freshly hung curtains. My children's only request is that I not discard the Chanukah piano.

The last thing to go is the family room couch and oversize chair, the furniture holding the most memories. This has been an intense undertaking, and I take solace in Yung Pueblo's words: "Before I could release the weight of my sadness and pain, I first had to honor its existence." I walk around the house, with its new palette and updated decor, feeling renewed. As if invoking God after each stage of creation, I think, *And it is good.*

Vivian and I work together to pick out the paint colors and new furniture, and as we do, I realize I'm not the same person who entered this house at twenty-six, newly married and imagining one kind of life, blind to the possibilities of what others might exist. When I eventually leave this home for another, it will be with Vivian—the emotional connection I always longed for—with a sharper lens through which to see the world, and with a greater understanding of myself as I consolidate my separate roles into the one person I uniquely am.

 **Chapter Thirty**

*"There remains in the atmosphere of an empty room
a little of the human soul."*
—EMILE VERHAEREN

Provincetown in June is the perfect proportion of warm
days, cool nights, and foggy mornings. I'm visiting my
daughter, who has been working here in between her semester
in Montreal and a six-week summer course she'll be doing in
London at Cambridge. The crowds are manageable, rainbow
flags are flying, skiffs and sailboats have returned to the bay,
and the gardens are in full bloom. Sitting on the brick steps of
our condo with my morning tea, the subtle scent of white dai-
sies opening for the day, I watch bees and butterflies siphoning
nectar from the flowers, glance up at mourning doves cooing
from atop leaning utility poles, and look for the red fox who
occasionally crosses the narrow street, her fresh catch still in
her mouth. Dogwalkers, bicyclists, and pedestrians always say
hello; some stop at the white picket fence to chat. At night,
I'll open the windows and listen for the baritone bullfrogs.
Provincetown never fails to wake my inner slumber, revealing
an energy I don't seem to have elsewhere.

My daughter and I are hiking the Beech Forest Trail, a
sand-covered footpath with a grove of gnarly trees flanking a
lily-covered pond on one side and beach dunes on the other. Ser-
enaded by whistling chickadees, we navigate over and around

dry leaves and pine needles to a steep sand dune sheltered by tupelo, beech, and oak trees. After climbing log steps, the setting for an impromptu photoshoot, we land on a wooden dock that juts out into a shallow beach pond scented by wet grass and dew. Our typically noisy worlds briefly muted, we embrace this quiet place of peaceful contemplation.

Back in the studio, my mom calls. My cousin, Jayne, has entered hospice care.

I fall back onto the couch as though shoved, even though I knew this was coming. Jayne is three years older than me, with a smile as contagious as a yawn. A woman I admire. I once asked her to be my kids' guardian if my husband and I were unable. Now she's losing the battle against a rare and aggressive cancer—an indomitable disease she's been fighting since around the time of my daughter's bat mitzvah. There was a brief remission at one point, but then it returned with a vengeance. Less than a year ago, her daughter got married—a beautiful Cape Cod wedding, though not knowing if it would be the last big event my cousin would attend made it bittersweet.

The outdoor ceremony overlooked the serene waters of the Nantucket Sound, where the blue water seamlessly met the clear sky at the horizon, yet what stole the guests' attention was a gray seal lingering by a stone wall just beyond the chuppah, as though he were a guest watching. Jayne's oldest sister claimed it was the spirit of their beloved dad, my uncle—the one whose death spurred such an intense reaction in me all those years ago.

We all knew this was coming, but it still feels too soon.

Days after Jayne passes—peacefully, shortly after transitioning to hospice, surrounded by her immediate family—we gather at her house. Pictures and flowers adorn the patio; no one is wearing black. Her siblings, children, and my aunt all wear attire featuring sunflowers, Jayne's favorite. My brain is a carousel carrying one recurring thought: *How will she never be here with these people again?*

Vivian and I, along with my mom and kids, stand on the perimeter of the yard, moved to tears and laughter by people's stories about my cousin. Her ex-husband approaches the makeshift patio pulpit. His own personal journey catalyzed their divorce, leaving my cousin to start over, but they remained amicable.

He stands before us, his second wife nearby, and talks about the conversation he and Jayne had before she died. Here he is, honoring her last request, reciting the lyrics to Five for Fighting's "Superman," bestowing a gift onto his children that strikes me so much in its simplicity. He showed up. He showed up for Jayne and for his kids, giving them a bridge to stand on, something to span their grief-stricken abyss.

I recoil from the realization that my children would not experience such a scenario, were the worst to happen. I only hope that when the time comes, they'll show up for each other.

A day later I'm driving to Provincetown to collect my daughter's belongings, since she left abruptly by ferry to return home for Jayne's tribute. The time alone in my portable sanctuary is welcome. I'm mostly lost in my sadness, but I do notice all the sunflowers along the way—have they always been there, or am I more attuned to them now?

I'll take these few days to understand how a person I've always known, a contemporary with two children like me, is gone. It triggers my fear of not being there for my children. I've been rehearsing this scene privately for years. I've written letters to them, "just in case," and of course stories fill the scrapbooks I've made. Losing Jayne brings death to life; imagining my kids' lives without me in it is a beat of a gong that reverberates through me.

I sequester myself in the studio, my refuge for peace and healing. Jayne's passing has brought all my accumulated grief to the forefront. I can no longer not see it, set it aside, or intellectualize it—it needs to be dealt with. Curled up on the couch, wrapped so tightly in a blanket that it feels like a second skin, I read, write, listen to podcasts, and try to make sense of the senseless. I'm no stranger to this work.

I stumble across a TED Talk by Nora McInerny about grief, a subject she knows well following the successive deaths of her father and husband. She suggests that we don't move on from grief, we move forward with it. She proposes that grief is more than a moment in time, it's chronic; she posits the idea that not all wounds are meant to heal.

I straighten up on the couch, contemplating this notion. Maybe it isn't a specific healing or closure that I need but rather acceptance of my current reality. Maybe closure isn't a box after all—not a construct you seal and leave behind—but rather a space you create and carry with you, a mini annex built onto your emotional house.

Mine is a different loss from death. My ex-husband is alive but off-limits; I feel his presence and witness my children's sadness at our circumstance. I have dreams about him in which it's impossible to know what's real and what isn't until I wake and realize that none of it is. He is a force surrounding me, swirling atoms in my private atmosphere, yet there's nothing tangible, nothing to hold on to; it's like grasping at wind.

I examine the Pandora's box that my ex-husband's choices opened. How my excommunication from his life launched me into single parenthood, forcing me to confront adolescent me and her deepest, time-hallowed fears. Navigating the emotional minefield along with the physical exhaustion was like climbing Mount Washington in winter. After a time, friends reprimanded me for not moving on, as though there were a statute of limitations for difficult feelings. But the grenades were still falling. My therapist, thankfully, disagreed with the laypeople's advice, advocating that no one can heal while still being wounded. I held on to those words like a flotation device but still felt like I was drowning.

Perched on the couch, I replay Nora McInerny's talk and consider packing up my grief and loss, along with those memories I've found hard to revisit. Instead of willing myself to move *on*, what if I try merely to move *forward*? The facts are these: My ex-husband and I shared many years. We have children together. He isn't physically present, but he isn't going anywhere. He's ingrained within me, our history, our children, reminders that find me wherever I go.

I recalibrate my thoughts, commit to accepting the uncomfortable feelings and empowering myself so they can't ambush me anymore. I take an index card and make a sign out of Maya Angelou's words: "I did then what I knew how to do. Now that I know better, I do better."

I peel myself from the couch and ride my bicycle through the winding streets of Provincetown, a village that is no stranger to loss. During the AIDS crisis, its population was decimated. The dead are honored, and the town's heart keeps beating. Biking through the streets, I imagine the spirits of the dead parting as I ride by. Absorbed in the town's energy, catching glimpses of the bay between aged buildings, I ride to the garden center and buy a sunflower.

Back at my condo, digging a hole in the sun-warmed dirt of my garden, it's as though I'm creating that space within myself. I plant the sun-worshipping flower—a task I'll do every year from now on in Jayne's honor—and then drive home in time to prepare my daughter for London.

Two days later, I'm at the airport. An ache swells deep within me as we near the departure terminal. Both our chins quiver as we hug.

After sliding back behind the wheel I grip it tight with two hands, bracing myself. I see my daughter in the rear-view mirror, watching me drive away. Images of a uniformed messenger at my front door delivering horrific news haunt me. I blink away tears and focus on the road, channeling my thoughts to the trip we've planned—Vivian, my mom, my son, and I—to visit her in London, followed by a mini-holiday in Paris. I think about the approaching weekend, when Vivian and I will return to Provincetown. The radio is white noise, a backdrop to my ever-present thoughts. I faintly hear the DJ say a name I recognize, but I'm not paying attention.

By morning, my daughter's plane hasn't landed yet. I'm in my office, preparing for the day, when the subject line of an email from my temple jumps out from the litany of irrelevant clutter in my inbox. I stare in disbelief at the words announcing the tragic news that the rabbi's daughter, who was my daughter's beloved camp counselor, has been killed in a car accident while riding her bicycle. She was twenty-eight. I realize this was the name I'd heard on the radio driving home.

My world goes static. I call Vivian, but she's in a meeting. The funeral is tomorrow. I must tell my daughter, who is somewhere over the Atlantic Ocean.

Twenty-four hours later, I arrive at temple. The main lot is full; I try recalling the last time I was here. I park in the back lot and take a minute to be still. I watch the cars fill in the empty spaces. I'm a stranger in this once-familiar place. Since I've been gone, the rabbi who led this synagogue for over twenty years has retired, but she's beloved by this congregation, so the funeral is taking place here.

I could never have imagined that the reason for my next return here would be such a somber occasion.

Despite arriving early, the crowds rival those of any high holiday. I wait in line for an hour to pay my respects to the rabbi and her husband. When I reach them, my words fail me; a hug is all I can offer. I find a seat on the far left of the standing-room-only sanctuary. I wish I had Vivian's hand to hold, but she couldn't get out of a work obligation.

I'm floating in this space as though not physically here, hearing the stories, absorbing the pain. Each embrace I witness, every sobbing mourner I see, fills me like strangers cramming into a packed elevator until there's no room to move and no air to breathe. Externally, I'm emotionless—until her father shares that he officially retired the day before his only daughter was killed. In that moment, as if the elevator door has opened, the pressure releases and stupor gives way to tears.

Scanning the congested room, the faces of people I once knew, I see my ex-husband. I wonder if this tragedy makes him think of our children the way it does me.

The rabbi approaches the podium. She's accompanied by her husband, whose hand she doesn't let go of. She had command of this space for two decades—teaching, inspiring, and occasionally angering the masses of people who came and went throughout that time. I listen to her speak, likely for the last time, and note how she glides between roles, from rabbi consoling her audience to a mom living every mother's worst nightmare. She finishes her eulogy, looks at the coffin holding her daughter, and in a broken voice says, "Rest, darling, rest."

I fidget in the cushioned folding chair. I sympathize with her as a grieving mom, imagining myself if a tragedy should befall either of my kids. The pain in the room is palpable; I stare at the coffin, thinking of Jayne. All the while, images of the horrific accident replay in my head. Despite being told not to watch the video footage that captured the street corner

accident, I watched it anyway knowing that it would trauma-
tize me but also knowing it wouldn't fully register otherwise.
Now I can't unsee it.

The contrast to the celebration of Jayne's life exactly one
week ago from this one couldn't be starker. Two women, each
in different chapters of their lives, both gone far too early.
But Jayne, knowing what was coming, at least was able to say
goodbye, to tie up the loose threads of her rich, albeit short,
life. Her family had an opportunity to leave no words unspoken. The rabbi and her family had no such outlet. A regret
over things left unsaid is evident in her oldest brother's eulogy.

I don't return to work after the funeral. Vivian picks me up at
home and takes me to Provincetown.

I'm skittish in the car; the traffic whizzes by faster than
usual, the sounds register more loudly. I wonder why I carry
my emotions the way I do, like a weighted knapsack. I'm so
heavily affected by events, especially loss. I recall when my
friend Johann cautioned, "Be careful of the rocks you put in
your own backpack."

My healing work continues; I labor to create space for my
grief, remove rocks from my backpack, and move forward.
Pema Chodron teaches, "the truth is that things don't really
get solved. They come together and they fall apart. Then they
come together again and fall apart again. . . . The healing
comes from letting there be room for all of this to happen:
room for grief, for relief, for misery, for joy."

Acute grief is like a phantom pain after amputation, at times
subsiding and then reemerging without warning. It engulfs
you, tingling your skin like static electricity while sinking deep
into your core like an anchor. The world looks different with
grief goggles on: It's fuzzy, as if you've been drinking. Your
eyes are heavy on your face, the taste of saltwater lingers on

your lips. Sounds are indistinguishable murmurs, as if you're under water.

With time, you breach the surface and adjust to a new normal; emotional scar tissue fills the void. But it's still there, embedded within you, like an old injury that aches before it rains.

 **Chapter Thirty-One**

"What if the world is holding its breath—waiting for
you to take the place that only you can fill?"
—DAVID WHYTE

Vivian Gornick said, "A relationship stays alive only if
people keep rediscovering themselves, if you keep experiencing yourself anew."

It's in this spirit that Vivian and I are at a wellness retreat in
Western Massachusetts. It's September, the outset of fall. This
wouldn't have been my first choice for a getaway weekend,
but Vivian, always interested in furthering her own growth,
registered for a course here, and she asked me to join her.

The Kripalu Yoga and Health Center is in the Berkshires,
an area sheltered within the Appalachian Mountains that boasts
tree-filled mountains and valleys, tranquil rivers and ponds,
and winding roads coursing through picturesque villages. I'm
hoping to see some early fall foliage.

It's the first night of the three-day workshop, for which
I pre-prepared since the subject matter, Inner Bonding, is a
bit abstract for me. We're sitting in metal folding chairs in
a cramped classroom, where we're encouraged to break into
groups of two or three to discuss a prompt. This instruction has
the predictable effect of reducing my body to a deflated balloon.

In the morning, Vivian steps outside to call her mother
and wish her a happy name-day—the anniversary of the

commemoration of the saint after whom a person is named, the Greek equivalent to a birthday. When she returns, I ask, "How do you feel?" knowing it can be difficult talking to her mother.

"Fine," she says, not offering more.

Vivian's family issues have risen to the surface these last couple years, triggering both of us. Vivian teeters between two worlds: her mother is unwelcoming of me, but she loves us both. In this moment, her cool response to my question lands like the rejection I feel from her mother.

We return to the sterile classroom and a topic I can't connect to. I come back to the room upset, which makes the environment feel intolerable. The room seems smaller, the chairs feel harder, and the people here are strangers with whom I have nothing in common. I mumble, "I can't do this," then grab my belongings and bolt.

I head down the hallway. It's a beautiful campus, so I set my sights on getting outside. On my way to the front entrance, a simple sign catches my attention. It reads:

Do you have a rich inner life and vivid dreams?

Are you conscientious, highly intuitive, and sensitive to noise, pain, and others' emotions?

If so, you are probably a highly sensitive person (HSP). Twenty percent of people are born with this trait.

Yes. And yes. I'm intrigued. I enter the spacious conference room and slip into a corner. My intention is to see what this is about, then go for a walk.

I settle inconspicuously into the back recesses of the large room and scan the space. There's a myriad of people scattered about. Many are in chairs, others are on the carpeted floor, a few have blankets, some are lying down with their eyes closed. There couldn't be a greater contrast to the room I just left.

A woman is speaking. I'll learn later she is Dr. Elaine Aron, a clinical research psychologist and author. She speaks about equanimity—I write the word down. She talks about the importance of self-care for individuals she calls highly sensitive people (HSPs). My curiosity is piqued at the notion that there is a name for the personality qualities with which I most strongly identify—that there are others, including the almost 200 people here, who share this temperament. I get more comfortable on the floor and listen more intently.

Dr. Aron reports that 15 to 20 percent of the population are born with this trait. She refers to HSPs as late bloomers, emotionally reactive, empathetic, easily overwhelmed—people who think and feel more deeply than most. It's as if I've opened a dilapidated gate only to discover an exquisite garden.

I no longer want to leave; it feels like a custom-made blanket has just been handed to me. I want to curl inside its softness.

During the first break I approach Dr. Aron's co-presenter, Alane Freund, and ask if I can join this session.

"Of course," she says warmly. She opens her laptop computer—my eyes are drawn to a rainbow sticker announcing, "You're safe here"—and shares with me the slides I missed from the first part of the morning. When I confide that Vivian once said to me, "Have you always been this sensitive?" she cringes, comparing it to asking a blue-eyed person, "Have your eyes always been *that* blue?"

I've stumbled over another threshold.

"How could I not have known this about myself?" I ask.

The look she gives me tells me that she's been on this side of the divide—has been the recipient of judgmental comments, is no stranger to feeling different. "You've been too busy trying to survive," she says gently.

The epiphany is as impactful as recognizing I'm gay was. The last several years have had me deep in the trenches, ducking and weaving but absorbing every emotion like a sock in a puddle.

I stay for the remainder of the workshop, scribbling notes on loose pieces of paper, mesmerized.

Back in the hotel, I reconnect with Vivian; I'm so excited about my discovery, I forget I walked out of the workshop earlier. She listens to me prattle on about HSPs and watches me take the twenty-seven-question HSP self-test (I score 100 percent). She's interested in what I'm sharing and sees how important it is to me. Her body softens; she discards her anger from our earlier fight. She agrees to accompany me to the conference room to watch a movie about HSPs.

The physiological explanation for this trait, called sensory processing sensitivity, is a heightened central nervous system that results in a tendency toward deeper thinking and feeling. HSPs are overstimulated by external stimuli, have stronger reactions to internal stimuli, transition slowly, and require more time to recover from traumatic or impactful experiences. HSPs think through everything, work hard to get things right, withdraw to regroup, and enjoy a special relationship with music, art, and nature. They are likened to orchids—beautiful flowers that thrive in certain environments—whereas non-HSPs can be compared to hearty species that grow everywhere, like dandelions.

This workshop is what Raia was to my sexuality. It's the key to a locked box I didn't know was inside me—one containing the instruction manual to my personality.

I return to the workshop the next day, and Vivian joins me after her class ends. She's supportive and curious and we find another same-sex couple in the group, one of whom identifies as HSP. They recommend an Imago therapy workshop, saying that it will provide us with the language and framework we need to navigate our difficult conversations. We are both intrigued and agree to check it out.

I'll later learn that sensitive people are a misunderstood cohort, often assessed unfairly. I'll gain a heightened awareness about the negative connotation the word "sensitive" evokes—not a valued trait in Western society. Being sensitive is associated with words like thin-skinned, weak, moody, and high-strung. It's weaponized in phrases like "You're too sensitive" and "Why are you so emotional?"

Sensitive people may take longer to arrive at their aptitude. They are often, in other words, "late bloomers"—a term that received increased attention following Rich Karlgaard's book *Late Bloomers: The Power of Patience in a World Obsessed with Early Achievement.* This is the same term, of course, for those who awaken to their sexuality later in life, so it resonates doubly for me. In both cases, with age or experience comes greater curiosity, resilience, self-knowledge, creativity, and wisdom.

Karlgaard concludes that blooming is not time-limited; we write our stories in pencil versus carving them into stone, and impermanence is the key underlying principle. He writes, "What we accomplish in the marathon of life depends on our persistence, our patience, and an ability to see ourselves as we really are."

How well do we see ourselves? How can we be expected to know ourselves when we don't have the words to describe our emotions and feelings, our intuitions about internal voids, sexuality, and the essence of our being? Language empowers us to reach beyond our imagination, both within ourselves and with others. When we close ourselves off, assuming we know all we need to know—when we stay on the tried-and-true path without ever venturing off or peering over the cliff—we cease to grow.

My accidental discovery is giving me the tools to see myself more clearly, to be more deliberate in my self-care. Armed with this new language to explain my behavior and express my needs, can I be better understood going forward? An alternate path has opened itself in front of me.

I remove more rocks from my backpack.

Away from those 200 other participants who shared my invisible trait, I return to being a square peg in a world of round holes. My thoughts replay: *another minority label, another characteristic about myself I can't change, I am different.* I attend classes, read books, and join a HSP social media site—diving deeper into learning more about sensory processing sensitivity. Discovering that others experience the same shifts from immediate gratification to grief in their self-realization pursuits that I do is validating, but it doesn't make the journey any easier.

Over time, I fill my personal tool bag with strategies for managing overwhelm and learn to anticipate situations likely to cause it. I incorporate self-care into my life, noticing which environments bring me closer to equanimity and which stir me up, tie me in knots, exhaust me. The downside of this process is recalling my worst parenting moments and wishing for a do-over.

Examining my journey with greater self-awareness, I revisit the teaching about hope that says what we've lost gets returned to us, although not always in its same form. I know I've been waiting for the wrong thing to return by expecting DH to show up. If I'm being honest, long before he morphed into an uncharacteristic version of himself, he watched me do the same. I remember sitting at the kitchen counter with him the summer before the bat mitzvah and him saying, "I have a feeling a year from now my life's going to look very different."

He was right, and we are two different people with different ways of processing. I sought restoration in reclaiming memories—holding on to the joy depicted in pictures of our family, the comfort of music that once held meaning for us. I didn't want our shared time together to have been in vain. I was trying to stave off my residual guilt and recapture a foundational part of my life by recalling what once made us good. When I think about what he might have needed and wanted, I imagine it was likely the exact opposite.

The eighteenth-century Jewish mystic Rabbi Baal Shem Tov said, "Remembrance is the secret of redemption." That was true for me, but likely was not for my ex-husband.

Summer is ending; another journey begins. The foyer is cluttered with boxes and bags, still-packaged sheets and blankets, desk supplies, and food. All the things my son will need as he starts college at the University of Maryland.

I sit on the hardwood step overlooking the piles and check my email again. I've been checking it routinely, expecting the "We regret to inform you" letter other universities have been sending out, canceling plans to allow students on campus because of the worldwide pandemic.

The first such letter announced a change from allowing roommates to single occupancy only. It feels inevitable. The virus rages on, the world is still essentially shut down, and schools have gone virtual. I haven't seen my daughter in five months; it'll be another six before I see her again.

My son, Vivian, and I have hunkered down in the house. He finished his senior year at home, graduated in his cap and gown while sitting at the kitchen table. My daughter didn't have a college graduation. The celebration of the achievement she'd planned for since she was eight years old was erased. I didn't get to see her off at the airport when she left for London from Canada to begin graduate school.

There's no email. We pack the car so full that there's no room for the dress shoes he wants to bring. I remind him that he won't be needing black leather shoes—that there won't be any formal activities for a while.

I back the car out of the garage and stop. This space is a storage unit of memories; its paraphernalia tell the story of the active children who grew up in this house. The pail and shovel peeking out from the unzipped OBX beach bag on the shelf, the *Toy Story* Woody costume my two-year-old son wore, the stack of skateboards, the fleet of bicycles, the plastic cart of bats, the variety of balls, the baseball gloves that no longer fit anyone's hands and have sat idle and untouched for years—all these are memories of a life that has floated by like bubbles from a wand.

I look at my son, who looks at me and says, "I can't believe I'm on my way to college."

"I'm so proud of you," I say, but in my mind he's the ever-smiling little boy with the Elmo backpack as big as him posing for his "first day" picture outside of the Y.

It's a quick turnaround once we arrive at his dorm; the rules are strict, they want to avoid crowds of people gathering. In what seems like seconds I'm driving north on the NJ Turnpike, my thoughts on what will happen next.

This time tomorrow, Sophie the cat and I will be in Provincetown. Time to exhale and take stock.

September in Provincetown is sweatshirt mornings, T-shirt days, and jacket nights. The galleries and restaurants are open, shows are running, and the summer crowds have gone. The deep red, orange, and yellow fall flowers are in bloom.

As summer turns to fall, the Jewish people welcome a new year. The Hebrew month of Elul draws to a close, signaling the approach of the High Holidays, a prescribed time for reflection.

It's Rosh Hashanah. I'm reflecting not only as a Jew but also as an official empty nester. I ride toward the breakwater, pull off the road before reaching the mile-long causeway. I walk my bicycle on the sand behind tall grass, then leave it and continue on a few more feet. Out of view of the road is a hidden alcove of a living art gallery. Anywhere you look you see the subjects of countless paintings and photographs—the massive granite boulders on the left, the Wood End lighthouse straight ahead in the distance, majestic sand dunes forming the border on the right, and the soft bed of the grassy moors filling the space in between.

Seated on a stone slab at the water's edge, I take in the view. People walk the dike to Long Point, minnows swim in the shallow water, the lighthouse flashes its red light every ten seconds. All these sights soothe my soul, ushering me into a state of equanimity.

My kids survived the turmoil of divorce and transition and are now stepping into the next phase of their young lives. Having escorted them to this point, I can take a baby step back. Vivian and I are living together in New Jersey and cherish our Lilliputian Provincetown sanctuary, which has been a gateway to community and friends these last years.

Standing on the edge of the salt marsh, I perform the Tashlich ritual of symbolically casting sins into moving water. Some do this with breadcrumbs or bird seed. I'm using pebbles. With each plop, I watch the ripples stretch out on the water's surface, reminding me of the swirly lollipops sold in old-fashioned candy stores. I remember Rosh Hashanah five years ago, when I was served divorce papers. Perhaps I always will on this day.

The gesture of tossing a tangible item into the water creates connection. In this act I am connected to all the Jews standing on their own shores or bridges casting bread, seed, or stones into flowing water, as well as to all the generations who've come before. The physical action invites mindfulness, consciousness of our actions; it encourages us to let go and refocus.

Soaking up the idyllic landscape before me, I recognize I've landed in a good place, even as my journey presses on. I throw one last rock, a wishing stone—gray with a white stripe encircling it—and renew my vow to continue becoming, just as that rock will allow itself to move with the changing tides. We are all in infinite motion. My wish is to heed the call of Teshuvah, an act of returning in which we circle back to ourselves, back to our authentic path.

Late Bloomer

I retrieve my bicycle and hear the hymn from morning service playing in my head:

> *Return again, return again, return to the land of your soul*
> *Return to what you are, return to who you are, return*
> *to where you are*
> *Born and reborn again*

And I return to the studio—to feeling whole.

Afterword

"If they don't give you a seat at the table, bring a folding chair."
—Shirley Chisholm

What finally helps me integrate my life with what I know about being an HSP is the pandemic.

I learn the value of quiet time, the importance of a light social calendar, and how overwhelming the daily grind of commuting and the toxicity of the political arena is to me.

Realizing I'm a hardwired introvert, I welcome opportunities to educate people about what that means. It doesn't refer to being shy or antisocial, but rather to how one recharges their battery. As an HSP, I've learned how quickly my battery drains, as well as the environments in which I thrive and best recover. Like many HSPs, I'm drawn to nature and art.

Provincetown is another calling into myself, one where all my homes—spiritual, emotional, and physical—seamlessly unite. In this place, echoes of my old soul reverberate in all that surrounds me—the wind, the trees, the sand, and the water.

Provincetown's uniqueness overrides the presence of the pandemic. Masks can't hide the array of individualism, the diversity, and the many types of love that exist.

There's a growing trend for support for LGBTQ equal rights and a steady increase in the number of people identifying as LGBTQ today. The latest Gallup poll reported that 7.1

percent of adults—an estimated twenty million people—identify as LGBT in the United States alone. Discrimination and danger still reign, though. Around the world, almost seventy nations have anti-gay laws in place; in ten of them, same-sex relations are punishable by death. Momentum grows within the US conservative movement to reverse the rights obtained by LGBTQ people, and there's been an uptick in violence toward the community.

When I came out, I straddled two worlds. Often, I failed to react when people—assuming I was straight—made inappropriate comments. Since then, I've become empowered to take a stand for myself and the community to which I belong. No longer do I remain quiet in the face of disparaging remarks about others' sexuality, nor do I allow for the perpetuation of stigmas regarding sensitivity or introversion.

In the end, I've learned about courage, and have come to understand that everything gets deposited into your emotional house, where hope, grief, loss, and joy reside. My journey has taught me about imperfection and impermanence, about the importance of releasing expectations and allowing our stories to unfold organically. It has shown me how to respond to my soul's calling, take the journey inward, and embrace the idea that growth may be more about releasing hold of a past than looking forward.

In the fullness of time, I've faced my old fears, banished unwanted ghosts, and made space for those who remain. I continue showing up for and nurturing my relationship with my kids, and I've found a passionate love, full of promise, with a woman committed to her own growth.

Above all, I've found me.

I'm in London, tending to my daughter's first broken heart. Yesterday, she read me a text from her dad about this being just one chapter in her life. *There are many other chapters waiting to be written*, he reminded her.

"Dad wrote that?" I asked, astonished.

She laughed and told me she and her brother had the same reaction.

Today, she tells me he sent another text recalling her at two years old, sitting on his shoulders, eating an apple as the juice dripped down his shirt. He said it's his favorite memory.

I smile as I recall the day he's referring to, envisioning the picture in the scrapbook.

I'm so happy he's showing up for her.

Months later, Vivian's mother asks her, "Are we celebrating this year?"

Vivian inquires about "we" and when her mother responds, "It's always been the three of us," Vivian says, "It's four of us now."

And just like that, after nine years, I am invited to join them for a family dinner.

Mark Nepo writes, "There are no wrong turns, only unexpected paths."

We're all on a journey—all finding our way home, that place where we feel safe, seen, and free to be our most authentic selves. Life is messy; we get a little muddy along the way.

 **Acknowledgments**

The journey to finding myself, and the journey of writing about it, share a commonality of needing time, patience, hope, and help. Both journeys would have been profoundly different had it not been for the presence of so many people who have impacted or helped me in a number of ways. For everyone who had a hand in either or both of my stories, I am eternally grateful.

Chani, Elissa, and Cantor Meredith responded to a stranger in need. I can't imagine where I'd be today had you not wrapped me in a cloak of compassion and gently guided me in those fearful early days.

Alison, you listened when even I was tired of hearing me. Thank you for knowing when to nudge me and when to hug me, for always responding when I needed to vent or was struggling to process it all.

Beth, for your steady hand and insight, I am filled with gratitude. Thank you for showing up and sheltering me in your loving friendship.

Michele—for cracking into my soul and being the emotional connection upon which I ultimately built a truer me.

J—for shining a light so I could see.

Michele and Johann—for enduring friendship, inspiration, and encouragement. When asked why I stayed at the cottage park, I know now it was so I could meet you.

Mari, for your friendship when I needed it most. Time spent with you is like touching base.

Lori, for making an indelible impression on me long ago. Still.

Li and LiPing, for fun hikes, brunches, dinners, and one day camping.

Anthony Abela, for years of generosity, support, and kindness.

Brady, Brad, and the team at Performance Physical Therapy, for always fixing my injury-prone family.

Tom, for your friendship and support for (almost) forty years.

Brooke, for taking me up the mountain, teaching me craft, and creating opportunities to dig deep. You helped me shed rocks from my backpack, and I'm a better person because of it.

Krissa Lagos, Addison Gallegos, Julie Metz, Rebecca Lown, and the entire team at She Writes Press, a thousand thank yous.

My SWP sisters, for welcoming me into a sacred community where I can learn, grow, and create.

Glenda—for helping me make sense of it, and for making sure I always feel heard. This is what it's about.

Jeannie, for putting us back together, you are the gold in our once-cracked vase.

Lyn, my ax editor and friend who encouraged me to find gold nuggets and put blood on the page. I am a better writer because of you.

Alyssa, for your friendship, expertise, and patience in helping this hardwired introvert get more comfortable with being visible.

Linda Atamian, for your generosity, expertise, and support.

Layne Mandros and the team at Books Forward for their dedication.

My father, for The Goodbye Girl and for allowing me to show up.

Robyn, for reinforcing the universality of the struggle between motherhood and self, and for your enthusiasm when I open the door needing a word.

Amy Ferris, Richard C. Morais, Julie Cantrell, Julie Barton, Carren Strock, and Michelle Theall, for your generosity of time, inspiration, and support and for allowing this newbie to benefit from your experience and to learn from your example.

To absent friends, thank you for being part of my journey. Big and little, it all made a difference.

Provincetown, for welcoming a stranger, embracing me, and being the still water in which I can see my reflection. For being home.

Tracy, for always turning the Rubik's Cube with me, for your honesty, humor, and insight. You know when to pull me off the ledge and when to sit beside me on it. I couldn't imagine taking any part of this journey without you; I wouldn't want to.

Mom, your unconditional love, and support has enabled me to write this book—which enabled me to heal. I cannot thank you enough.

Vivian—for sheltering me during my storms, for loving me when it isn't always easy, for pointing your compass north so I can be whole, or for waiting patiently while I recover and recharge. Thank you for your generosity and permission in allowing me to share our story. In a room full of countless women, all I see is you. I look forward to falling in love with you over and over for the rest of my life.

To the ones for whom any of this mattered as much as it did, my children:

Jillian, who told me *Diamonds are made under pressure,* you are as unique and brilliant as any diamond, the one who taught me to re-engage when my body says retreat. Your love is a steady stream of comfort that fills me with gratitude.

Justin, the little boy who once called me a princess grew into a man who loves me even with my quirks. You'll never know how those random kisses on my cheek carried me through my darkest times. Like you, they're priceless.

I love you both so much. Thanks for your patience when I dig deeper, drive farther, pull back or love harder.

A special shout out to Sophie, my co-pilot and companion on countless trips to Provincetown, a constant source of comfort and an attentive audience to my stories. Sophie brought beauty and softness to my days, countering the harshness of a life that no longer fit. She is sorely missed but forever loved (July 2004-October 2021).

 **About the Author**

Melissa is a late bloomer, a highly sensitive introvert, and a proud mama bear to two children. She has published articles in *Kveller, Dorothy Parker's Ashes, Highly Sensitive Refuge, Journal of Expressive Writing,* and *The Boston Globe.* She received an Honorable Mention in the Memoirs/Personal Essays category of the 91st Annual Writer's Digest Writing Competition and her essay, "Art is the Antidote," appears in the anthology, *Art In The Time of Unbearable Crisis* (June 2022). Melissa is living her authentic life with her partner Vivian, and their two cats; together, they split their time between New Jersey and Provincetown, Massachusetts.

Author photo © Giulianna Pistolesi and Flo Inciardi

SELECTED TITLES FROM
SHE WRITES PRESS

She Writes Press is an independent publishing
company founded to serve women writers everywhere.
Visit us at www.shewritespress.com.

I'm Still Here: A Memoir by Martina Reaves. $16.95, 978-1-63152-876-7. Martina Reaves weaves the story of her early life—coming of age in the 1960s, living and working in various small towns with her hippie husband, coming out in 1980, and eventually having a son with her life partner, Tanya—with that of her 2008 tongue cancer diagnosis, after which she fights to maintain hope even as she accepts that death might come.

Queerspawn in Love by Kellen Kaiser. $16.95, 978-1-63152-020-4. When the daughter of a quartet of lesbians falls in love with a man serving in the Israeli Defense Forces, she is forced to examine her own values and beliefs.

Affliction: Growing Up With a Closeted Gay Dad by Laura Hall. $16.95, 978-1-64742-124-3. Laura Hall was born in a small city on the San Francisco peninsula to a straight mother and a gay father who lived in the shadows. This is her tender, frank account of how her father's secret became her inheritance and, ultimately, the path to her own healing.

You Can't Buy Love Like That: Growing Up Gay in the Sixties by Carol E. Anderson. $16.95, 978-1631523144. A young lesbian girl grows beyond fear to fearlessness as she comes of age in the '60s amid religious, social, and legal barriers.

Once a Girl, Always a Boy: A Family Memoir of a Transgender Journey by Jo Ivester. $16.95, 978-1-63152-886-6. Thirty years ago, Jeremy Ivester's parents welcomed him into the world as what they thought was their daughter. Here, his mother—with Jeremy's help—chronicles his journey from childhood through coming out as transgender and eventually emerging as an advocate for the transgender community.

The Buddha at My Table: How I Found Peace in Betrayal and Divorce by Tammy Letherer. $16.95, 978-1-63152-425-7. On a Tuesday night, just before Christmas, after he had put their three children in bed, Tammy Letherer's husband shattered her world and destroyed every assumption she'd ever made about love, friendship, and faithfulness. In the aftermath of this betrayal, however, she finds unexpected blessings—and, ultimately, the path to freedom.